MODERN ENGLISH PAINTERS

MODERN
ENGLISH
PAINTERS

*   *   *

WOOD TO HOCKNEY

John Rothenstein

MACDONALD:LONDON

Copyright © John Rothenstein 1974

First published in Great Britain in 1974
by Macdonald and Jane's,
Macdonald and Company (Publishers) Ltd.,
St. Giles House, 49 Poland Street, London W.1.

Printed in Great Britain by
REDWOOD BURN LIMITED
Trowbridge & Esher

ISBN 0 356 04608 7

CONTENTS

LIST OF PLATES

25 LUCIAN FREUD: *Mike (Michael) Andrews and June.*
    Marlborough Fine Art (London) Ltd.
26 LUCIAN FREUD: *John Minton.* Royal College of Art.
27 MICHAEL ANDREWS: *All Night Long.* Collection Felton Bequest,
    National Gallery of Victoria, Melbourne.
28 MICHAEL ANDREWS: *Good and Bad at Games II.*   *192 and 193*
    Privately owned.
29 MICHAEL ANDREWS: *Lights III: the Black Balloon.* Privately owned.
30 BRIDGET RILEY: *Movement in Squares.* Collection Arts Council.
31 BRIDGET RILEY: *Fall.* Tate Gallery.

32 DAVID HOCKNEY: *The Second Marriage.*
    National Gallery of Victoria, Melbourne.
33 DAVID HOCKNEY: *Henry Geldzahler and Christopher Scott.*   *224 and 225*
    Privately owned.
34 DAVID HOCKNEY: *Still life with TV.* Privately owned.

PREFACE

Since the last volume of these studies appeared I have been engaged on writings of a different kind. But the aims and principles of this volume are identical with those of its two predecessors. It is my considered view that groupings of painters are in reality more fortuitous and more conditioned by extraneous factors than they appear in the systematizations of art history. Nor do I hold any kind of evolutionary (or other) model for the construction of this kind of history. This book is a series of studies of particular painters about whom I have wanted to write because their work is of high quality and because I admire and enjoy it. I am also unrepentant in my conviction that judgement of aesthetic quality is not reducible to subjective factors or even to a consensus.

No doctrine was more false than the view of Roger Fry and Clive Bell that to the contemplation of a work of art we need not and should not bring any of the emotions of everyday life. It is no less false of the production of works of art, and this is why these studies are also biographical.

John Rothenstein

Newington,
Oxfordshire,
1973

ACKNOWLEDGEMENTS

My gratitude is due to the artists, for permission to reproduce examples of their work and for their ready help. Wherever possible they have checked the relevant chapters to enable me to avoid error of fact and misinterpretation of motive, and in several cases have sent me photographs. In the case of Christopher Wood, the only one who was personally unknown to me, this has been done by his friend Mr Rex Nan Kivell. In that of Robert Colquhoun, with whom I was barely acquainted, by his friend Mr George Barker whose help has been invaluable and who has allowed me to quote the poems he wrote in memory of Colquhoun and his lifelong friend MacBryde. Likewise my thanks are also due to Mr John Malkin for allowing me to make use of the account of their early lives in Scotland given in the brochure he prepared on the occasion of opening of The Colquhoun Memorial Gallery, Kilmarnock. For information about Colquhoun I am also indebted to Miss Prunella Clough, Mr Michael Ayrton, Mr Robert Frame, Mr Keith Vaughan, Mr Sebastian Barker and Mr Benny Creme. For information about Edward Burra I am grateful to his sister The Hon. Mrs Colin Ritchie, Mrs Barbara Ker-Seymer, Mr William Chappell, and Miss Beatrice Dawson, besides the artist himself.

Many thanks are also due to the owners, both public and private, for permission to reproduce works in their possession.

For the loan of photographs I am greatly obliged to Marlborough Fine Art, the Rowan Gallery, Mr James Kirkman (as well as for useful information), the Lefevre Gallery, the Arthur Tooth Gallery, the Colquhoun Gallery and the Kasmin Gallery.

I am, too, deeply grateful to Father Vincent Turner, S. J., for his invaluable help in correcting the proofs.

If among those to whom I am indebted there are any to whom I have not made acknowledgement here I offer my heartfelt apologies.

In view of the increasing prevalence of burglary I have not given, as I did in the two previous volumes, the names of private owners.

MODERN ENGLISH PAINTERS

CHRISTOPHER WOOD
1901–30

There was nothing in the early boyhood of John Christopher Wood to suggest that he was in any way unusual. He was born on 7 April 1901 in Knowsley, Lancashire, the son of Dr Lucius Wood, a doctor on the Earl of Derby's Knowsley estate, and his wife Clara, born Arthur, a member of a respected Cornish family, which for several generations had served the Church of England or the Navy. He attended Freshfield preparatory school, where his chief interests were cricket and golf, as they were during most of his single term at Marlborough School, until at the age of fourteen he suffered an attack of polio which rendered him physically helpless for some three and a half years, and left him with a slight limp and recurrent pain in the affected leg. His mother nursed him throughout his illness: the relations between them, already close, became closer still. To her he remained uniquely devoted, and after leaving home he wrote to her constantly. 'You are the only person I care about,' runs a sentence in one of his letters, and expressions of the same sentiment frequently recur.

At the age of eighteen he went to Malvern College, where he was allowed to work in special conditions, lying, for instance, on a couch instead of sitting at a desk. No longer able to play cricket or golf he played the flute and sketched. It seems that he had always liked to draw: his mother preserved some of his first drawings, made when he was three — which are no better than those of the average child — and she recalled that three years later he wrote a letter to Father Christmas asking for a box of paints.

Dr Wood wished his son to follow him into the medical profession, but the idea of constant contact with pain repelled him and he refused. Instead he briefly studied architecture under Professor Reilly at Liverpool University, where, according to the testimony of a fellow student, they used to make drawings together of the Liverpool docks. Whether his interest in architecture flagged or for some other reason difficult to ascertain, he

went to London in 1920 and was apprenticed to a dried fruit
merchant, whose speciality was the import of prunes and figs.

Two encounters in London stimulated his growing interest in
painting and drawing. Augustus John saw him sketching at the
Café Royal: they met and John praised what he was doing — and
remained his lifelong admirer. The other encounter, with the
celebrated Alphonse Kahn, was more decisive in its effects. In the
second of his many hundred letters to his mother[1] that survive he
wrote from Paris (19 March 1921):

> Alphonse, with whom I am staying . . . said whenever I was free, to come and
> so I came. . . We spent the evening looking at his paintings. . . Tomorrow we
> go to the Louvre, which by degrees he is going to show me, he being one of
> the greatest (if not the best known) connoisseurs of art in Paris. . . He is going
> to introduce me to all the artists of note here, so I am absolutely in the heights
> of heaven. I honestly believe I was born under a lucky star.

In this belief he was justified, for in an incredibly short space of
time this entirely untaught, strictly conventional young man from
Knowsley, recently the apprentice of a dried fruit importer, was to
enjoy a position in the art world of Paris, then beyond question
predominant, approached by no English artist of his generation
and by very few others.

It was only two years later that he won the friendship and
regard of Picasso, besides many others among the leading
painters, writers and musicians, and was widely considered the
most talented British painter alive. His social success was more
spectacular still. 'I had royalty for tea yesterday, His Highness the
Infant of Spain came up,' he wrote in the October of the same
year. 'He's a good fellow and I have met him at dinners before.'
The letters show that he was sought after by a number of the most
prominent hostesses of Paris.

When he arrived in Paris he had not painted a single picture —
he was given his first paint-box the autumn after his arrival —
and he was without innate sophistication. For instance, he could
describe Augustus John (in December 1922) as 'very refined and
a gentleman to his fingertips'.

How was it that this young man, without achievement to his
credit and, although a member of a most respectable family,

[1] The letters from which quotations are taken are those written to the artist's mother unless
otherwise indicated.

lacking both background and connections, was so quickly qualified for the position he won?

The answer is that he was given, by circumstances, unique opportunities and that he was enabled, by certain innate characteristics, to take advantage of them. His second opportunity arose, after an autumn visit to Italy, with a meeting with Antonio Gandarillas, a Chilean diplomat with houses in Cheyne Walk, Chelsea, and the Avenue Montaigne, Paris, a man of unusual charm and cultivation with a wide, international circle of friends and a zest for travel. The two men became intimates at once. Wood stayed with him often, in both Paris and London, and accompanied him on his constant travels. The extent of Wood's travels in Europe was probably greater than those of all the other painters together who figure in this book.

Christopher Wood had rare and extraordinary charm and a capacity for friendship with men and women in equal measure. There was little or perhaps nothing of the courtier about him in spite of his awareness of the extent to which his career as an artist would be helped by influential social connections. His manner was direct but gentle, he had the advantage of conspicuous good looks, and his disposition was simple and affectionate. Given the good fortune to meet Alphonse Kahn, he had the sense to listen to his encouragement to be a painter so attentively that he telegraphed to him as soon as he was free to accept his invitation to stay and was with him in Paris immediately after receiving his affirmative reply. He had the further good fortune to meet Gandarillas, to whom few doors were not open. It would be wrong to suppose that without these he would not have made many friends useful for his career and enhancing of his life: the contrary is the case. But the protegé of Alphonse Kahn and the intimate of Gandarillas had a ready-made position which his qualities of heart and mind, expressed with his boyish and all but irresistible charm, enabled him first to justify and quickly to enhance. He became not only a social figure much sought after, but, what is mysterious, a notable figure in the art world as well. Where allusion was made to his qualities of *mind*, it was not to suggest that he was an intellectual; this he never was. The most notable feature of his intellect was zestful curiosity: the people he knew, the places he visited, literature, music, to a lesser degree politics, and of course painting, evoked in him a passionate response. It was as though he were aware, quite early in life, that he was to die young and that no moment must be wasted, even though there is no reason to suppose that he had any such intuition. His letters to his mother are full of vivid evocations of people and places.

Wood constantly tells her of progress he is making, and of the praise he receives. For instance (29 November 1926): 'There are one or two modern French people, two painters among them, who think I am already a far better painter than anyone in England except John, who doesn't come into it at all and who is too old fashioned now.' Nevertheless Wood was a modest, even a humble man. 'My life,' he wrote to her on 2 May 1926, 'is almost too interesting, surrounded by people so very superior to myself in intelligence that I feel as if I were in the centre of a whirlpool.'

Once he had decided to be an artist he worked extremely hard and systematically, studying at Julian's, later at the Grande Chaumière, concentrating first upon drawing.

> I know I am improving in my drawing [he wrote in the summer of 1921] because I am getting it right with infinitely less trouble and worry over measurements etc., than I did when I first started. I am not troubling at all with the painting yet awhile as I am so determined to try to and be a master over the drawing part of it before I do anything else.

But by the 20 April of the next year he wrote:

> Now that I have learnt to use my Oil Paints and do just what I want with them, my painting, I think, has taken a big jump in the right direction and it pleases me greatly to see the results I am getting.

Christopher Wood's intense responsiveness to everything he experienced enhanced in some respects and in others frustrated his evolution of an individual way of looking at the world and setting down what he saw and felt. This power of response, when he was able to focus it directly upon his favourite subjects — flowers, landscapes (ports and coasts in particular) and figures — enabled him to see them with an eye both lyrical and penetrating. The weakness of so many of his paintings was due to his frequent inability to see his subject except through other artists' eyes. In the almost comprehensive exhibition of his work arranged in 1938 by the Redfern Gallery at the larger, now defunct, New Burlington

Galleries in Burlington Gardens, it was easy to pick out works which closely resembled those by the artists whom he had currently admired — so closely that a number of them would not have appeared incongruous in exhibitions of their work. Number 41 (in the catalogue) might be a Segonzac; number 111 a Dufy; number 116 a Van Gogh; number 117 an Utrillo; number 152 a Braque; number 124 a Vlaminck; number 181 a John. It was easy, too, to find others in which the characteristics of more than one other artist are conspicuous — a street scene of 1925 which might be the fruit of the collaboration, in a bad moment, of Vlaminck, the Douanier Rousseau and Utrillo, or of Rousseau and Modigliani. The influence of Marie Laurencin is also to be detected, likewise that of his friend Jean Hugo. And in his work, as in that of painters all over Europe and America, that of Picasso. 'Madame Errazuriz has invited me to dinner tomorrow with the Picassos which I shall enjoy,' he wrote on 6 July 1923; 'Picasso is the greatest painter of the day and I admire his work immensely, more, I think, than anyone else's, the more I learn the more I see in it.'

Wood was very conscious of the temptation to follow the example of other painters and determined to overcome it. 'My greatest difficulty in my work with this almost suffocating influence of modern art,' he wrote on 22 February 1924, 'is to be very true and just', that is to say, quite simply to be himself.

It was not surprising that this young and unsophisticated beginner should imitate artists who were the most illustrious in Europe. What was surprising was that a man with such a potentially personal way of viewing the world should have remained an imitator for so long. Various critics spoke and wrote about his capacity to assimilate what he took from other artists; Eric Newton, for instance, in the informative essay published in connection with the Redfern Gallery's exhibition, argued that 'his habit of borrowing another man's vision was less remarkable than his power to outgrow that vision', and he described how an experimental essay in another man's style was followed by a series in which it had become absorbed in his own. My own impression of the exhibition was of the extent to which, over so large a part of his brief career, he did in fact remain an imitator. Nor was it easy to discern any evolution at all — only an ultimate, shortlived, tragic flowering.

Much of his work, even the most derivative, does reveal one highly personal quality: a basic simplicity of outlook. A number of those who spoke and wrote about his painting, aware of the extreme sophistication of the society in which he moved, were inclined to treat this simplicity as something deliberately assumed, as artifice masking its opposite. 'Fashionable clumsiness' was the expression applied to it, for instance, by one sensible ,critic, Gwen Raverat, in *Time and Tide,* 11 April 1936. It must not be forgotten that in their recoil from the elegance and finish of academic art the products of many 'progressive' movements, most particularly perhaps those of the German expressionists and the fauves, were marked by a conscious roughness, a 'clumsiness', a quality that owed much, too, to the growing admiration for primitive art. 'Fashionable clumsiness' was, so to speak, very much in the air, and Wood, ever susceptible to his environment, was not untouched by it. But to dismiss its presence in his work as mere conformity to a pervasive tendency is, in my belief, to do him an injustice and to overlook the fact that the vein of simplicity in his art is a direct reflection of something basic in his character. To this his intimate letters to his mother amply testify, and no less the evidence of his friends. He did indeed move in one of the most sophisticated circles in Europe and at times he derived much pleasure from doing so, but it is arguable that the revulsion that he constantly experienced against it made him value simplicity. 'I have no friends I want to see' and even 'I hate my friends' are sentiments that often recur in his letters. In one of them (21 May 1923), succinctly expressing his 'love-hate' feeling for the social life he led, he wrote:

> I hate staying with people. I always prefer my liberty and I am afraid of becoming very unsociable . . . I never go out. I think I shall go to the ball given by the Count de Beaumont.

Wood was in fact an exceptionally devoted and loyal friend and although there were times when he withdrew from social life he never became habitually unsociable. But the intensity of his periods of sociability, the insight they afforded into the corrupting effects of dissipation and idleness, as well as corruption of a still more positive kind, fostered in him increasingly the desire for simplicity of both being and environment. And as was inevitable with a man so quintessentially an artist this desire was reflected in his art. Some sentences in a letter of 28 July 1922 show how early he was preoccupied with the concept of simplicity.

> Do you know that all the great modern painters . . . are not trying to see things and paint them through the eyes of experience of a man of forty or fifty or whatever they may be, but through the eyes of the smallest child who sees nothing except those things which would strike him as the most important? To the childish drawing they add the beauty and refinement of their own experience. This is the one explanation of modern painting.

In the letter, already quoted from, in which he tells his mother of his impending dinner with the Picassos he wrote, 'I am reducing my colours in everything I do now to very few in the same pictures. . . I am making everything simpler and simpler.'

Another indication of his response to simplicity is his attitude to Alfred Wallis, the primitive painter of sailing ships and imaginary Cornish landscapes. Wallis, born in 1855, went to sea at the age of nine and in 1890 he opened a marine rag and bone shop in St Ives; to relieve his loneliness after his wife's death he began to paint, at the age of seventy. Three years later Wood and Ben Nicholson discovered his work. There was an amusing contrast between the impressions that Wood and Wallis made upon each other. To a friend Wood wrote:

> I am more and more influenced by Alfred Wallis — not a bad master though: he and Picasso both mix their colours on box-lids! I see him each day for a second — he is bright and cheery. I'm not surprised that nobody likes Wallis's paintings; no one liked Van Gogh's for a long time, did they?

But when somebody sent Wallis some paintings by Wood he returned them with paintings on their backs; he had seen in them nothing more than good surfaces to paint on. In one of Wood's later paintings ('Seascape, Brittany' of 1929) there is a boat on the shore that might have been painted by Wallis himself, so totally are the lines of perspective ignored.

The basic simplicity of Wood was recognized by Cocteau, who perhaps was the more clearly aware of it since it was a quality he entirely lacked. In his own introduction, *Les Toils ou l'Etoile de Christopher Wood,* to his first London exhibition, held in 1927 at the defunct Beaux-Arts Gallery, he wrote:

In Christopher Wood there is no malice, there is something straightforward and naive, the freshness of a puppy who has not yet had distemper (or the disease of the period). . . This unaccustomed straightforwardness gives the love of life and the wish to know well this young painter whose eyes are not in keeping with his harlequins' sweater, for they reflect nothing false.

(The 'harlequins' sweater' is the one he wears in the Self-Portrait painted that year and included in the exhibition.)

This evidence — and there is much more — miscellaneous though it is, is sufficient to suggest that the notion that the simplicity in Wood's pictures is 'fashionable clumsiness', affected naivety masking sophistication, is quite simply nonsense, even though his indiscriminate adoption of the styles of others makes it on occasion difficult to perceive until he was nearing the end of his career.

I have emphasized the derivative element in Wood's painting, but from time to time something characteristic of himself emerged — it is discernible, for instance, in a watercolour of 1925, 'The House of Raphael, Rome'. This something was evidently not only discernible to his friends and acquaintances in Paris, but even impressive. Evidence of Cocteau's admiration has already been cited. Picasso admired him. In a letter of 2 February 1926 he tells of Picasso's first visit to his studio. After describing an enjoyable luncheon with his friend Madame Errazuriz he continues:

After, we went with her to look at a new house which Picasso thinks of buying, enormous where he will have a huge studio. After Picasso asked her what she was going to do she said she was going to my studio; it would have looked so silly not to have asked P. also who was charming and came. It was a terrible moment for me as it is what I have dreaded for a long time, but it had to happen before I could make any headway here. He never as a rule says whether he likes the things or not, and I was very nervous, naturally. But he seemed to, very much, and Tony [Gandarillas] and Madame E were surprised at how much he said. It was much better to take him by accident like that without any preparation for him, and looked better too. I feel as if a terrible weight had been lifted off my shoulder. Curiously enough it has given me enormous confidence, the fact of his having seen them, and I feel better disposed towards the future. . .

Picasso is charming to me and said he couldn't understand why Diaghilef had not taken my ballet, that it couldn't have been better or more beautiful. He loves it and simply couldn't make out why it had been refused.

The ballet reference was to some designs he had been encouraged by Diaghilef to make but which, in spite of Picasso's advocacy, were eventually declined.

Five years later his ambition to design for the theatre was gratified by C.B. Cochran's commission of both scenery and dresses for 'Luna Park' or 'The Freaks' in his '1930 Revue'.

It was Wood's usual practice to paint direct without first making a drawing on the canvas, but he varied this habit for the Cochran ballet, making finished preparatory drawings.

Easel painting and watercolour, however, remained Wood's most intense preoccupations. He worked, in spite of the constant distractions of his social life, often until two or even three in the morning and was up always by half-past eight.

No one of his generation ever wasted less time: when he was not painting he was looking at paintings and sculptures (for instance he made many drawings of Greek sculpture in the British Museum) and he particularly studied Leonardo. He read constantly. 'Reading fine works,' as he rather quaintly put it, 'keeps one's morals and intellect up to a certain high standard.' He translated, for the benefit of his mother, a poem by Michelangelo, which he included in a letter of 8 May 1924. 'If I want advice I look in Bacon's Essays', and he quotes from Voltaire. But he is very conscious of his shortcomings as a reader, partly as a result of exhaustion after a long day's work. He writes that 'the difficulty to be a well-read person when I read with such difficulty and forget it the minute after is exasperating. I have to write everything down before I can remember' (23 April, 1924). He went often to concerts: Brahms and Wagner were his favourite composers. The company of the intelligent gave him particular pleasure. 'I have a painter friend called Wyndham Lewis who is one of the cleverest men alive, he is also an author' (20 October 1923). Of his various intellectual friends the one whom he admired the most was Cocteau. 'He is not only the greatest poet alive,' he wrote on 1 November 1924,

> but I suppose the greatest genius. He is a wonderful craftsman also. He is looked on as the greatest conversationalist in France and everything he does is a chef d'oeuvre. . . He and Picasso, the painter, are great friends and admire each other intellectually and they are the two outstanding genii of this period, perhaps the only two, in the world of art.

And on the 14th:

Jean Cocteau has drawn a beautiful profile of my head. . . It is really beautiful and too classic for my puffy face. Of course Jean like Picasso has the last word in good taste, and the two together have created the modern art of this century. Picasso has created the colour and the drawing and Cocteau the modern literature and philosophy, and the modern school of music although he is not a musician. . . He is a god.

This ardent but indiscriminate praise of Cocteau gives an intimation of the simplicity of Wood's heart.

Although it is not easy to discern anything approaching consistent progress in the work of his first six years he was accorded ever-increasing recognition in both Paris and London. He held a second exhibition, of drawings only, at the Claridge Gallery in 1928; a third the following year at Arthur Tooth's gallery and a fourth, with Ben Nicholson, at the Galerie Georges Bernheim in 1930.

This recognition brought him both delight and apprehension. 'It is a very drastic moment now at the beginning of my career,' he wrote on 13 June 1926:

. . . and I must think of nothing but my work, as the more I see of English people the more I am given to understand that I am the only young English painter who is expected to carry on. I pray to God I may be able to carry on this terrible responsibility.

Poor Kit Wood! 'The beginning of my career', when he had only fifty months to live. But there is a sense in which he was only approaching the beginning of his career, and the end of his apprenticeship. For him, it may be said, his end was his beginning. It was about three years later that his passionate apprenticeship — an apprenticeship not only of the eye and the hand, but of the intellect and the ear — began to earn its reward in such paintings as 'Evening, Brittany', 'Lighthouse, entrance to Tréboul Harbour', 'La Tremouille Church, Tréboul', and 'Boat in Harbour, Brittany' (Tate Gallery), all painted in 1929.

But it was only in the last remaining months of his short life that his work culminated in an extraordinary blossoming — extraordinary not only in the lyrical intensity of his paintings and drawings but in their number, for during those six months he made at least a hundred.

It was the coasts of Celtic France and England, Brittany and Cornwall, that seemed to ignite his ultimate creative blaze. In a letter written in August 1929 from Douarnenez — the little Breton fishing-port which, with nearby Tréboul, provided themes which evoked a poetry quintessentially his own, lyrical, gay, yet sometimes with an undertone of menace — there occurs a sentence which helps us to understand how he looked at his chosen subjects.

> I have a little sailing boat which I adore, I sit in it and glide along looking quietly at all the things I love the most, I see the lovely fishing boats with their huge brown sails against the dark green fir trees and little white house, instead of always against the sea and an insipid sky.

In Brittany he was happy. In *Christopher Wood, A Souvenir* his friend Max Jacob wrote that he used to say: 'The Bretons make one believe in Paradise' — and these words give an indication of how happy he was during the summer of 1929. According to this touching tribute the Bretons were no less fond of him. 'I can remember,' continues Jacob, 'the humble and pious Breton women who used to wait on us at the Pension Cariou drying their tears on their aprons at the news of his death.'[1]

That summer Wood gave, in his landscapes, clear intimations of the highly individual poetic quality that was to emerge with such splendour the following year. Regrettably his portrait of Jacob (acquired by the Musée du Luxembourg) with its head of exaggerated size and its small collapsed boneless body reflects the mannerisms of several East European artists in Paris.

The following June he was back in Brittany, staying at the Hotel Ty-Med until towards the end of July. Here and during a brief visit to St Ives, Cornwall, the previous March, there occurred the extraordinary and tragically brief blossoming of his art. Among all his earlier works — with the exception of some of those made in Brittany the previous summer — the derivative far outnumbered the original, but with those done during his last two or three months the opposite is the case: almost everything he painted is the emanation of a very rare spirit. One could name such works almost at random. 'P.Z. 134 Cornwall' and 'The Yellow Horse' **(PLATE 1)**, 'La Ville Close, Concarneau' (Fitzwilliam Museum, Cambridge), 'Decorating the Sanctuary, Tréboul', 'The Yellow Man', 'Nude Boy in a Bedroom', 'Mending the Nets, Tréboul',

---

[1] *Christopher Wood, His Life and Work* by Eric Newton, 1959

'Breton Woman at Prayer' (Southampton Art Gallery), 'Douar-nenez' and 'The Church at Tréboul' (Tate Gallery), and his two last paintings 'Zebra and Parachute' and 'Tiger and the Arc de Triomphe'. All these and a number of others are pervaded by the gentle radiance of colour, expressing happiness as 'Nude Boy in a Bedroom' or an undertone of menace as 'The Yellow Man' **(PLATE 2)**, occasionally expressing surrealist fantasy, as 'Zebra and Parachute' and 'Tiger and the Arc de Triomphe'. Although it is the colour in these paintings which most strongly affects the spectator, they are lucidly and logically composed.

Wood's power of sustained hard work, always conspicuous, attained in these last months of his life an extraordinary pitch: he scarcely slept; he allowed the meals placed on a tray beside his easel to grow cold, and such was his passion of creativity that in at least two instances, running out of canvas, he painted over a complete painting. One of these is 'Zebra and Parachute'. Fantastic as it seems, it was in fact painted in front of the motif, a Corbusier house in the outskirts of Paris. Leaving Tréboul for the last time on his way to England he arrived in Paris on a Sunday, and unable to buy a canvas, he sacrificed a Tréboul landscape that he had brought with him, intending it for the exhibition of his work at the Wertheim Gallery in London. 'Tiger and the Arc de Triomphe' was painted — also over another picture — on the same last passage through Paris, the tiger and leopard at the Zoo and the Arc on the site.

Many of the works produced in this ultimate lyrical outpouring were painted in ripolin and, like their forerunners, they were carried out with ease rather than at high speed, though he liked to finish a picture on the same day as he began it.

Wood makes references throughout his correspondence with his mother to his confidence that he is making progress. This he does in his last letter from Tréboul (dated 11 July), but there follows a sentence which suggests an awareness of the unique character of the series of paintings he had just completed.

> I have almost worked myself to the end, for the time being, and begin to feel I want to leave this place. It is rather much to be alone all the time and the only thing is to work, and now I have done as much as I want I am waiting for some money to come to be able to go.

A letter of eleven days later does indeed say: 'I have done a lot in

Tréboul and am pleased.'

Whatever is to be read into these words, he had in fact worked himself 'to the end'; although references to the future suggest that he was unaware of it, for him this was the end. Augustus John wrote to Mrs Wood (in an undated letter) that Kit's last months seemed to have been passed in such a flame of creative energy that he burnt himself out — gloriously.

The following month he returned to England to prepare for his exhibition at the Wertheim Gallery then scheduled for October (it did not, in the event, take place until the following year), and after a brief visit to his London house, at 3 Minton Place off the Fulham Road, he went to Salisbury in order to see his family, in particular his mother. (The Woods had left Lancashire and were living in the village of Broadchalke, near Salisbury.) Rex Nan Kivell, whom Kit had known since 1925, came down on 21 August to have lunch with Mrs Wood and her daughter Betty at Sutton's restaurant, prior to meeting Kit at Salisbury station. After lunch Rex Nan Kivell left. At the station they found Kit in an intensely agitated state: he maintained that he was being watched by some strange Algerians and insisted that he must go back to London. Instead he fell under a moving train. On an envelope in his pocket were written in his own hand these two enigmatic sentences: 'Are they positive?' and 'Throwing away is not big enough proof.' He was buried at Broadchalke: the flat stone over his grave was carved by Eric Gill.

Christopher Wood was widely mourned as both painter and friend. In death he became more than ever a legendary figure.

During his life, in spite of the high reputation he enjoyed, he sold relatively few pictures and those for modest sums. Eight years later, according to a newspaper report, one was bought for £3,000 — an immense sum for a work of a young contemporary. Wood's well-deserved posthumous reputation owed much to the devotion of his mother and the admiration of his friend Rex Nan Kivell, the director of the Redfern Gallery, which showed his work consistently from 1936. After holding an exhibition of oils that year and of watercolours and drawings the following, the Redfern, in 1938, took the audacious step of showing, at the spacious New Burlington Galleries, what was believed to be the complete works of Wood — five hundred and thirty oils, watercolours and drawings — and sponsored a book based on the catalogue with a substantial prefatory essay on his life and work by Eric Newton. This exhibition, for the most part received with admiration, established him, momentarily, as a major figure in twentieth century British painting. Owing to the Second World War its effects were less enduring than would otherwise have been the case, for the art world underwent radical transformations and Wood was little remembered by emerging generations, but the respectful interest evoked by an exhibition of a hundred and thirty-four of the paintings, drawings and watercolours held at the Redfern Gallery in November 1965 suggests that the time is approaching when Wood will be accorded the place he deserves.

Very few young artists, whatever their stature, would emerge with their reputations intact from the exhibition of virtually their entire production. The fact that the comprehensive exhibition of 1938, which included his work as a student and as an uncritical disciple of many other painters, should have impressed many people of acute perception, shows that it was imbued with rare qualities. Lucien Pissarro spent an hour there, expressing ardent admiration. 'Dead at twenty-nine!' he exclaimed, 'How long had he been painting?' Eight years, he was told. 'And nothing from my own first ten years survives.' Augustus John also paid it a long visit and, scrutinizing 'The Plage, Hotel Ty-Med, Tréboul', said that the tree on the left constituted one of the remarkable passages in modern painting. Paul Nash, of the last pictures when shown in 1932 at the Lefevre Galleries, wrote of the 'gay easy swing of Wood's manipulation of paint, free but never showy or slick, above all his ability to keep his canvas alive from corner to corner, yet leaving restful spaces for the eye'.

All but his most derivative pictures were invested with a spirit of radiant purity, guileless, gay, yet aware of the dark, confusing forces that shadow human life, expressed in terms of lyrical colour (especially yellows, which he believed artists had been prone to neglect) with occasional sombre overtones in blue-black seas and iron skies. It was, I believe, this quality that so much moved the perceptive visitors to this exhibition of almost the whole of Wood's life work. The exhibition also enjoyed a vast popular success: it had drawn some fifty thousand visitors before it closed.

The aura of legend around Kit Wood was due in part to his being an artist of rare talent, who had died tragically and young, who within a few years of beginning to paint had made a respected position in what was then the undisputed capital of the world of art and in particular had won the admiration of such as Picasso and Cocteau. But this aura was also due to his qualities as a man which had won him not only the admiration but the friendship of Picasso, Cocteau and other illustrious figures with whom, in those days, few British artists were even acquainted.

Nothing published about Wood expresses so movingly the sense of loss felt by his friends after his death as a paragraph in Max Jacob's *Souvenir*. 'Under those trees and by the rocks of the Bay of Douarnenez,' it runs:

> Kit lived for two months; his last, alas! Neither the October storms nor the horrible recollection of his death could deter me from returning there. The wind was howling against the door of his room. I did not dare enter nor cross the threshold which now seemed like a tomb . . . this landing which used to ring with our laughter! There on the table could no longer be seen the wet canvases, the brushes and pots of paint. No longer on top of the high wardrobe were the paintings which he had first completed in the space of a few hours with such vigour and which he surveyed with maybe melancholy. I shall never see again the larch tree beneath his window hiding the sea and the minute chapel which he loved to paint.

STANLEY WILLIAM HAYTER
b. 1901

Most artists who on account of parental pressures or other circumstances begin their working lives in a different profession regret the time thus spent as time wasted. Hayter is one of the rare exceptions. He early showed artistic inclinations, he had a painter for a father and other artistic antecedents, but nevertheless he devoted himself for almost ten years mainly to scientific research, painting and drawing only in his spare time. Rigorous training as a scientist, although its effect on his painting was relatively slight, was stylistically appreciable and contributed radically to the ease with which he mastered the intricacies of the various techniques of print-making and to his powers of lucid exposition, which have won him recognition as its greatest living teacher.

Such is his celebrity in this field, both as artist and teacher, that there is a disposition to overlook his achievement as a painter. Although it is primarily with this that the pages which follow are concerned, it is no more possible entirely to separate the two than it would, for instance, to treat of Turner's oils without reference to his watercolours.

Stanley William Hayter was born on 27 December 1901 in Hackney, the son of William Harry Hayter and his wife, Ellen Mercy, born Palmer, a school teacher, of a Lincolnshire family. His father was a painter whose family had produced several artists. The first to be recorded was Charles Hayter, who was born in 1761 and died in 1828, miniaturist, portrait draughtsman and writer, who published in 1813 a treatise on perspective and who was Professor of Perspective to Princess Charlotte. Two of his sons were painters — George the elder, who was appointed on her accession by Queen Victoria as her Portrait and History Painter, and John the younger, who was the great great-grandfather of Stanley William. Like many artists of his generation W.H. Hayter shared the recoil from academism; his sympathies were with the impressionists but he did not join the New English Art Club or any other groups, progressive or otherwise.

Stanley William Hayter began to paint in his father's studioin Croydon when he was fourteen, and no doubt following his father's example his earliest works were impressionistic studies in light and colour. At the time he did not aspire to be an artist but painted, as he has said, 'for the fun of it'. His enjoyment was enhanced by frequent visits with his father to the National Gallery. The artists he most admired were Uccello, Boltraffio, Zurbaran and El Greco.

In 1913 he won a scholarship to the Whitgift Middle School in Croydon, where he remained until 1917; his main preoccupations were scientific and he was given charge of the laboratory. After leaving school he worked in the research laboratory of the Mond Nickel Company while also working part-time for an honours degree in chemistry at King's College, London. The following year, after the Armistice, he left Mond Nickel to work full-time at King's, where, three years later, he took an honours degree in chemistry and geology. That year, 1921, was a significant one: besides graduating with honours he made his first prints. In the meanwhile he pursued research into organic sulphur compounds under Professor Samuel Smiles at King's. In 1922 he joined the Anglo-Iranian Oil Company with which he remained for three years, spent mostly in Abadan in the Persian Gulf, where his duties were both technical and administrative. He made visits to the north Arabian desert, to Basra, Baghdad, Ispahan and elsewhere. With his departure from London the academic life lost its hold upon him. In Abadan his hours of work were irregular, and during his hours of leisure he began to paint and draw, eventually doing so every day, making landscapes, seascapesn pictures of the refinery, as well as some hundred and fifty portrait drawings of his fellow workers. Painting and drawing gave him such intense delight that shortly after his arrival in the Persian Gulf he decided to resign on the completion of his contract at the end of 1925 and to become an artist. He accordingly returned (by way of Egypt) to London, where the paintings and drawings he had made in the Middle East were exhibited at the Anglo-Iranian headquarters.

The following April he went to Paris where, although he has travelled widely and frequently and retains his British nationality,

he has made his most constant place of residence, settling first in
the rue du Moulin Vert, his workroom adjoining Giacometti's.
For three months he attended the Académie Julian (studying
under Paul-Albert Laurens), a place to which innumerable British
and American students have gone to escape the academism of
their native schools. Hayter went there for the opposite reason.
Owing to the anti-academic sentiments of his father and his own
total lack of contact with the academic world, his attendance at
the relatively traditional Julian's was prompted mainly by
curiosity. The principal advantage he gained there was the lasting
friendship of a fellow student, Anthony Gross; also of Balthus.

It would seem that about this time Hayter received what in pious
circles would be termed a 'call' to make prints. His father had
made none and Hayter does not recall knowing anyone who did.
But at the age of sixteen or seventeen he became interested in
prints and bought two or three. As already noted, he
experimented in engraving while reading chemistry at King's; he
also visited Frank Short, the head of the school of print-making
at the Royal College of Art.

    In the course of the year he made a number of dry-points and
aquatints; several of these, together with some paintings, he
showed at the Salon d'Automne. Unlike many foreign students,
Hayter entered instantly into the art life of Paris, making a wide
variety of friends including Alexander Calder and Joseph Hecht
the engraver (who taught him the use of the burin). How rapidly
he mastered the art of draftsmanship is apparent, for instance, in
'Bottles', a soft-ground etching on zinc he made during his first
year in Paris.

The following year, 1927, when he was only twenty-six years old,
he took an audacious step that had decisive consequences not only
for Hayter himself but for the art of print-making: he established
a school, the celebrated Atelier 17. (Julian Trevelyan suggested
that it should be known as '17' after the number of the house it
occupied in the rue Campagne Première.)
    Like many another significant event it came about by chance.
Two women called at his studio one day (where he had installed
a printing press) and bought one of his prints. A week later they

Plate 1: CHRISTOPHER WOOD: *The Yellow Horse* (1930), oil on canvas, 20 × 24 in.

Plate 2: CHRISTOPHER WOOD: *The Yellow Man* (1930), oil on canvas, 20 × 24 in.

Plate 3: STANLEY WILLIAM HAYTER: *Chrysalis* (1970), oil, 64 × 51 in.

returned and asked him if he would teach them. He answered that he would not teach only two and that two more were needed. A week later they returned with the needed two, and Atelier 17 — though as yet unchristened — was in being.

So intense had Hayter's preoccupation with print-making become, and so eager was he to share his knowledge, that it was almost certain that, even had the original two ladies decided to pass by his door, something like Atelier 17 would have been established, sooner rather than later. 'I don't believe it was arrogance that made me start Atelier 17,' he said to me, 'it was that I was overwhelmed by the prevailing neglect of print-making, the failure to be aware of its immense potentialities. In short by the sense of *things to be done* with a new etching, a new engraving. In any case there was no question of a master and pupils relationship, but of one of harnessing talent in a collective venture, of "Let's see what's going to happen". I was convinced that in the course of working together new ideas would emerge.'

At least one feature of his method of teaching has a parallel in his approach to print-making and painting, namely his consciousness of the relation between intellect and inspiration or 'imagination-unconscious' as he prefers to call it. 'Starting from an arbitrary position,' he wrote, 'action is continued in consecutive stages, at first rational but later becoming intuitive, in the absence of a concrete project . . . The reason for this is that a plan can only be made of what is already known, but an experiment of this type can lead to matters completely unknown.'[1]

The art of Hayter has a classical clarity together with elements deriving from the unconscious. As a consequence of his association from 1929 in the surrealist movement, these elements came to play a larger part. (He helped to organize the Surrealist Exhibition held in London in 1936 and was represented in it.) They are more conspicuous in his prints than in his paintings, in such, for instance, as 'L'Apocalypse', an album of six plates published in 1932.

Artists in whose work the unconscious plays a part have had widely different approaches to it. De Chirico, for instance, wished to express the workings of the unconscious in poetic terms, and

---

[1] Chapter on 'Methods of Teaching in Atelier 17' in *New Ways of Gravure*, by S.W. Hayter, 1966.

Dali, with scientific accuracy, evolved what he called a 'spontaneous method of irrational knowledge based upon the interpretative-critical association of delirious phenomena'. Hayter's approach is that the unconscious is most effectively invoked through the process of work itself. The following gives an indication of his attitude:

> . . . the reciprocal effect of imagination/execution will generally decide the next stage in the development of the design. The first strokes on the plate set up a train of consequences like the ripples from a stone dropped into a still pond, and the factors of experience in the artist determine the number and succession of possible consequences offered to his choice . . . just as a master of chess can visualize from an opening a great number of moves to a mate while a beginner can see only a few immediate moves . . . In my own manner of working I would consider the selection among these consequences rather to be unconscious than deliberately conscious.[1]

Hayter believes, like many post-Freudian artists, in the participation of the unconscious in their work (though not all use the same term: 'chance' is that which Bacon, for instance, prefers), and that the simple act of beginning work with no more than a general plan may effectively invite it.

Hayter's procedures as a painter differ technically from those as an engraver, but their objects are the same. Instead of making, as on the plate, 'first strokes that set up a chain of consequences' he makes preliminary drawings, intended rather as tentative trials of ideas and sensations than complete in themselves. 'If a drawing is complete,' he said to me, discussing his methods, 'what need to say the same thing in paint?' The drawings are put aside and he begins to paint, the brushstrokes themselves providing clues as to how to proceed. He cannot visualize the finished painting when he first faces the virgin canvas: the painting develops as he goes along. He is moved to paint by his frequent impulse to work on a larger scale than the print conveniently allows; I have heard him quote Gauguin: 'A square metre of green is *greener* than a square centimetre.'

One all but invariable characteristic of the art of the surrealists and of the others who call on the unconscious is its lucidity. Considering the shadowy, elusive character of the unconscious, this lucidity I have never seen convincingly explained.

[1] *Op. cit.*, p. 279

In spite of Hayter's surrealist affinities and his friendship with Eluard (who wrote a poem about him, *Facile Proie*), Mirò, Tanguy and Arp, he was not, even in the 'thirties, as committed to surrealism as Dali or any of the other painters just named. Its effect for him was to strengthen his predilection for avoiding too detailed a plan when he begins a painting or a print in order to give full scope to brush or burin to open up possibilities, to invite ideas. It would be misleading, however, to suggest that there is a sharp distinction in his mind between the initial plan — product primarily of the intellect — and the role of the hand, in stimulating the imagination. Indeed he believes it erroneous to separate the functions of intellect, inspiration and execution, convinced that all three are integral parts of the creative act. It is, however, useful to the understanding of Hayter's work to emphasize the part played in it by the 'imagination-unconscious', in that it has nothing of the look of 'spontaneity' often to be associated with work in which this plays a crucial part: for Hayter's work, especially his prints, is distinguished by a look of calculated precision and finish that belies it. This is in part due to his mastery of line. The line is of course used by most painters and print-makers, but few, at least in our own day, have explored its possibilities so fully, in theory as well as practice.[1]

Atelier 17, through Hayter's eagerness to share his knowledge, his rare gifts of exposition, both verbal and written — his *New Ways of Gravure* and *About Prints* became classics when first published in 1949 and 1962 — was quickly recognized as possessing unique authority. The result of the collaboration between an inspired teacher and generations of pupils — drawn from all over the world — many of them with exceptional talent, has been to revivify the art of making prints: the discovery of new processes, of neglected potentialities in old ones and a new confidence in the print as a medium the equal of painting, drawing and sculpture. Hayter has been able to give technical help to, among others, Picasso, Mirò, Ernst, Masson, Tanguy and Giacometti, Pollock, Rothko and de Kooning and a number of other illustrious figures.

The first exhibitions of the work produced at Atelier 17 were

[1] *Op. cit.*, chapter on 'Theory of Line'

held at the Galerie Pierre in Paris and the Leicester Galleries in London in 1934.

On the outbreak of the Second World War Hayter returned to England, where he was one of a group engaged in research into camouflage, and a number of their findings were adopted by the British government. In 1940 he went to New York, setting up Atelier 17 at The New School of Social Research, moving it five years later to Greenwich Village, where it remained until 1955, although Hayter also re-established it in Paris in 1950.

So great was the impetus given by Hayter and Atelier 17 to the world-wide revival of gravure, and so extensive and detailed the writings of Hayter himself on a wide range of technical procedures, that his painting has suffered relative neglect. As recently as 1967 (and only ten years after his Whitechapel retrospective) when an exhibition of a hundred and fifty of his engravings — about a third of his production — was held at the Victoria and Albert Museum, and a smaller exhibition of his paintings at the Grosvenor Gallery, I remember hearing a person much concerned with the visual arts observe: 'I didn't know Hayter painted.'

It is accordingly worthwhile to give some account of his technical procedures as a painter, for they are almost as original and ingenious as those he employs as an engraver, although far less influential.

Hayter works at the same time on one, two or even three canvases of semi-absorbent linen placed upon the floor, the easel in his workroom being used only for the scrutiny of the completed paintings by himself and his friends. Round the canvas or canvases are placed the preliminary drawings. These are invariably tentative in order to leave open every possibility that the work may offer as it proceeds. Not all the possibilities, however, are suggested by the actual doing of it, for he makes use, too, of drawings made at the promptings of the unconscious, although corrected and developed by the conscious mind. It was his belief in the potentialities offered by the tapping of the unconscious that first drew him, in the late 'twenties, into the surrealist orbit. It was this belief, too, that led him to experiment briefly, in association with Miró and Masson, with a 'drip' technique; also with applying paint with string. Hayter told me, incidentally, that Jackson

Pollock had said to him that he was well aware of these experiments by Mirò and Masson, yet Hayter praised Pollock 'as a great originator all the same'.

The preliminary drawings are in fact a series: the earliest on the backs of envelopes or scrap paper, the later suggesting not the completed design but rather aspects, especially contrasting aspects, of it, some emphasizing, perhaps, red forms, others white, then yellow and so forth and yet others the black framework. These preliminary studies are sometimes in pencil or more usually made with one of his set of felt-tipped flow-master pens, each filled with a different coloured ink.

For medium he uses a thick whitish fluid of his own invention — 'mayonnaise' is what he calls it — an emulsion composed of white-of-egg, poppy oil, damar varnish and water — preserved in gallon wine bottles. The paint is mixed on a glass palette. Recently he has sometimes used acrylic and fluorescent colours.

He begins his painting with a linear arabesque suggested by one of the later drawings over, perhaps, a yellow ground. Two or three days later when it has dried he applies a colour wash mixed with 'mayonnaise', emphasizing the white forms. When this has dried a second arabesque is superimposed on the first, say in cadmium red. After two or three weeks of intensive work what he terms the oppositions and ambiguities of his (say) red and yellow images have crystallized and been enmeshed in a net of black enamel paint. The original images, part products of the unconscious, part of an acute consciousness, have been transmuted by trial and error, are then enlarged and animated, and Hayter realizes that his painting is complete.

They are in a sense abstractions (in what sense I will shortly attempt to establish) but they do not in any way resemble those works in which the artist takes a figurative image which he reduces to an abstract entity. With Hayter the process is, on the contrary, one of growth in complexity and in ambiguity — but in essence one of growth not of reduction.

For Hayter the prevailing practice of dividing art into 'abstract' or 'non-figurative and figurative' categories results in impoverishment.

> The term 'abstract' is unfortunate, [he writes] as it suggests the abstraction or removal of a part of experience — the attempt to show less of the

phenomenon and not more: the non-figurative label again suggests a pre-tension to deny to the observer the association or comparison of the work with latent images in his own brain — a pretension which it is impossible to sustain. . . . I would suggest that to replace the opposition of 'figurative' and 'abstract' it would be wiser to employ the contrast of specific and general.[1]

Although on casual reading Hayter seems to be concerned with terminology, he is concerned with it not for its own sake but as fostering the concept of an unreal and therefore deleterious dis-tinction between two points of emphasis in the work of art. He has pointed out, both in his writings and his teaching, that however uncompromisingly an abstract artist may attempt to exclude the phenomenal world, his work can in fact be no more abstract than the perception of it by the spectator, who will interpret any closed round as a head and a bifurcated form as a human figure. (His negative attitudes to abstraction caused him to decline the invi-tation by Mirò and Arp to join the Abstraction-Creation group.)

Later in the same paragraph he elucidates his own vision:

> The artist of the present is abstracting only in the sense of generalizing experience and not of restricting his field. It is of the climate of existence and not the weather; of motion rather than of that thing there and now fast; not the momentary appearance of the stream at one place but the sense of motion in liquid or air which (to mention one of my own preoccupations) links with the almost infinite implications of the medium in which we live.

A number of the most rigorously abstract painters habitually give their pictures titles, drawn from mythology, history, landscape and the like, to which they have no resemblance whatever; this for several reasons, the chief of which derives from the difficulty of titling works which can in fact represent nothing in the world of natural appearances. Many of Hayter's pictures look like abs-tracts, but their titles give clues to their subjects, such as — to take examples at random — 'Deliquesence' of 1935 (at the Tate) or 'Labyrinthe' of 1953. Without such clues the subjects of many of his pictures, both paintings and engravings, would be difficult to make out, and even with their guidance they remain, in certain cases, obscure. But for all that the titles are never arbitrary.

There is one particular theme, which he mentioned in the paragraph quoted from just now as one of his own preoccupa-tions, namely 'motion in liquid or air', to which he frequently

---

[1] *Op. cit.*, p. 285.

reverts. Preoccupation with movement has marked his work since the 'thirties but from 1951 conspicuously. In that year he bought a house at Alba, in the Ardèche. Near the house flows a small river, the Escoutay. Water, he realized with delight, especially sunlit water, was a subject that offered scope for his most intense preoccupation: brilliant colour, density, rhythmic movement, contrasts and ambiguities. (Hayter's love of water is not only aesthetic: he enjoys sailing and used to sail in the Mediterranean with Hillier and the Greek painter Varda.) In an interview in the Parisian periodical *Arts*, entitled 'Quel paysage avez-vous choisi?' he said in reply to a question about water: 'The trajectory of movement is more clearly defined in water. I can follow the laws of space better in the substance of water which is dense and at the same time fluid.' Asked whether this trajectory indicated pursuit he replied: 'Naturally, life is a pursuit. It is not the goal that impassions me but the pursuit towards a creation, the value of which is indifferent to me.' The interview was illustrated by one of the first of his pictures to be inspired by the neighbouring rivulet and was captioned 'Poissons de L'Escoutay'. It was painted in 1951 and bought the following year for the Tate. At the same time he began to use contrasting metallic colours (though he had experimented with these in 1929) in order to enable the spectator to obtain alternative views of the painting — a positive and a negative, so to say — according to the angle from which he looks at it. From that time onwards, as many of their titles remind us, he was profoundly fascinated by water, fish and aquatic birds. This fascination was also expressed in a number of engravings.

Hayter's painting and engraving form essentially a single art, although they do in one respect differ. The engravings give greater scope for what has been called the whiplash character of his line; for the expression of convulsive energy by lines of a rare purity and rhythmic harmony. These linear qualities are achieved more readily with the burin than the brush.

Although his outlook has remained consistent in his 'abstracting only in the sense of generalizing experience and not of restricting his field', he has become preoccupied less with mythology and more with water, landscape and atmosphere, represented with a serenity of spirit which seldom animates his earlier work. Of his many qualities perhaps the rarest is his power of transmuting some visual experience — ripples on a river suffused by sunlight, for instance — so that it is no longer specific but transformed into a general human experience, but, unlike most generalizing art, Hayter's is decisive, subtly arresting and exquisitely precise.

Hayter's complex and highly-charged imagination, scientific knowledge (and where engraving is concerned a technical command) unapproached by that of any other artist of his time, his capacity to learn continuously from nature, from the masters and even on occasion from relatively inexperienced students, have combined to create an art which is an enthralling combination of the ambiguous with the elegantly lucid. It is alive with a rhythmic vitality of its own. Two characteristic examples are 'Chrysalis' of 1970 and 'Cheminements' of 1971-2, Collection Musée d'Art Moderne de la Ville de Paris **(PLATES 3 and 4).**

Since Hayter is so precisely articulate a man it is proper to accord him the last word about his art. In the brief preface to the catalogue of the exhibition of his paintings at the Grosvenor Gallery in 1967 he wrote:

> All our perception reaches us in terms of rhythm; the slow turn of the seasons, the beat of the heart, the microcurrents of the mind, vibration of waves of sound and light. Hence our adoption of a language of rhythm is justified. Some acquaintance with the sciences, the language of mathematics, is of aid to the painter and still more the pursuit of irrational consequences. Since the sciences have abandoned the pretext of disinterested observation of nature as impossible and absurd and have undertaken the study of the fluid patterns of understanding in the mind, the artist and the scientist have found common ground.

Not all these statements are of universal and some not even of wide application, yet together they illuminate the sources and the character of Hayter's own art.

CERI RICHARDS
1903–71

As a man Ceri Richards was direct and accessible; as an artist he was elusive. The names Henry Moore, Francis Bacon, Pasmore and Freud evoke images clear-cut and solid, even when, as in the cases of the last two, the 'early' is sharply distinct from the 'later'. But the name Richards evokes no such image, but rather a succession of images — some concrete enough, others ambiguous — difficult to envisage as a single entity. Critics accordingly were apt to treat him with circumspection. Two of them, both perceptive and well-informed, reviewed his achievement in substantial appreciations with contrary emphases: one upon the relief constructions of the middle 'thirties and the 'Cathedrale engloutie' paintings begun in the later 'fifties,[1] the other upon the 'organic exuberance' of the work of the intervening years.[2] These differences are characteristic: the work of Richards is widely admired but there is little consensus of opinion about its essential character. This diversity is not difficult to account for. As the spectator surveys in his mind's eye the long succession of Richards's works in many media, he sees images close to nature, others so remote from nature as to border on the abstract, images that are massive and still, others in a state of violent animation; some of them of a rare originality and others directly absorbed from those of other artists (Richards was at times an avid borrower but far too honest a man to disguise what he borrowed in the least degree). In the face of such variety it is not surprising that critics, his fellow artists and others should focus rather on selected aspects of his work than on the diverse and elusive character of the whole. That there is an integral whole the spectator must, however imperfectly, be aware.

[1] *Ceri Richards* by David Thompson, 1963.
[2] Introduction by Robert Melville to catalogue of the Ceri Richards retrospective exhibition at the Marlborough New London Gallery, 1965.

Ceri Geraldus Richards was born on 3 June 1903, the eldest of the three children of Thomas Richards and his wife Sarah, born Jones, at Dunvant, a village about five miles to the west of Swansea. Thomas Richards was a rollerman in a small tinplate works nearby. Both he and his wife were Welsh-speaking, although they used many English words, and Welsh was Ceri's only language until he was five or six. Ceri's father was an avid reader of poetry, especially Welsh, who rehearsed poetry recitals and produced a number of English and Welsh plays, and was conductor of his Congregational Chapel's choirs. Ceri responded early and ardently to his father's passion for music and poetry and he became the chapel organist and played the piano at concerts. Music and poetry, especially music, remained lifelong passions often reflected in his art.

Ceri's first ambition was to become an engineering draughts-man, which stimulated an early preoccupation with drawing. Drawing came easily to him and won him prizes at local eis-teddfods. In the meanwhile he bought books on engineering draughtsmanship. He recalled his fascination when a mining engineer who lodged next door allowed him to watch him at work on plans; he was, he said, 'an embryo artist without knowing it'.

Although he was fascinated by drawing from childhood, he did not, all the same, think of his drawing as independent of en-gineering. It was otherwise with several of his friends: they did not presume to assess his talent, but they considered that, as he was always drawing, it was possible that he was intended to be an artist. Believing that he should at least be given a chance they took him to see the principal of the Swansea School of Art. In the meanwhile he himself had come to realize, and with intense excitement, that drawing was indeed his vocation and he became, in 1920, a full-time student at the school.

The relative belatedness of this realization — considering his early and persistent passion for drawing — was due to his en-vironment: his home and his country. If his had been a philistine home, it might, paradoxically, have come to him earlier. But it was a home in which interest in art was ardent — but it was directed exclusively at poetry, music and drama. For the Richards family these *were* art. Nor did his wider environment suggest otherwise. For a people so imaginative, so ready to communicate their emotions and ideas, so delighting in spectacles, the Welsh have produced surprisingly few painters of note and even these have drawn minimally upon Wales as material for their art. Richard Wilson, Augustus John and J.D. Innes have indeed painted Welsh landscape, but so have innumerable English artists; 'sketching tours' through 'Picturesque Wales' were frequent occurrences in the eighteenth and nineteenth centuries, taken, among many others, by Turner and Samuel Palmer. Wilson, John and Innes drew upon Wales only for a small minority of their subjects. David Jones — born in Kent, son of a Welsh printer and an English mother and a very infrequent visitor to Wales — in his illustrations to the Arthurian Legend is more expressive of the Celtic and the specifically Welsh spirit than anything by Wilson, John or Innes. (Several of them, incidentally, have intimations of the landscape at Capel-y-Ffin in Breconshire, where he studied with Eric Gill in the middle 'twenties.) But the Welsh subjects of these four illustrious Welsh artists afford not the merest shadow of Welsh men or women, or the environment, social and architectural, that they have created for themselves. In Welsh painting there is nothing remotely comparable to Dylan Thomas's *Under Milk Wood*, that portrait, so brilliant, so racy, so witty, so touching and so quintessentially Welsh, of the many-sided life of one region of Wales. The paucity of Welsh painting and the relative scarcity of painting of any kind, and therefore of concern with painting, almost everywhere in Wales, combined with the powerful presence of music, poetry and drama, explains Ceri Richards's belatedness in recognizing painting as his profession. While still at school he had met an artist who told him of the Glynn Vivian Art Gallery and the School of Art at Swansea, but the information seemed to strike no chord. Even when he had taken the decision to be an artist he 'did not know', to quote him, 'what great painting was'; he had made copies of reproductions of pictures by Landseer and Lucy Kemp-Welch. The teaching at the Swansea School of Art was arid, but the principal, W. Grant Murray, quickly discerned his talent and was instrumental, eleven years after he entered the school, in securing for Richards, at the Glynn Vivian Gallery, his first one-man exhibition. In 1923 he was one of a group of students who attended a summer school at Gregynog Hall, Newtown. This was conducted by Hugh Blaker (who advised

Gwendoline and Margaret Davies on the formation of their fine collection of paintings), Fred Urquhart and Robert Maynard.

The effect of this visit to Gregynog was transforming: 'I was staggered,' he said to me, 'by the sight of the superb impressionist and post-impressionist paintings hanging on the walls, and the bronzes by Rodin. I was fascinated most of all by Monet. Imagine their effect on someone who'd dreamed of great painting but had seen none at all.' He listened eagerly to the talks about the impressionists and their successors. He left Gregynog in an exhilarated state of mind.

The following year, 1924, he went to the Royal College of Art, remaining there until 1927. By this time his decision to be a painter was definite, but his preparation to enter the School of Painting was inadequate — there being offered at Swansea only 'a derelict painting course which', he said, 'none took' — so he was placed in the School of Design, from which the professor would not give him permission to transfer.

During his first term at the Royal College he was confused by the strangeness and variety of prevailing styles, having seen few important works later than the impressionist and the few post-impressionist paintings at Gregynog, and he had at first no one to guide him through the labyrinth. One of the college staff, Randolph Schwabe, made him aware of Picasso and lent him books, including Apollinaire's *Les Peintres Cubistes*, which he read with avidity, likewise Kandinsky's *Concerning the Spiritual in Art*.

The award of a prize for drawing afforded encouragement to a still confused student — confused not on account of any deficiency of perception but by the intensity of his response to painting of many kinds. While at the Royal College he attended evening classes at the Westminster School of Art, where he was taught life drawing by Bernard Meninsky.

In spite of the zest of his response to life in London and the years he spent in English-speaking society he remained very much a Welshman. He told me, for instance, that when my father (then principal of the College) criticized his work or addressed the students he used, as he listened, to translate his words into Welsh in order to have the fullest understanding of them.

Leaving the College in 1927, and needing to make his living, he was uncertain how to set about it. Determined, however, to remain in London, he resisted an attempt by one of his former professors to induce him to take a teaching post in Liverpool. Through the influence of the distinguished typographer Stanley Morison he was commissioned to illustrate a book *The Magic Horse*, stories from *The Arabian Nights*, which was published in 1929. The drawings were admired by a director of the London Press Exchange, where Richards was consequently employed as an illustrator for the year after he had left the Royal College.

At the College he had become friendly with Frances Clayton, a highly gifted fellow student, whose interests were in pottery and wall painting. They were married in 1929. The following year she gave him a copy of Florent Fels's book on Matisse, which heightened his interest in this painter's audacious use of colour and led to several portraits in the manner of the master. But by the early 'thirties he was — to use his own expression — 'trapped by Picasso', especially by his draughtsmanship. For Richards it was an inspiring encounter. In 1933 he began on a succession of relief constructions which he continued to make through the greater part of the decade.

Ceri Richards, who had been so hesitant in recognizing his vocation and who had already won admiration at the Royal College, especially as a figure draughtsman, made, in the finest of these constructions, works comparable with the best of his English contemporaries. The first few of them, in metal, he destroyed, but by 1934 the series of relief constructions in wood, with paper, paint or metal was under way. Twelve of them survive.

They were primarily inspired by the wooden reliefs with collage made by Picasso during the First World War, but the variety of media he used — wooden planks, pieces of newspaper and found objects — shows that he was aware not only of the cubists, but of the dadaists and their preference for discarded material previously regarded as unfit for inclusion in a work of art, and the eerie originality of some of them — the very original 'Variable Costerwoman' of 1938 for example — reflects his excited response to the London Surrealist Exhibition of 1936. (Henry Moore, from early days a consistent admirer of his work, described him to me a few years later as the finest draughtsman of his generation.) As always, the sources of his inspiration were undisguised. But as always, too, diverse influences were assimilated and fused into entities which were enamations of his own spirit alone. These constructions are more than personal: all are original creations of a rare order, and unlike anything else done in Britain at the time. In them Ceri Richards not only attained maturity but a high place among his contemporaries.

With the two last the series comes to an impressive culmination. These are 'The Variable Costerwoman' and 'Two Females' **(PLATE 5)**, the latter begun in 1937, briefly abandoned, and completed the following year, and acquired in 1959 by the Tate Gallery. The artist told us that it represents two contrasting concepts of the female form, the one virginal, the other reproductive or proliferating, the 'vegetable' or sexual aspect. Both these constructions owe much to surrealism. 'The Surrealist Exhibition of 1936 helped me to be aware of the mystery, even the "unreality" of ordinary things,' the artist said to me. 'It was there I saw Ernst's "Loplop presente une jeune fille", and the Tate's "Two Females" was made under its influence, and although less evidently by Picasso's "Femme en chemise" at the Tate — but then I'm always stirred by Picasso.' These constructions were admired by Mondrian and Arp, who were brought by Julian Trevelyan to Ceri's studio at 26 St Peter's Square, Hammersmith. Arp invited the artist to visit him in Paris; he felt honoured, but the visit never took place. 'I was not influenced,' he said, referring to surrealism, 'by the uncontrolled, subconscious element, though I felt it bracing and adventurous, giving a sense of "barriers down". But the metaphysical element enthralled me.' The value of 'some sort of accidental quality', he freely acknowledged, gave him a heightened awareness. He deeply admired Max Ernst's work of the 'twenties and 'thirties. It was owing to his example that he used to drop string onto a wet canvas, not with the intention of revealing the workings of his unconscious mind but of exploiting accident to suggest ideas. The painting in which this procedure was most fruitfully employed is his fine 'Paraphrase after Delacroix's Lion Hunt', a painting of 1944 in which the shapes made by the dropped string suggested this highly complex subject.

Confident that he was in no danger of becoming a disciple of any of them, he felt free to expose himself to a variety of movements, among them futurism. As his interest in the surrealists was not excited by their preoccupation with the unconscious, so his interest in the futurists was not excited (in spite of his abiding interest in engineering) by their obsession with machinery but by their sense of movement and glitter. However avid his interest in contemporary movements, Richards took from them precisely what he needed for the enrichment and diversification of his own vision and often disregarded those very elements which their practitioners regarded as crucial.

In the later 'thirties he began to achieve a quality not conspicuous in these two strange and majestic constructions, namely colour. 'Costerwoman', oil of 1939, for instance, reveals a muted harmony of many colours and tones that gives the fantastic figure a mysterious and compelling quality. 'Flowers', painted the previous year, although without the exuberant fantasy of 'Costerwoman', is marked by a similar muted harmony of colour and a composition strangely combining ambiguity with lucidity.

Of the many prevailing movements there is one that has not touched him. This is abstraction. 'Subject is a necessity,' he has flatly declared. 'Working through direct from visual facts to a more sensory counterpart of reality of my subject I hope that as I work I can create later on an intense metaphorical image for my subject.'[1] The effect of this procedure is often one of exuberant proliferation of the subject rather than abstraction from it. The remoteness of his art from an impulse so powerful and so pervasive that many people treat it as virtually synonymous with the basic 'progressive' movement of the century, accounts in part for the respectful ambiguity with which the art of Richards has often been treated by the critics. 'The Variable Costerwoman' and 'The Costerwoman', and other works with a similar theme, fantastic though they are, were based upon a number of drawings, some of them detailed, that he made of costers in the early 'thirties, in particular of a Pearly King and Pearly Queen whom he sought out and persuaded to sit for him. He was in fact circumspect about the effects of too exclusive a reliance on the imagination. The equilibrium between fact and imagination he assiduously maintained by close observation of his environment, by making still-lifes, portraits and an occasional landscape in which he intensively probed the complexities of natural form.

By the late 'thirties Richards had shown, in the constructions

[1] Artist's statement prefacing *Ceri Richards* by David Thompson, 1963.

and paintings referred to and a number of other works, rare imaginative power and technical mastery; although the significance of his achievement was not widely understood, it was recognized as a contribution to the modern movement that gathered momentum in Britain in the 'thirties. Besides being given the exhibition in Swansea he was invited to show with the Objective Abstraction Group at the Zwemmer Gallery in 1933, with the Surrealist Group in 1936 and 1937, and in the latter year he was elected a member of the London Group. Then came the war, which disrupted his creative life: he taught design and book illustration at the Cardiff Technical College from 1940 until 1944; he served in the Home Guard and worked for ten months on the land; in Cardiff he felt isolated and lonely and he was happy to be back in London in 1944 where he settled in 1945 at 54 West Side, Wandsworth Common, moving in 1958 to 12 Edith Grove in Chelsea where he lived for the rest of his life. 'But throughout the war,' he said, 'I painted between times.' He painted in fact to such good purpose that he was given his first London exhibition at the Leger Gallery in 1942 and a second — the first of nine at the Redfern Gallery — two years later.

The response of British artists to both world wars was ambivalent. When they were commissioned to represent aspects of them they made some of their finest works. When they were not commissioned, war was a subject which they mostly ignored. Although it had little appeal for Richards he showed his independence by making a few paintings about war in 1939 and 1940. Characteristically the theme he chose for the most important of them, 'Blossoms', had been germinating in his mind for several years. Indeed it was originally suggested by an incident in a previous war. 'Blossoms' (1940, oil) was bought by the Tate from his exhibition at the Leger Gallery and in response to a request for information about it he wrote (30 November 1958):

I remember the impression made on me when I read a description (brutally factual but observant) by a well-known Italian [Count Ciano] about an air attack on Abyssinians during that unprovoked war, and the title 'Target Blossom' stems from these impressions and later ones, when air bombardments broke out here in earnest. These paintings, obscurely maybe, make flowers into explosions or vice versa, aeroplanes look like insects, aggressive plants and an incendiary sun rises over the landscape.

Two related works in the same exhibition, an oil painting and a drawing, were more explicitly titled 'Target Blossom', and others 'Incendiaries in a Landscape' and 'Explosive Plant'. Another painting on a similar theme was 'Falling Forms (Incendiary Landscape)' made in 1944.

The big exhibition of Picasso and Matisse — both already long and ardently admired — held at the Victoria and Albert Museum shortly after the war, besides celebrating peace and his re-establishment in London, he found an exhilarating occasion, which launched him into a second period of intense creativity.

Musicians and musical instruments had been the subject of many of his pictures ever since he began to paint in the late 'twenties, but after the war he returned to them with enhanced delight, expressed, for instance, in 'Interior with Figures and Piano', 'Interior with Violinist and Pianist', both of 1946, in pen, ink and watercolour, and at the Tate, where there is besides, an oil, of four years later, 'Cold Light, Deep Shadow', also an interior with two figures seated by a piano, and 'Interior with Music by Albeniz' (1949, oil). This last clearly reflects, too, particularly in its colour, the effect of the renewed spell of response to Matisse resulting from the Picasso-Matisse exhibition. (From a distance it might almost be a Matisse, but the figures on the wall, related to those in his series of paintings, 'The Rape of the Sabines', begun two years earlier, identify its author.)

Such works as this and the closely related 'Red and Green Interior' (1951-3, oil) led naturally to one of his major achievements, the 'Cathedrale engloutie' series. Musical themes figure frequently in his art; indeed it is doubtful whether music has played so large a part in the work of any other painter of this century. He continued to play the piano and while he was a student at the Royal College he served as organist on Sunday mornings at the Catholic church in Wandsworth Bridge Road. Pianos, musical scores, feature constantly in his paintings and drawings and even in one of his constructions; he made, in the 'fifties, sequences on 'Homage to Beethoven' (Cardiff University College of Music and Drama), 'St Cecilia', and a 'Hammerklavier' theme (one of them is in the Glynn Vivian Gallery, Swansea). The 'Cathedrale engloutie' series, their culmination, begun in 1957, illustrates Debussy's music on the theme of the

Breton legend about the cathedral of Ys which had sunk into the sea but on calm days rose up to the tolling of bells and the chanting of priests, and then sank once more into the depths. The element of metaphor marks many of Richards's paintings, but nowhere, I think, more consistently than in this series. None, in effect, are remoter from the actual world. The sea is a constant element, in which violence contrasts with calm. In the study in chalk and wash of 1961 (The British Council) the rippled surface is explicit, but in most of the others, especially the sombre, impressive triptych, 'Augmentez Progressivement', of 1960-61, the spectator is aware chiefly of the conflict and interplay of powerful natural forces, though rose windows may be seen rising from the sea. Others afford glimpses of pointed gothic arches, of piano keyboards, of sea-worn bases of columns, of blocks of masonry, of the remote sea-bed. Of those alluding to masonry there is one at the Tate, entitled 'Circular Bases', an oil also completed in 1961. About it the artist wrote to the Gallery a letter that throws light on his method: 'These canvases are hardly completely complete — I never know how many manifestations of painting acts a canvas should have on it — there is always another shot at achieving the right number of marks for the right occasion.' This suggests that it is not only his obsession with successive themes that impels him to make series of paintings of them but the sense that each one represents a stage in the search for — to quote from the same letter — 'the successful mutation', the most precise, the most intense 'metaphorical image' of his subject. The 'Cathedrale engloutie' series is wide and various: in one of them, a gay relief construction and collage, of 1960, actual bells tinkle as they seem to float on the surface of a tranquil sea.

Richards's obsession with his subjects and the urge to explore them more and more deeply is often, then, expressed in successions of paintings, drawings or constructions. Another of these subjects was inspired by his admiration for the poetry of his fellow-countryman Dylan Thomas, whom he met only on one occasion when he visited his house at Laugharne in 1953, not long before his death. Richards enjoyed the meeting in spite of the tension between Thomas and his wife, who was critical of his impending visit to the United States — which resulted in his death — so that both were almost silent. Dylan Thomas's poetry inspired a number of paintings as well as a dropcloth, 'Homage to Dylan Thomas', made for the Memorial Reading organized by the *Sunday Times* and given at the Globe Theatre, London, on the evening of 24 January 1954. For this he made several designs, one of which is at the Tate; it is in crayon, ink, gouache and cut-paper collage. There are others at the Cecil Higgins Art Gallery, Bedford, and at the Glynn Vivian Art Gallery.

But the most impressive of the works inspired by Dylan Thomas, the last of three oil paintings illustrating his 'Do not go gentle into that Good Night' **(PLATE 6)**, was made two years later and also belongs to the Tate. Richards was asked by John Berger to make a drawing based upon this poem — written for his father — and he made several others. It was at the suggestion of Mr Berger, who admired the drawings, that he undertook the Tate's painting.

Although his admiration for Dylan Thomas's poetry was intense, and for this poem in particular, he was no more willing to interpret it literally than Blake was Dante's *Divine Comedy*. He did not accept the validity of the injunction to 'Rage, Rage against the dying of the light', which, he conceded, might be an injunction to protest, but he chose to interpret it instead as an affirmation of the futility of protest. His figure does not represent, as has been supposed, an old man, perhaps the poet's father, but, he declared, 'just man — the poet maybe', for the owl is holding a shroud (which in some preliminary drawings is covered with handwriting) and from this shroud the figure falls into the deep unknown. The man, already a corpse, does not — or cannot — rage as the poem commands but falls helplessly into the Night, while the owl flies off with his winding sheet. Richards has, I believe, painted nothing more moving than this. It is not surprising that he should have responded so ardently to Dylan Thomas, certain of whose poems, especially *Under Milk Wood*, express the Celtic spirit and give a memorable picture of Welsh life. Richards did not portray Welsh life, perhaps because he did not live his creative life in Wales, but in his work the Celtic spirit flowers as it does in the poetry of Thomas. The close affinity between painter and poet — of which the painter has been aware ever since he came to know the works of the poet — has often been remarked, in particular the preoccupation of both with what Richards terms 'the cycle of nature', birth, love and death, and their subtly exuberant imagery. Although the theme of birth, love and death had long preoccupied Richards, the series of paintings entitled 'The Cycle of Nature' (one, of 1944, is in The National Museum of Wales) — like so many of his works — was undertaken as a result of exterior prompting. In 1955 the Contemporary Art Society commissioned a number of artists to paint pictures representing 'The Seasons', which were shown at the Tate Gallery that year. Richards titled his contribution 'The Cycle of Nature', which he himself described as one of 'two attempts to include the sequence of all four seasons, Birth, Life, Death Cycle — if you like . . . interpreted figuratively and by the sonority of colour'. This painting, acquired by the Tate, was followed by others, of which one, wrote the artist, 'expresses this cycle more obscurely (maybe) and more interestingly by colour', and still others, of a more formal character, in the middle 'sixties. 'Underlying everything that Richards touches,' Bryan Robertson perceptively observed, 'is a tough, wide-eyed, almost innocent awareness of the fundamental elements of human existence', words particularly applicable to 'The Cycle of Nature'. Another series, but one which allowed less scope for the exploration of these deeper preoccupations, was promoted by a collective commission of a similar kind. In 1950 the Arts Council, by way of celebrating the Festival of Britain to be held the following year, commissioned sixty artists to make pictures for an exhibition 'Sixty Paintings for '51'. For his subject Richards chose 'Trafalgar Square'. After the painting (made the previous year) had been acquired by the Tate he wrote a letter about it to the Gallery (14 July 1959) which throws light on his procedures:

> I made numerous small notes from and away from the motif — in order to discover the inner themes, and also to feel the appearance of some sort of dynamic rhythm in design — to find ideas for shapes and spaces and movement — after involving myself in these ideograms for some time I then painted instinctively straight on to the large canvas [59 × 96] — colour was resolved as design created sense of reality. Everything changed in many ways, the all-over blueness, as well as being used spatially and achieving simplicity in the saturation quality of blue, was finally an expression of the all-over greyness of the Square itself.

Richards was an artist with an insight into a wide variety of subjects and for each he had an appropriate technical method. It would not be easy to think of works by the same artist more different than the constructions of the 'thirties, with their fantasy and detachment, their static, and at their best majestic character, and the series made in the following decade of the 'Rape of the Sabines', expressing a surging erotic violence. Yet each expresses an intrinsic aspect of a vision which, however various its manifestations, is fundamentally consistent.

It is a vision constantly preoccupied with both the natural world in itself and as interpreted by the poet and the musician. 'A subject,' he has stated on more than one occasion, 'is a necessity.' He has himself lucidly defined his procedures:

> Discovering a subject — which for me means one that haunts me — I make masses of the speediest notes to catch at all sorts of evocations. This foraging is stimulating because the speed of drawing spills out a spate of unpredictable images . . . I take advantage of all my experiences of events or objects, and to use the observational faculty in the graphism of drawing is of special delight and importance to me . . . Working through from visual facts to a more sensory counterpart of reality of my subject I hope that as I work I can create later on an intense metaphorical image for my subject. Temperamentally I feel attuned to the movement and dynamism that lies in nature and events, and in my forms I like to realize this subtlety and complexity.[1]

The work of Richards, in its remoteness from both realism and from the academic tradition, has long been accorded an honoured place among that of the avant-garde, but it is nevertheless, in spite of its profusion of features drawn from or suggested by that of other pioneering artists, independent of any movement. His place there is ambiguous. Few generalizations about art, especially about art as various as that which flourishes today, are valid and none is of universal application. It is however more often, far more often than not, characterized either by a total exclusion of natural phenomena or by a radical formalization. In short it is either abstract or reductive of natural phenomena to highly simplified 'equivalents'. The art of Richards is, of course, not abstract, and rarely one of simplification. On the contrary it reflects the artist's passion for the 'movement and dynamism that lies in nature and events' and as he works 'through from direct visual facts to a more sensory counterpart' of his subject, the subject grows in animation and complexity. The longer he pondered a subject the more

[1] *Op. cit.*

perceptive was he of its subtleties of form, and of its sheer profusion. Figures and objects blossomed under his hand (which does not mean, as in 'Do not go gentle into that good night', that the blossoms may not be sombre). It is the strange combination of ebullience, sparkle, animation and profuse complexity with obliqueness and metaphor, often obscure though never illegible, that makes the art of Richards one of the most elusive but one of the most fascinating of our time.

Just as Richards was attracted and exhilarated by a wide variety of masters, most conspicuously Matisse, Picasso, and Ernst, as well as by movements such as cubism, surrealism, futurism, so too was he proud to regard commissions as incentives to invention and exploration. In one instance at least he was prompted by a commission to achieve a noble simplicity, a quality not conspicuous in his work since the constructions of the 'thirties. (Certain of the 'Cycle of Nature' paintings of the 'sixties and some others appear to share this quality, but if their forms are sometimes simple their meaning rarely is.)

A commission to which he responded wholeheartedly was to design the tabernacle, reredos and two windows for the chapel of the Blessed Sacrament in Sir Frederick Gibberd's Catholic Cathedral of Christ the King in Liverpool, consecrated in 1967. This evoked a capacity, minimally apparent before, for classical design. All these, in particular the reredos and tabernacle, are austere and grand. Richards, like Moore when he was given his first ecclesiastical commission in 1943 to make his 'Madonna and Child' for St Matthew's Church, Northampton, was greatly concerned to create figures which, without sacrifice of any conviction of his own, would be acceptable to the congregation. It was not Richards's first commission of the kind, which was to paint an altar frontal for the chapel of St Edmund Hall, Oxford, but the Liverpool commission was a far more ambitious undertaking. He combined and brought into being a tabernacle, reredos and a pair of windows of rare beauty — and in startling contrast to the garish shoddiness so widely prevailing in ecclesiastical art. (There are, of course, other notable exceptions, in the cathedrals of Coventry, Chichester, and Westminster, as well as Liverpool itself, Campion Hall, Oxford, St Aidan's Church, East Acton, and elsewhere.) In another branch of ecclesiastical art, the design of vestments for Chichester Cathedral, he has been free to work in his accustomed animated, scintillating style. Yet they reflect a glowing purity appropriate to the sacred office of their wearers.

Much of his later work shows a greater simplicity of both form and colour, expressing, among other themes, equilibrium or tension between conflicting or contrasting entities: stability and flux, flowering and decay, the male and the female, or the seasons.

The pervasive metaphor, and the ambiguity of much of Richards's work, which often calls for close scrutiny if its themes are to be fully understood, the zestful delight in complexity and exuberant proliferation evident in much of it, at a time when a predominent aim of many of the most serious artists active today is the reduction of natural phenomena and of ideas to their simplest 'equivalents', place it outside the main current of creative art. But it continues to command the same admiration that it won in the 'thirties and, in addition, it becomes ever more widely understood and more intensely enjoyed. The achievement of Richards is formidable in its volume and variety: besides numerous paintings and innumerable drawings, and many prints and book illustrations, he has made mural decorations, in 1937 and 1954, for ships of the Orient Line, for the Shakespeare Festival in 1965 and for the Europa Hotel, London in 1951, costumes and décor for the English Opera Group's productions, Berkeley's *Ruth* in 1956 and two years later for Britten's *Noyes Fludde* at Aldeburgh.

The work of Richards is a compelling harmony of qualities various and even, in other contexts, contrary: metaphor and reality; lucidity of form and its exuberant proliferation — A Cycle of Nature ardently explored, gravely meditated, and ambiguously recreated for the delight of the observant eye.

On 6 July 1971 Ceri and Frances came to a dinner given by our son-in-law and daughter to celebrate my imminent birthday. I never remembered him in higher spirits: he charmed his fellow guests with his wise, gentle humour accompanied by his light, crackling laughter. Saying goodbye he invited us to dinner 'any time'. I had to explain that we were going shortly to New York, remaining until Christmas. There, in November, opening a London *Times* in a club, I was grieved to read of Ceri's death.

It appeared that, returning from a holiday in September, he was disturbed by the spread of weeds in the garden, rooted out a number of them, and had a heart attack. This made him depressed and listless. He had been engaged on a series of seven lithographs, illustrating Roberto Sanesi's *Journey towards the North*, to be published in Milan in Italian and English. (Sanesi, an ardent admirer, was also making a catalogue of his prints.) Ceri's state of mind had caused him to work only intermittently. On 9 November Frances encouraged him to make the last plate of the series. This he did — and shortly afterwards died from another heart attack on the same day as Dylan Thomas had died, the fellow-countryman whom he so greatly admired and with whom he had so much in common.

The following passage from *The Forge of the Solstice* by Ceri's friend, also a fellow countryman, the poet Vernon Watkins, was prompted by his work:

Another, curbing vigour on his page
To movement, makes the abounding life his own
And rhythmic finds in a discordant age,
Singing like living fountains sprung from stone,
Those unifying harmonies of line
Torn from creative nature . . .
Love gives their art a body in which thought
Draws, not from time but wisdom, till it bend
The solstice like a bow, and bring time round
White with young stars, quick from the forge they have found.

GRAHAM SUTHERLAND
born 1903

One of the most conspicuous differences between artists is the way in which they discover the language best suited to express their imagination, or their observation of nature. Riley, for instance, in spite of the talent evident in her early life drawings, remained a frustrated searcher after a language until her ideas were clarified, largely by constant discussion and study with a learned and highly intelligent mentor. Houthuesen, Collins, Colquhoun and Freud made the discovery early in their careers.

However different his earliest engravings from the paintings of his maturity, Sutherland belongs in essence to the second category, in that there is a steady consistency in his evolution. Steadiness and consistency were not inconsistent with moments of exhilarating discovery, of new subjects — one of particular importance — or of his discarding one medium in favour of another. From the time — it would hardly be an exaggeration to say from the moment — of this discovery, he formed a vision of his subject which, whatever he absorbed from other painters, was unmistakably his own, and so remained. His subject, too, in characteristically logical fashion, became more varied and wide-ranging, although reaching, at a certain time, a point when, in essentials, it changed little.

Graham Vivian Sutherland was born in South London on 24 August 1903, the elder son of George H.V. Sutherland, a Civil Servant, and his wife Elsie. He went to preparatory school in Sutton, Surrey, in 1912 and two years later to Epsom College, where he remained until 1919, spending his holidays at Merton Park, Surrey, and Rustington, Sussex. After leaving Epsom College he served as an apprentice in the engineering branch of the Midland Railway works at Derby. During the year he spent there he became convinced that he had no vocation for engineering; he had already begun to draw and to feel the first stirring of artistic aspiration. Accordingly he returned to London in 1921 and became a student at Goldsmiths' College School of Art. During his five years there he worked with a zest often denied to the student who has done sufficiently well in the art classes at school to go, as a matter of course, to a college of art; he drew diligently, drawing from casts and from the life. Owing, perhaps, to the influence of two highly respected teachers of this subject, Malcolm Osborne and Stanley Anderson, engraving became, and for several years remained, his chosen medium. The aptitude he showed attracted the notice of the eminent engraver F.L. Griggs, who befriended him and fostered his enthusiasm for an artist who became the principal influence over his early work, Samuel Palmer.

It is not surprising that Sutherland should have regarded engraving as his chosen medium, for it is difficult to believe that anything so assured and accomplished as his 'Barn Interior', a drypoint, was the work of a student; it was in fact made the year after he went to Goldsmiths'. By 1925 Palmer's influence was ascendent, as is apparent from etchings such as 'Peckham Wood' and 'Cray Fields' (both made that year) and 'St Mary Hatch' and 'Lammas' (the next), in which the romantic pastoral spirit of Palmer and his friends at Shoreham is vividly recalled. But by 1930, in another etching, 'Pastoral', there is a change of style which clearly anticipates his future course. The earlier prints referred to are sharply and minutely linear, but 'Pastoral' is broader in treatment and seen at a distance could easily be mistaken for a wash drawing.

The following year the market for etchings collapsed as a result of the calamitous 'slump' in the United States, and the career that had won him high respect came to a sudden end — he had held two exhibitions, in 1925 and 1928, at the XXI Gallery, had taught engraving at the Chelsea School of Art since 1926 (where he remained until 1940, teaching, from 1935, composition and book illustration). Even though he had begun to think that he had 'said his say' as an engraver (he had made, since 1923, some thirty etchings) and to feel the need to liberate himself from the per-vasive influence of Samuel Palmer, the abrupt ending of a career which had achieved much and promised more was an em-barrassment, more especially as he had been married not long before, in 1927, to Kathleen Frances Barry, who had been a fellow-student at Goldsmiths', and had taken a house at Far-ningham in Kent. Accordingly he accepted, during the 'thirties, commissions to design posters from Shell-Mex, the London Passenger Transport Board and the Post Office. In the meanwhile he was increasingly attracted by the wider possibilities offered by painting over engraving and, by 1932, if not a little earlier, he began to paint, making landscapes in Cornwall and Dorset. Later on his perception was enhanced by new surroundings, but these early landscapes appear to have been destroyed, except 'Dorset Farm' (1932, oil on hardboard), a well-composed, sober but conventional work, which would be unlikely to be recognized as by Sutherland even by someone familiar with his painting. But before long his painting was marked by a greater fluency. It was also — not unnaturally during this period — marked by echoes of the work of other painters whom he admired, 'Men-an-Tol' (1931, pen and watercolour), by that of Paul Nash, whose example did much to emancipate him from the conventional tradition to which 'Dorset Farm' unequivocally belongs; and some of his fallen trees derive, though more remotely, from Henry Moore's reclining figures.

By the middle of the decade he was on the way to evolving his own pictorial language. One of the most conspicuous and permanent features of it was aptly described, in the first book[1] on Sutherland, by Edward Sackville-West. Writing of 'the linear exactitude which — all appearances to the contrary — in fact supplies the structure of all his mature paintings', he continues, 'you will observe that a discreet but tough thread of black cotton stitches the design . . . ' and he later refers to darker passages as 'made of that same black thread, rolled into a mass and pulled out again to define . . . the centre of visual interest'. The black thread, which, viewed casually, may appear to sag, to wander, even aimlessly, in fact holds together the various elements in his designs. In spite of the sunset radiance of his earlier paintings and the brightness of the later, Sutherland, like Moore and Collins, for example, is a linear painter as distinct from, say, Francis Bacon, who is a 'painterly' one.

During the early 'thirties he still had not quite found his way.

[1] Penguin *Modern Painters*, 1943.

It was in 1934 that, wishing finally to free himself from the still-lingering influence of Palmer, difficult as long as he lived in Kent, he decided to visit the most westerly part of Wales and wandered along 'the arms of land which embrace the great area of St Bride's Bay' in Pembrokeshire. The quotation comes from a long letter that he wrote to an early friend and patron Colin Anderson. It is an important letter for our understanding of Sutherland. 'It was in this country that I began to learn painting,' he forthrightly declared. To quote from another passage, which reads like a description of some of his finest landscapes,

'I wish I could give you some idea of the exultant strangeness of this place . . . the left bank as we see it is all dark — an impenetrable damp green gloom of woods which run down to the edge of low blackish moss-covered cliffs — it is all dark save where the mossy lanes (two each side) which dive down to the opening, admit the sun, hinged, as it were, to the top of the trees, from where its rays, precipitating new colours, turn the red cliffs of the righthand bank to tones of fire. Do you remember the rock in Blake's Newton drawing? . . . Cattle crouch among the dark gorse. The mind wanders from the contemplation of the living to their dead ghosts. It is no uncommon sight to see a horse's skull or horns of cattle lying bleached on the sand . . .' [This 'sketchbook' throws light upon both his methods and his way of seeing.] 'At first I attempted to make pictures on the spot. But I soon gave this up. It became my habit to walk through, and soak myself in the country. At times I would make small sketches of ideas on the backs of envelopes, and in a small sketch book, or I would make drawings from nature of forms which interested me and which I might otherwise forget . . . sometimes . . . I would lie on the warm shore until my eye, becoming rivetted to some sea-eroded rocks, would notice that they were precisely reproducing, in miniature, the forms of the inland hills'.[1]

The sentences quoted evoke his forms and their radiant but sombre sunset illumination; they show how he worked from notes made on the spot, especially of individual objects, and something of the way in which he used small objects, closely observed, to represent greater.

Also he refers to fields 'each with a spear of rock at its centre'. This too is significant, for although spearlike forms are not common in the work of his early maturity, they quickly became so, and whether in the form of palm-leaves, horns, thistles, thorns and the like, the spear form occurs in numerous works. To West Wales where he 'began to learn painting' (to which he applied himself

[1] Published under the title of 'A Welsh Sketchbook' in *Horizon*, April, 1942.

intensively from 1933) he returned during his vacations from Chelsea for the five following years, only ceasing with the outbreak of war.

Sutherland differs from painters such as Lowry or Stanley Spencer, who drew inspiration from their native environment or from wherever they have made their home, as being most strongly affected by the elements of strangeness he discovers in the unfamiliar. He never settled in Wales, and accordingly these elements affected him strongly, more especially as he visited different parts of the region, among others, Dale, Solva, St David's and Haverfordwest. Kent, on the other hand, where he made his home as long as he remained in Britain, moving from Farningham to Eynsford in 1931 and to Trottiscliffe five years later, had little effect upon his painting, apart from that, dwindling in any case, inherited from his early discipleship of Samuel Palmer.

By the late 'thirties he had found a way, impressively his own, of expressing his perception of the strangeness of nature. To this time belong several of his most memorable paintings, among them 'Entrance to Lane' (1939, oil, Tate Gallery), 'Gorse on Sea Wall' (same date and medium), 'Green Tree Farm', 'Interior of Wood' (1939, pen and watercolour,) and 'Small Boulder' (1940, gouache), which show how effective was his power of observing something small and depicting it as the 'equivalent' — to use a favourite expression of the artist's — of something far larger in scale.

No sooner, however, had he attained the stature as a landscape painter shown by these and a number of other works than, like that of almost everyone else, his life was transformed by the war, and from 1940 until 1944 his employment as a war artist occupied the greater part of his time.

Sutherland has shown from time to time a predilection for the sinister, even the ferocious. One of the finest of all his drawings, 'Blasted Oak' (1941, pen and wash), resembles as much an open-jawed ravening beast of prey as a damaged tree. There is no ferocity of outlook evident in any of his war pictures, but the scenes of devastation he often chose to depict themselves gave wide scope for this predilection, which also shows itself in subjects of a quite different kind, such as his several 'furnaces' which also are pervaded by an infernal aura. This, in representations of almost any aspect of the most devastating war in history, was all but inevitable. War paintings evoked a feature in the art of Sutherland scarcely evident before, namely preoccupation with his fellow-men. In several of the early etchings of Palmeresque themes, such as 'St Mary Hatch' and 'Lammas', a Palmeresque figure or two wanders; but their absence would hardly be noticed. They are mere adjuncts to romantic pastoral scenes. When human beings figure in the landscape of the 'thirties (which they rarely do) they are trivial, such as the man running in 'Road and Hills in Setting Sun' (1938, oil), who is a mere accent. A more significant, though perhaps unconscious, indication of his interest is apparent in the human qualities in some of the studies, for instance 'Green Tree Farm', but far more clearly in 'Association of Oaks' (1940, gouache) in which two trees closely resemble sparring boxers. These examples are far from isolated. There are also works in which landscape features resemble birds or animals or insects. In 'Landscape with Mounds' (1943, pen and wash) the mound in the foreground might be taken for a strange sitting bird, but the resemblance of 'Blasted Oak', already mentioned, to a ferocious animal, is unmistakable.

Sutherland's work as a war artist began the liberation of his urge to depict not only men and women but from time to time animals, birds and insects. But it only began it: the figures in the war pictures are as anonymous as figures in a crowd. The head in 'Man and Fields' (1944, chalk and watercolour) and 'Woman in a Garden' (1945, pen, chalk and gouache) are unconvincing and even a little absurd. The focus on animate life, later to become so lucid, was curiously slow to develop, especially in an artist generally very conscious of his aims, as his *Welsh Notebook* and other writings and interviews show. But however subordinate and anonymous the human being in the war pictures, his destructiveness is shown with a dramatic power; they have, as Eric Newton wrote while they were actually in progress, 'a wild, crucified poignancy'. The knowledge gained during his apprenticeship at Derby gave Sutherland a particular interest in devastated machinery. The finest of his machines are those sharply focussed. 'He is best,' as James Thrall Soby observed, 'when he peers rather than scans.' The virtual compulsion to portray a wide variety of subjects and at relatively high speed expanded his field of interest and increased his technical resources. Although he worked fast, it was never on the spot but, like his earlier work, always from notes and memory. And unlike many other painters, who can impose their particular way of seeing on whatever happens to be at hand (though they may prefer something else), Sutherland has to seek out a particular subject, or else to come upon it unexpectedly, to set in motion the creative process.

Service as a war artist resulted in a number of memorable works, but in several respects its benefits were long-term, for the ending of the war left him somewhat at a loss. The element of urgency, the obligation to record without time for reflection, proved — as it did with some other war artists — disturbing in its immediate after-effects. (I recall Paul Nash, in the same situation, describing himself as 'a war artist without a war'.) Sutherland continued to paint landscapes but compared with the earlier they seem summary and the outcome of experience less deeply felt. In a number of his thistle and horn paintings and drawings there were overtones of cruelty. In these years he had been made uncertain of his direction, not only by the war but by his increasing attraction to the art of the continent. Since 1947 — when he visited the Picasso Museum at Antibes — he has spent a part of every year in the South of France (and since 1956 he has lived there almost entirely, though keeping his house at Trottiscliffe).

Many of his paintings of the later 'forties show this temporary loss of direction by their formlessness, indeed their lack of significance of any kind. To take examples, 'Estuary with Rocks' (1946, gouache, British Council), or 'Chimère I' (1946, oil) and 'Chimère II' (1946-7, oil) are confused in composition and unconvincing in theme. But an artist should not be judged by his failures. At the same time he painted a number of thorn trees which combined complexity and harmony in their design, brilliance in colour, and which sparkle with energy — paintings which can bear long scrutiny. Of these, which number among his finest works, 'Thorn Tree' (1945, oil) and 'Thorn Trees' (1946, oil, British Council) are outstanding.

Even by 1950 he had not entirely recovered from the effects of his service as a war artist and the relatively sudden impact of the art of the continent. His first visit to Paris did not take place until

1944, considerably later in life than most of his artist contemporaries, and the impact of continental art was accordingly more deeply felt. Moore and Bacon had not yet won world acclaim (indeed Bacon painted his first serious work only that year) nor had British art of both the nineteenth and twentieth centuries become the subject of international interest, even in Paris, the capital city least responsive to its qualities. On the contrary, it was regarded, not least by many British artists and critics, as provincial and even negligible. In the 'forties and 'fifties it was a far more disturbing experience for a British artist to settle in a country which was still generally considered to be the creative centre of Western art than it would be today.

This, following the effects of the war, accounts, I believe, at least in part, for the disparate quality of his creation. Even as late as 1950 he could paint 'Armoured Form' (oil), a confused pastiche of de Chirico, and the fine 'Standing Form against a Hedge' (oil, Arts Council), a massive enigmatic 'presence' — to use another of the artist's favourite expressions — standing against a background of bougainvillea. A more elaborate and complex and still more impressive painting, surely one of his very best, is 'Three Standing Forms in a Garden' (1952, oil), composed from studies of roots, trees and hanging maize. Paintings such as these two — in the opinion of the present writer — constitute the outstanding expressions of the artist's power of creating forms, part primitive, part sophisticated, based, however remotely, on objects observed.

Two developments mark his later work, a brightening of colour and, as already noted, preoccupation with animate life. The glowing yet sombre colour of his Pembrokeshire and war pictures has been replaced by colour of a lucid brilliance, due in part, no doubt, to residence in a region that is clear-aired and sunlit. On occasion he has created compositions of an extraordinary though highly disciplined complexity, such for instance as 'Variation on a Theme II' (1953, oil) or, to an only slightly lesser degree, 'Thorn Cross' (1954, oil, Galerie des 20 Jahrhunderts, Berlin).

It was in the 'forties that the intimations, usually tentative or oblique, of Sutherland's interest in the figure became explicit. This might eventually have happened as a consequence of innate impulse, but, as so often in the lives of artists, changes are precipitated by external circumstance. In this decade he accepted

Plate 4: STANLEY WILLIAM HAYTER: *Cheminements* (1971-2), oil,
137⅘ × 118 in.

Plate 5: CERI RICHARDS: *Two Females* (1937-8), painted wooden relief
construction with strip brass and two brass ornaments nailed on, $63 \times 46 \times 3\frac{1}{2}$ in.

Plate 6: CERI RICHARDS: '*Do not go gentle into that good night*' (1956), oil on canvas, 42 × 28 in.

Plate 7: GRAHAM SUTHERLAND: *Tree with G-shaped form* (1972), oil and
gouache, 19⅝ × 15¾ in.

commissions to portray figures — figures both divine and human.

The divine came first. In 1944 he was invited by Canon Walter Hussey — the highly discriminating patron of the arts — to paint an 'Agony in the Garden' for St Matthew's Church, Northampton, for which he had commissioned Henry Moore to carve a 'Madonna and Child'. Sutherland preferred the Crucifixion and Canon Hussey agreed. Between 1954 and 1957 he designed an immense tapestry, representing 'Christ in Glory in the Tetramorph', for the new Coventry Cathedral, and in 1960 he accepted the invitation of another of the few enlightened patrons of ecclesiastical art, Father James Ethrington, to paint a Crucifixion for St Aidan's Catholic Church, East Acton, London.

The execution of these three commissions caused him more stressful self-questioning than any other of his works. Before undertaking the first of them he had painted natural phenomena, creating 'equivalents' for these in response to their action on his imagination. His work as a war artist, he realized, must constitute a record of actual scenes, but although he would have preferred longer periods of contemplation than circumstances allowed, they caused him no undue anxiety. In brief he had been, although not in quite the sense in which Constable used the term, a 'natural painter', not associated with any group or movement; clearly a 'contemporary' but untouched, for instance, by such influential movements as cubism or surrealism.

In accepting commissions to represent precise traditional subjects, already represented, century after century, by generations of painters and sculptors, he knew that he would be submitting himself to severe limitations; he knew, too, that his images were intended for specific places and specific purposes. And of course he was painfully aware of the growing, indeed all but absolute, alienation of the churches from serious art.

Before beginning work on all three undertakings he studied the portrayals of the subjects by a number of the old masters and made studies derived from them, in order, as he told a friend, 'to eliminate them from his mind' and leave him the freer of traditional conventions to reinterpret them as though seen for the first time by an artist of the twentieth century.

All three were formidable tasks and Sutherland achieved them in a manner unmistakably his own, though in each case echoes of earlier masters are easy to identify: in both the Northampton and Acton paintings the spirit of Grünewald, for instance, is present, and the former reveals memories of the de Maistre 'Crucifixion' of 1942-4 in the Leicester Museum, of which, indeed, he took some photographs. All three are images not easily forgotten. In the handling of undertakings so formidable it is perhaps inevitable that there should be features which invite criticism. In both the Northampton and Acton Crucifixions the head of Christ, without a neck, grows out of the upper part of his chest, leaving exposed, where the neck should be, a functionless curving ridge of flesh. In the Coventry tapestry the lower part of Christ's garment forms an almost featureless oval that distracts the spectator's attention from more significant features. This and other weaknesses are perhaps due in part to the great disparity in scale between the preliminary study and the completed tapestry. But how easy to discover weaknesses in the treatment of subjects which present such manifold difficulties! It is more relevant to be grateful to the authorities concerned that they commissioned an artist of Sutherland's gifts and gave him an almost entirely free hand, thereby proclaiming — though not, of course, for the first time — that the present alienation of the serious artist and the churches is not inevitable.

Sutherland's portrayals of mortals were less complex. In the middle 'forties he painted a few heads, lacking in sense of character, of anatomical structure, and more serious still, of evident purpose. Then there occurred the external circumstance that made him a painter of portraits. In 1948 he received an invitation from Somerset Maugham, whom he had met occasionally at St Jean Cap Ferrat, and who enjoyed having himself painted and drawn, to paint his portrait. The invitation was eagerly accepted. It is rare that a painter of portraits does not make his first portrait until he is in his middle forties and the portrait of Maugham was accordingly an adventure. 'As a person sits so I tend to accept him,' Sutherland has written, and instead of imposing a posture on his sitter he waits until he or she assumes, perhaps unconsciously, the one most revealing of character.

The portrait was completed in the March of the following year, after some two months' work, Maugham giving him about ten consecutive sittings of an hour a day, the artist making only drawings. While at work on the definitive portrait he also made a few oil studies from the sitter. (The portrait was presented by Maugham to his daughter Lady John Hope, who two years later presented it to the Tate.)

Painters have criticized the 'Maugham' on the grounds that the emphatic modelling and the strong colour of the clothing distract interest from the head and that the narrowness of the stool on which he sits gives the whole a top-heavy look. There is some justification for the first, but the very narrowness of the stool surely draws the spectator's attention upwards to the prime focus of interest, the face. Unlike landscape or still-life, portraiture has a primary function: to achieve likeness. In his 'Maugham' Sutherland has achieved a searching likeness: bone structure, expression and habitual pose are precisely as those who knew him remember them. It is, incidentally, something of a feat, even for an experienced painter, as a first portrait.

His second portrait, 'Lord Beaverbrook' (the Beaverbrook Foundation, Fredericton, New Brunswick, Canada), is less penetrating as a likeness and somewhat coarse in execution, but these shortcomings are due, at least in part, to the sitter: unlike Maugham, Beaverbrook did not particularly care for being painted or drawn, and he was physically restless and, when he sat, he simply slumped into his chair. Sutherland, true to his belief that he should accept the pose which the sitter assumed, accepted this. But the difference in characterization constitutes the basic difference between these two portraits: Beaverbrook wears a characteristic but transitory expression, one, merely, of many. No portrait can reveal the whole of a man's nature, but Maugham's portrait reveals much more about him; there is something basic about his expression. Beaverbrook, incidentally, liked the Maugham portrait and when the staff of his newspapers wished to present him with his own portrait on his seventy-fifth birthday, he asked Sutherland to undertake it. It is my belief — having known all three subjects — that Sutherland's most searching portrait is one of the two he made of the Hon. Edward Sackville-West, namely the oil, made in 1953-4. (The smaller preparatory version, also oil, in the City Art Gallery, Birmingham, completed from memory, in 1959, is marred by the exaggerated depth of the skull and the clumsy shoulders.) But the first-mentioned is a portrait of rare insight and, were it hung between the Beaverbrook and the Maugham, it would highlight the coarseness of the first and give the second, fine though it is, a slightly over-emphatic, almost caricatural look. Sackville-West's intellectual distinction, sensibility, pessimistic outlook on life, absence of personal ambition and even the withdrawal, over the immediately preceding years, from social life and from a number of his friends — all are shown with a lucid sympathy. It is surely an impressive portrait and, for anyone who had the privilege of friendship with its subject, a very moving one.

Sutherland has painted since then a number of portraits which show a high degree of perception, but none, I suspect, with such understanding of his subject as his 'Sackville-West', although in offering this opinion it is right to say that several of the subjects of his later portraits are unknown to me.

A fine example of his increasing preoccupation with animals is 'Toad II' (1958-9, oil), where the creature's character is observed with the same perception as the artist's human subjects.

Since the early 'sixties his subjects have undergone no radical change or extension. Rocks, thornlike forms, the occasional portrait, the animal, the bird, the still-life, but above all, landscape, have remained his continuing preoccupations. Their treatment, however, has undergone conspicuous changes. Instead of being held together by the tough thread of black cotton that Sackville-West wrote of they are looser in construction; the sharp outline tends to be replaced by one that is broken and easy, suggesting rather than defining. More radical still is the change in colour. With many exceptions — the 'Thorn Trees' earlier referred to for one — the glowing sombreness that pervaded the painter's earlier work has been replaced by a greatly heightened palette. These changes can be observed, for instance, by comparing such works as 'Study Landscape 1968' (gouache and indian ink) with several of the Pembrokeshire landscapes made thirty years before, which in subject it closely resembles, but which, in drawing and colour, is very different indeed.

But Pembrokeshire, the place where he 'began to learn painting', has remained a source of inspiration — where landscape is concerned the principal source, as exemplified, for example, by

'Tree with G-shaped form' **(PLATE 7)**. Especially since the late 'sixties, he has returned to Wales two or three times a year, twice spending Christmas there; indeed during his relatively infrequent visits to Britain Wales has seen him more often than Trottiscliffe.

Sutherland has moved from delicate, highly proficient discipleship of Palmer to the exhilarating revelation of West Wales, through the disturbing yet fruitful experience of the war, through a period of experiment and reassessment resulting from this and the impact of continental art, and emerged as an occasional portrait painter of exceptional insight at his best but, above all, as a landscape painter whose work has much in common with that of his inspired Pembrokeshire years, yet without its sombre overtones, lighter in tone and touch.

ALBERT HOUTHUESEN
born 1903

The frailty of his health has compelled Albert Houthuesen to conserve all his energies for the practice of his art: his life therefore has been unadventurous and marked by few noteworthy events, though he has known tragedy and privation. He is happily married and deeply attached to his Camberwell house which he rarely leaves.

However uneventful his personal life, his life as an artist has been one of a conspicuous strangeness. At the age of fourteen, for instance, before receiving any professional instruction, he painted several still-lifes so accomplished that were they hung in the company of any but the greatest of the Dutch masters of the seventeenth century they would not be easy to distinguish. Yet it was not until he was fifty-eight years old that he began to receive a measure of the recognition that he had for so long deserved.

Albertus Antonius Johannes Houthuesen was born on 3 October 1903, the eldest of the four children of Jean Charles Pierre Houthuesen and his wife Elizabeth Emma Petronella, born Wedemeyer, at 263 Albert Cuyp straat, Amsterdam. (Cuyp, it so happens, is a painter for whom he has a particular admiration.) He was baptized at the Catholic church of St Willibrordus. Among his ancestors, both paternal and maternal, the Houthuesens, the Wedemeyers, the Houlliers and the Wittenbergs have numbered artists and musicians active in Holland.

Albert's father was a pianist who, in the last ten years of his life, turned to painting. Such, it seems, was the innate artistic sensibility of the family that he painted pictures which offer no hint of the fact that he was self-taught. He was an able pianist but he had always aspired to be a painter. The family's capital, however, consisted of a legacy from his wife's maternal grandfather, the conductor Nicholas Wedemeyer. When Pierre Houthuesen on his marriage abandoned the piano in favour of painting, his wife

70

responded resentfully, feeling that she had the right to object to his taking up a profession that offered such dubious material prospects. By 1911 Albert was painfully aware of rising tension between his parents. This erupted suddenly with tragic consequences for the family. For Albert these were radical and lasting.

One day in October that same year, when his father was giving him a drawing lesson, his mother exclaimed angrily: 'Not *another* artist in the family!' 'He can do better than I,' his father answered. Albert had scarcely left the room when he heard anguished groans and rushed back, where he saw his father staggering and shouting: 'My head! My head!' It was plain that his mother had struck her husband with one of her shoes and its high heel had penetrated his temple. Presently he subsided on to his bed and she seemed demented. Albert could neither move nor speak. 'Take this,' said his father to his wife, holding out his purse, 'I shall never need it again.' And to Albert: 'Look after your mother, sister and brothers.' After Albert had left the room agonized cries echoed through the house. On 5 November, aged thirty-three, his father died, without having been able to speak during the three weeks he spent in hospital.

The following year the widow took her four children to London, where her mother lived and where they settled permanently, first at 7, later at 20 Constantine Road, Hampstead.

For Albert the effects of these events were almost catastrophic: unable to speak English he was entirely dependent on a mother whose guilt it was agony to recognize, and who insisted it was while playing with Albert that his father had struck his head against a chandelier.

In Amsterdam he had enjoyed the ardent encouragement of his father in his determination to be an artist and the accessibility of innumerable paintings by the Dutch masters, of which he acquired a precocious knowledge. Suddenly, fatherless, exiled from a civilization of which he had been conscious of being a part and from ubiquitous beauty, he was living in subjection to a mother whose fears impelled her to sever every link with the past, unable to speak with anyone except members of his immediate family and living in an environment of unredeemed drabness. (In order to make the break absolute, as soon as the children had learnt the rudiments of English they were discouraged from speaking

Dutch.) The boarding house their mother kept was a failure and they became ever more abjectly poor.

Every other morning he stood in the stale bread queue before school and every Friday he went with his mother to the pawnshop where all their possessions of any value were delivered, his father's watch among them, which however was redeemed. His years from eight until twenty-one I have heard him describe as 'unmitigated hell'.

When he first attended Fleet Road, a London County Council school, by way of compensation for his inability to speak English to the other boys, Albert drew a thrush on a blackboard, which was applauded by his class. The teacher showed it to a colleague and he to the headmaster: all three admired it; the drawing was not erased for several days. This was his first recognition as an artist. But in spite of this auspicious welcome he was unhappy at school, horrified, in particular, by the savage canings for trivial offences of many boys by a sadistic master which the others were compelled to witness, and he feared for his own hands but was never caned. Nor did his mother's constant visits to voice a wide variety of complaints fail to intensify his unhappiness.

At fourteen he left school without prospects, but continued to work, as he had for the past two years, as a grocer's delivery boy. Later he served as an assistant to an engraver, a furniture decorator (mostly restoring red lacquer) and an architect. It is fortunate that he was unable to find the £25 he would have had to pay to be formally indentured to the engraver — Vintner, of Holborn — as this would have bound him for five years. The time he spent at the engraver's was not wasted, for he came to know and revere the engravings of Dürer, in particular his 'Adam and Eve', 'Death on a Pale Horse' and 'Melancholia'. In the meanwhile as often as his circumstances allowed he visited the National Gallery and the British Museum, and every evening from 1917 until 1923 he worked at the St Martin's School of Art. From here he made three yearly applications for a London County Council scholarship (of £80 a year) to the Royal College of Art; on each occasion it was rejected. Two students with whom he had become friends at St Martin's and who had gone on to the College, Barnett Freedman and Gerald Ososki, were deeply concerned at what had happened. Together they explained the situation to my father (at the time principal of the College), saying that they believed he would be interested in their friend's work and expressing the hope that he would see the portfolio he had submitted in support of his application. My father immediately took a taxi to County Hall and after looking through the portfolio angrily insisted on Albert's being awarded the scholarship.

Accordingly he entered the College in 1923, where he remained for four years, becoming one of a group that included Henry Moore, Edward Burra, Charles Mahoney, Barbara Hepworth, Cecil Collins and Ceri Richards, as well as the two friends so largely responsible for his presence and a number of other members of an outstandingly gifted generation. Also Catherine Dean, to whom he became engaged in 1926 and married five years later. No marriage could have been more fortunate, for she was a painter of rare but reticent talent, able to sympathize wholeheartedly with Albert's aspirations. The quality of Catherine's painting is attested by 'Cat asleep in High Backed Chair', still in her possession, and 'Sheep's Head and Skull' at the Tate. She taught painting at St Gabriel's College, Camberwell, from 1939 until 1967.

At the Royal College Albert's attitude was different from that of most of his fellow students, who were high spirited and often rowdy, in the degree of his sense of the privilege of being an artist: he had seen his father die for it and he himself had suffered exile and privation. In spite of his highly developed sense of humour he was never for a moment forgetful of the, to him, scarcely believable fact that he was free at last to devote all his time and all his energies to his chosen vocation.

Before he entered the College he had achieved a technical command which most students lack when they leave. This command is apparent in his three earliest surviving paintings. The first two, made when he was fourteen, are 'Apple' and 'Potatoes and Onion', in oil on lids of his father's cigar-boxes brought from Holland, and 'The Candlestick', in oil on canvas, all still in his possession. These and other paintings were made in secret in a bedroom that was 'his' only when unoccupied by a boarder. As the work of a schoolboy who, apart from lessons from a self-taught father, had received no instruction, they are remarkable not only for the skill they show, but for the knowledge of the Dutch masters. The 'Apple' and 'Potatoes and Onion' are highly realistic, yet the blackness of their background is an intimation of the symbolism that was to be a cardinal element in his work: the blackness referring to the secrecy in which they were painted. In 'The Candlestick' (which shows some resemblance to the work of his father) symbolism is explicit: the candle is burning; its flame represents the gleam of hope which circumstances seemed so grimly to deny — but the last match has been struck. The painting bears the marks of the jabs of his mother's scissors: he caught her, just in time, in the act of destruction.

As though his circumstances were not sufficiently sombre, a further misfortune occurred in about 1920. One night Albert thought he saw a fire burning in the house next door; it quickly emerged that this was the reflection of a fire in their own. All the accommodation he was allowed for his possessions was a single drawer in a table. Beneath stood a laundry basket; its contents had been set on fire by his mother, perhaps by accident, for she habitually carried a lighted taper, and the table was damaged, and all Albert's early drawings and a portrait drawing by his father were destroyed. Fragments survived of copies of an illuminated manuscript in the British Museum and of some lettering by Edward Johnson. After this occurrence Albert asked his mother to sit for him for a drawing. It was impossible for her to sit or for him to draw: neither could bear to look at the other.

At the Royal College he made the fullest use of the opportunities offered him by good teaching, official encouragement and exhilarating companionship — to what purpose may be seen in the two versions of his diploma painting: 'The Supper at Emmaus' made in 1927, the second of which was bought by the Duveen Fund.

They are not, like the two still-lifes of ten years before, virtuoso pieces. They show the same command of form and colour, but that is not what impresses, but rather the originality and intensity of the treatment of the subject: the risen Lord, followed by two disciples, enters by a narrow gate a garden of a kind still to be seen in Hampstead (except that the house on the left with a step-gabled roof is reminiscent of Amsterdam) and approaches an ordinary table on which supper is being laid, but the chair on which He is about to sit is surrounded by an aura of gentle light, and wild roses blossom against the red-brick wall behind. The unearthly character of Christ and the chair are thrown into gentle relief by the convincing ordinariness of their setting — an ordinary garden, an ordinary serving-man, mildly surprised at the emergence of the haloed white-robed figure, not even noticed by the other manservant, concerned only whether the table is properly laid. Figure and chair are thrown into relief without in the least impairing the unity of the work as a whole or diminishing the credibility of the scene. One does not expect to see Jesus emerge from a garden door, but this painting persuades us that if He did, this is how the scene would present itself.

Rembrandt is the master whom Houthuesen has most ardently and continuously revered and in this picture, as in a number of his other works, the influence of the master is apparent, for instance, in the treatment of the servants' sleeves. But here the influence of Rembrandt also reveals itself in terms deeper and more pervasive. Unlike many of his contemporaries and successors who placed the events of the New Testament in what was imagined to be, or in the case of Holman Hunt actually was, their true setting, Rembrandt did not concern himself with archaeology or with the actual appearances of the Holy Land. Instead he observed the people of the Bible as they went their ordinary way in the Jewish quarter in Amsterdam. Houthuesen has set the event not, indeed, in Whitechapel but in a pleasant English garden, contemporary but not aggressively 'modern' in the manner of certain religious painters of today who make their representations of comparable events look forced and artificial.

Life after leaving the College, in spite of the happiness of his marriage, was something of an anticlimax. At 20 Abbey Gardens, St John's Wood, where he and Catherine settled in 1931, they endured abject poverty and eventually debt. As an artist he suffered almost total neglect, and the Depression made work of any sort difficult to obtain. Every evening for nine years, however, he taught at the Mary Ward Settlement and later at the Working Men's College. Nine years of such a way of life resulted for him in prolonged and serious illness. They moved in 1938 to a studio in nearby 37 Greville Road, which was damaged two years later by a bomb and had to be abandoned. Kindly neighbours rescued his work and stored it in their house. But it was later moved by a maid into a damp cellar where it remained for three years and some forty canvases were destroyed. At the same time he was rejected for the armed forces on medical grounds, and placed in category Grade IV. From 1940 until 1944 he worked as a tracer in the draughtsmen's office of the London & North Eastern Railway in Doncaster — when he lived for a short time in the village of Letwell, in Nottinghamshire, and a succession of lodgings near Doncaster — which resulted in his complete collapse. They returned to London in 1945 without money and still without prospects, and accepted the offer at nominal rent of three rooms in a vicarage at the Elephant and Castle, in return for acting as wardens to students billeted there. But their enforced unhappy wanderings were almost ended. After living for two years with friends in a house in Oxted, Surrey, they went as tenants of part of a house in Camberwell, 5 Love Walk.

In spite of the harassments of ill-health and acute poverty as well as the distress which the war brought to most of the inhabitants of these islands, Albert continued — almost miraculously — to work, and after the war daily when not frustrated by illness. For some sixteen years, however, he worked in almost total obscurity. He had a few admiring friends, some of the fellow students at the Royal College (where his work had been held in high regard), friends he had made during his years in Yorkshire, and a handful of others. One of his Yorkshire friends, Lady Matthews, bought several examples of his work, and I myself persuaded, when I was their director, the Leeds and the Sheffield Art Galleries, and later on the Tate, to buy or accept a handful — the two former a painting each, the latter four — but the chilly indifference of their respective governing bodies was undisguised. At Leeds the painting was demoted to the cellar after my departure in 1933, where it remained - subject to constant disintegration for thirty-six years, being eventually repaired, with minimal success, on the initiative of the artist himself. This circumstance I relate not by way of reflection upon my successors — all men of quite exceptional ability who brought about radical improvements — but to illustrate the degree of Albert's neglect.

This neglect he philosophically accepted; his fastidiousness would have forbidden the least attempt at self-promotion. (Those who are strangers to the hardship of most artists' lives may not understand the temptation to try to attract public notice, which is no loss when their work has been done without the slightest concern for popular appeal. Even so respected an artist and honourable a man as Paul Nash praised his own work in a periodical in reviews pseudonymously signed.)

Albert Houthuesen's existence as a painter might even now have scarcely been recognized had it not been for the enterprise and perseverance shown by a lifelong friend in the late 'fifties in interesting dealers in his work. The friend was Elizabeth, my wife. There was a meeting with Victor Waddington, who offered him an exhibition of his sea paintings. This in turn led to a discussion with Graham Reid, which resulted in his first exhibition of paintings and drawings which was held in 1961. Its timing — entirely by chance — was propitious. In the course of his forty-odd years of life as a painter his outlook had changed scarcely at all. It often happens, with the passage of time, that a painter's brushwork becomes freer and more fluent (Turner's and Corot's are conspicuous examples of it). Of course the brushstrokes are as precisely controlled as ever, but they can assume an audacious, spontaneous look. This was the case with Albert's, and the effect was to bring his painting for the first time into relationship with that of a number of his contemporaries. In spite of his paintings being, as always, figurative, their seeming audacity and spontaneity made it possible to see them in terms of paint applied in a certain way and even to relate them, however superficially, to those of certain of the action-painters. The resemblance, entirely accidental though it was, obscured the fact that Albert was as solitary a figure as he had ever been. His command of resonant and dramatic colour as well as his impassioned brushstrokes impelled many who had not known or had discounted his work to scrutinize it with close attention. A growing number recognized it as the expression of a rare spirit: exalted, highly imaginative, yet intimately conversant with the natural world.

The high praise with which this exhibition was received gave him a wide measure of recognition — and it enabled him to subsist, and for the first time, by his painting and drawing alone. For his friends, for decades painfully aware of his almost total neglect and his consequent poverty, who happened to be present, the opening night was one of those occasions when they were tempted to doubt the evidence of their eyes and ears: the densely packed, attentive crowd; the information that there was neither a painting nor a drawing left unsold. A second exhibition was held at the Reid Gallery in 1963 and when it closed the following year Albert was taken on by Victor Waddington.

In 1967 he transferred to the Mercury Gallery (like the Reid and the Waddington, in Cork Street) where an exhibition was held that year, followed by two others in 1969. All were attended by the same success. The Mercury also published a finely produced book in a limited edition, illustrated mostly by recent work, by way of a tribute to an artist so long and so unjustly neglected. One result of his success was that he and his wife were able to buy the house in Love Walk, not long after the landlord had given them notice. The interior of this house, although they had until the 'sixties not pounds but shillings (and not always these) to spend on furnishing and decorations, puts one in mind of one of Vermeer's.

But in spite of his success - of recent years there have been around fifty collectors eager to buy any example of his work that might become available — his position has remained in one sense anomalous: the establishment still ignores him and nothing was acquired from these exhibitions for any public collection.

Ours is a time when many, possibly even most, artists are preoccupied exclusively with formal problems and relatively few consistently express an attitude to life. Their art is addressed to small groups of initiates and some is sheer soliloquy.

Even Houthuesen's two earliest surviving still-lifes already referred to, in spite of their look of objectivity, are expressions of nostalgia for the art of his native land and of the hopelessness of a miserable boy. Almost all, perhaps all, his painting and drawing is the expression of a highly personal, a passionate outlook.

Were it possible to express this attitude precisely in words there would be no need to do so in paint or crayon. It may, however, be approximately defined as one of intense responsiveness to the beauties of the natural world, shadowed by an awareness, at times almost overwhelming, of their transitoriness and vulnerability. The theme to which he constantly reverts, implicitly or explicitly, is tragedy: the tragedy of disappointed hope; the destructive power of hurricanes, sea, jagged projecting rock, the chaos always threatening mankind, the transitoriness of everything precious, especially the fruits of creative effort. I recall his telling me that often, before beginning a painting or a drawing, he is overcome by the awareness of their inevitable destruction, and sees canvas or paper as already disintegrated into dust. (He has invariably done his utmost to delay the disintegration of his work by using the very best materials he could afford. In the later 'sixties he began to use acryllic, as the most durable paint.) Tragedy, however, may be redeemed by its acceptance with sublime indifference or else by a gleam of hope, as in the early 'Candle' — painted at a time of abject misery — for though the matchbox is empty the candle is alight.

For Houthuesen there is no conflict between the pursuit of formal values and the expression of a theme, whether seen or imagined. Form, tone, colour, composition, are never ends in themselves but, unless they are as perfectly realized as his dedication and technical command can make them, they cannot effectively serve their purpose.

However radically his technical procedures have changed, from the minutely articulated, minutely finished still-lifes of his boyhood to the audacious evocations of stormy sea, windswept landscape and sky, fierce sunlight, menacing rock, his outlook has changed hardly at all.

The change in his methods is not easy, indeed impossible, to chart precisely, owing to his practice of resuming work on a painting or drawing often after the passage of years. 'If I go on with a drawing or painting,' he wrote to me, 'it means that it had not been carried as far as possible. Certain paintings I wouldn't dream of altering because it would be a lie to alter them.' He allows no work to go from his studio unless he is convinced that he can carry it no further. 'The Somnambulist', for instance, a watercolour about which I will have more to say later, was reworked from 1943 over a period of twenty years.

Although, difficult to trace in detail, the evolution of his method from the smoothly finished (which he used on occasion up to the 'thirties) to the broadly audacious has been fairly consistent. Nor has this evolution related only to the application of paint. Earlier he made use of studies from life but later, for figures, land- and seascapes, he has drawn upon memory or imagination and, for still-life, he has the subject on the table before him, constantly observing but freely interpreting what he sees. To quote from another letter: 'As one gains experience, so one understands how to use it and model it — freely — selectively.' Without preliminary studies he paints straight onto the canvas, after putting in with a few touches of blue the chief features of his design.

After he left the Royal College, disillusioned by current tendencies in English painting, he responded to the poetic earnestness of the preraphaelites, but this highly informed student of Van Eyck and Rembrandt was also conscious of their defects and the response was brief.

> So much of their painting is coloured drawing [I recall his saying]. The preraphaelites could admire Van Eyck, who also painted minutely, but unlike them, in tone. And he saw life naturally and as a whole, but with, say, Holman Hunt, life was *arranged*. One could walk around Van Eyck's 'Arnolfinis', but Hunt finished his 'Scapegoat' from the wretched animal tethered to a tray of salt, and what a world of difference there is between the two!

This transitory response, scarcely reflected in his work, was followed by the reassertion of the strongest and most lasting influence of his life: that of Rembrandt. Perceptible, as already noted, not only in the 'Supper at Emmaus' but in a number of other pictures, it is more explicit and pervasive in such, for instance, as 'The Butcher's Block' (chalk) in the City Art Gallery, Leeds, 'Farm on Fire' (pen and ink) at Tullie House, Carlisle, and 'Deserted Tin Miners' Cottages' (chalk); made in 1928, 1931 and 1932 respectively when the preraphaelite response was growing fainter.

Albert has studied Rembrandt not only in the original and in reproduction but also his methods. (How, in his studio in his house in St Anthonies Breestraat, known as The Joden Breestraat, where he lived before his ruin, he must have manoeuvred each of the four shutters of its high windows — one wide open, another almost closed, the two lower closed entirely — until he had created the marvellous light he wanted, but with his own eyes shaded.) If with the passage of years the spell of Rembrandt has become less evident, this is not because it has diminished but because it has been completely assimilated, still pervading the spirit of his work rather than specific features.

There was another fructifying element which first took a hold upon his imagination as a child in Amsterdam, namely the sea. Memories of the Zuider Zee, the high long dyke, sea on one side, the roofs of houses on the other; of the sea at Sandvoort, at Scheveningen, have remained with him all his life. One of his many sea pictures is 'Rocks and Sea-spray II',1960, oil. **(PLATE 8)**.

Years passed before he saw the sea again, as in 1931 after an illness, at Birling Gap, other than briefly; but he and Catherine visited North Wales in 1932, staying with relatives in a cottage near Holywell, returning annually until 1938 and intermittently until ten years later. They also took holidays with relatives in Devon and on the Sussex coast. His visits to North Wales resulted in a series of landscape paintings and drawings. 'A wonderful landscape, wherever one looked,' he wrote, in a letter to the Tate about 'Maes Gwyn Stack Yard', an oil of 1935 which was presented in 1939. In some of these landscapes the influence of Rembrandt is apparent. One of them, 'Windswept Tree and Cottage' (chalk), made in the middle 'thirties, affords the first intimation of the violence that animates much of his later work, in particular the seascapes.

At Maes Gwyn farm, Llanasa, he painted not only land- and seascapes. Two or three miles from the coast is Point of Air colliery and he became fascinated by the colliers. He painted a portrait of the first collier he met (which was acquired for the Graves Art Gallery, Sheffield). In another letter to the Tate he described the sitter of 'Painted in a Welsh Village' (an oil of 1933 presented to the Gallery by his doctor in 1938):

> One day I saw a really fantastic figure carrying a great bundle of wood on his back, and later this young man, Harry Jones, came to sit for the portrait you have . . . four times . . . A village funeral was a procession with the coffin on a farm wagon, but alone, quite alone and leading the way, in a long black overcoat and bowler hat, carrying a bunch of wild flowers which he had gathered from the hedges, was Harry Jones.

Allusion has already been made to Houthuesen's solitary position. This is due largely to his use of symbolism, never a common feature in British art, which has now virtually disappeared. The only others of comparable stature active today in whose art symbolism plays an integral part are David Jones and Cecil Collins. Houthuesen's refers to some aspect of the manifold tragedy of the human lot.

Usually the symbolism's meaning is explicit, as it is in 'The Wreck of the Early Hope', an oil of 1960, in 'Icarus', a casein tempera made between 1962 and 1967, and in 'The World Upside Down', a series of drawings of the middle 'sixties. 'The Wreck' alludes immediately to the wreck — by homicide and exile — of his own early hope of a happy initiation in his life as a painter by a father to whom he was deeply attached and by the presence of works by the masters whom he most ardently revered, in an environment of extraordinary beauty. The picture refers, too, to the frustration of hope as a universal human experience. Symbolic elements even less easy to interpret are the luminous radiating outlines — reminders that even among the wreckage hope still glimmers, however faintly. The theme of 'Icarus' is also the frustration of hope, but in a special, one might say in a professional, context. Artists of exceptional talent, however modestly disposed, are sufficiently perceptive to be aware of it; they are also aware of the wide gulf that separates achievement from aspiration. 'Icarus' suggests that Albert must be painfully aware of such disparity, for Icarus is the artist, attempting to fly to the sun, being burnt up and his paintings and drawings falling with him to destruction. It carries intimations, too, of Albert's often expressed sense of the vulnerability of what is precious to the destructive forces in nature. 'The World Upside Down' series, expressive of a world gone mad, still emphasizes hope. They do indeed recall the misery of his boyhood and youth (the boots which figure in one of them refer to those which as a schoolboy he did not possess until a pair was given to him by the London County Council, the folios of drawings to those of his own destroyed by bombing; likewise the collapsing houses).

In spite of these and similar distresses and calamities, the artist — in every one of the series — remains at work, representing the artist in every man who continues, come what may, to create.

Sometimes his work is done at the prompting of impulses more obscure, and it is correspondingly more difficult to decipher; in a few cases a clue from Albert's life is necessary. But it always refers to specific events or situations, experienced or observed. One such is 'The Somnambulist', already mentioned, which was inspired by an incident which took place during the war when for a time he had to walk daily along a path of cinders leading from Letwell, the village where he was living, to Langold coal tip. One day a stranger walking the same arid path in the opposite direction made him a gift of roses. Another, entirely incomprehensible without a clue, is 'A toute à l'heure' (PLATE 9), a work with a near tragic genesis. In 1961 he underwent an operation. Lying in the ante-room of the operating theatre he overheard a conversation in French of which 'à toute à l'heure' were the last words he heard before losing consciousness under the anaesthetic. After the operation he returned home and during a long period of acute depression in convalescence he cut up several of his pictures. This act afforded a release from tension and saved him from suicide. Much later, again returning to his workroom, he found it thickly covered in dust. As he picked the scattered fragments up, each one left a clear silhouette on the floor or worktable. The sight inspired him to reassemble, re-arrange and add to the fragments of one of the paintings he had cut up. To the new work he gave as a title those last words overheard. This oil and collage was not completed until six years afterwards. A similarly esoteric work, of which the symbolism, though obscure, is less difficult to make out, is 'Here and Now', 1963 (chalk), where a clown is represented as creator with tiny seeds — symbols of hope — which can just be seen scattering from his hand.

Clowns, artists and poets have always had for Albert a very close affinity, deriving perhaps partly from the fact that the mother of the celebrated Dutch comic actor, Johannes Busiau, was a Houthuesen. His professional acting he was too young to see but he remembers his clowning and the happy laughter evoked by his presence in his parents' home.

Albert's interest in clowns (of whom he had made his first drawings in Doncaster towards the end of the war) and the theatre was stimulated by his residence in the second half of the 'forties in the Elephant and Castle, where he went often to the theatre, and made a number of drawings — some of them among his finest — of clowns, dancers and other performers. He continued to represent them after he had left the district. 'Young Dancer and

Old Clown', in red and black pastel, was not made until 1954 or
'56, and the much reworked 'Song of the Cat', in indian ink, wash
and black chalk, was not finished until 1960. His attitude towards
clowns is suggested by some words he wrote on the back of a
photograph of one of his oil paintings titled 'Poet': 'Poet clown:
Clown Poet'.

There is inevitably something sad, even tragic, about a clown,
since his function is to make his fellow men momentarily forget
their sorrows, and this element is marked in Houthuesen's clowns.
The dancers he made at the Elephant and Castle and from the
memories of his days there, like his still-lifes of fruit and flowers,
are expressions of his delight in the beauties of the natural world.

For all his compassion Albert, like Turner or Brueghel, views
humanity from a distance, rather than, as Renoir or Van Gogh
did, by close identification with it, and during the 'sixties his chief
preoccupation was with land, sea and sky rather than with his
fellow men. One feature of his skies is notable. He belongs
inalienably to the north, and he sees the sun not, as Mediterranean
man does, as the source of intolerable heat, but as a visionary
essence, not to be sheltered from but exultantly faced. Innumerable painters have shown the rising or the setting sun, but
relatively few, like Houthuesen, the sun high in the heaven. In
most of his landscapes and seascapes he directly faces the source
of light.

It is the continual beauty of the natural world that precludes
ultimate despair, and for him this beauty is a symbol of hope.
Response to the beauty of the natural world precedes his impulse
to interpret it. He and Giacometti (they never met or communicated) expressed themselves to me, although in different
languages, in terms strangely identical:

> 'Do you know anything more repellent about an artist than his referring to
> "my art"? My own hope, given propitious circumstances, is to do justice to
> *my subject.*'

The painters who figure in these pages are, as painters, mostly
solitaries, but none as solitary as Albert Houthuesen, never a
member of any group, or a participant in any 'movement', deeply
grateful for what other artists have taught him yet the disciple of
none, going his own way, against the way of the world, the

complex of ideas that dominate it. His way does not lead back to any tradition: he is as independent of the past, for all his reverence for Rembrandt, Van Eyck, Turner and other masters, as he is of the present. In spite of its wide variety of theme and treatment his work reflects a rare consistency of vision: humane, delicately perceptive, and above all tragic, yet offering its gleam, however faint, of hope.

JOHN PIPER
born 1903

The early environment of John Piper, unlike that of many artists, prepared him well for the pursuit of his chosen vocation, including even one circumstance that threatened to prevent his becoming a professional artist at all, and in fact delayed it.

John Egerton Christmas Piper (the 'Egerton' was taken from Thackeray's *Newcomes* which his father particularly admired) was born on 13 December 1903, the youngest, by six years, of the three sons of Charles Alfred Piper and his wife, Mary Ellen, born Matthews. His birthplace was 'Alresford', a villa in Ashley Road, Epsom, Surrey, named after the town in Hampshire where the Piper family had lived for several generations. It was demolished, and a larger one, similarly named, was erected in its place, but this, too, was demolished. Charles Alfred Piper was a solicitor, a partner in the firm of Piper, Smith & Piper, with offices in Vincent Square, Westminster, and a visual man with wide-ranging interests and the author of an autobiography, *Sixty-Three: Not Out*, published in 1925. He was a man of strong convictions, disapproving, for instance, of boarding-schools, and leaving his children to choose their own religion. His visual aspirations led him to attend art classes at St Mary's School, Vincent Square. 'My own special inclination,' he wrote, 'has been towards drawing and architectural work, and I made one or two attempts in this direction without success.'

Charles Piper's father had begun life as a boot-maker and eventually became a Westminster City Councillor; he was a militant radical. One of John's uncles was an amateur artist who made a set of architectural drawings; it was this that first evoked John's lifelong passion for architecture. For a time his family assumed that he would make it his profession, but his father, by taking him on frequent expeditions from his offices in Vincent Square to the nearby Tate Gallery, aroused a still more ardent passion: to become a painter. In particular he was obsessed by the watercolours of Turner. In the meanwhile, by walks and bicycle rides through Surrey and Sussex, he extended his knowledge of landscape, but in particular he studied parish churches, their architecture, sculpture and glass.

While still at school at Epsom — where he was a day-boy from 1917 until 1921 — he became a local secretary of the Surrey Archaeological Society. On his way to Switzerland, where the family used to spend their holidays, he visited the Louvre. On a visit to Italy with his father in 1921 he made drawings in Venice, Siena, Volterra and San Gimignano. Revisiting his English parish churches he was able to study them with more sophisticated eyes. But 1922 seemed a year fatal to his hopes: his father, who had done so much to foster his enthusiasm for painting and drawing, decided that the life of an artist was too precarious to be risked and insisted on his studying law in his office as an articled clerk, with a view to becoming a partner in the firm. There he remained for five years, able to leave only in 1926 after his father's death. His law studies, however, were not so demanding as to prevent him from drawing and writing: he wrote verse, and a volume of it, entitled *Wind in the Trees*, which he illustrated, was published in 1924.

These five years intensified his already ardent desire to devote his life to painting and made him value the liberty to do so when it came to him far more than if he had merely graduated from an art school to become an artist as a matter of routine. Piper was in his twenty-third year, an age when many students graduated, when he went to the Richmond School of Art. Here he studied painting under Raymond Coxon, a zestful Yorkshire intimate of Henry Moore. 'It was Coxon,' Piper says, 'who really taught me how to *look*.' It was at Richmond that he met Eileen Holding, a fellow student, whom he married in 1928, when his mother had a house with a studio built for him at Betchworth in Surrey. Their marriage was dissolved five years later. In the meanwhile he entered the Royal College of Art, where he was introduced by Coxon to Henry Moore who taught there. Piper recalls with gratitude the sympathetic helpfulness of two fellow students, Charles Mahoney and Morris Kestelman, with a variety of technical problems; he learnt, he recalls, more from these and other students than from the College staff. He received no particular encouragement from my father, then principal, who however praised one of his landscape studies as being 'like a Conder'. To my father he confessed that he was acutely bored by the lectures of one of the professors; he responded by giving him permission, instead of attending these, to make a copy of Cézanne's 'Aix: Rocky Landscape', which had just been given to the Tate by the Courtauld Trustees. At the Tate he met H.S. Ede, then working there as an assistant, who praised the copy and otherwise encouraged him, and the two became friends. One day Ede invited him to his home in Hampstead where, to his delight, he met Braque. In 1927, while still a student, he held, with David Birch, an exhibition of wood engravings. Assiduously as he applied himself to the study of painting, drawing and engraving, his interests were not confined to these: he attended concerts, the Diaghilef Ballet — and he played the piano in an amateur dance band at Epsom.

By the time he left the Royal College, John Piper, already painter, draughtsman, engraver, archaeologist, musician, poet, art critic, anticipated what he was shortly to become and has since remained: beyond comparison the most versatile British artist of his time, and after Michael Ayrton the most articulate. He wrote book reviews and notices of exhibitions for *The Nation* and *The Listener*, in which he gave discerning praise to such contemporaries, then little known, as Hitchens, Pasmore, Richards and Coldstream.

The paintings and drawings he made for the next five years also anticipate — clearly in their subjects and even in some degree in their treatment — the work of his maturity. Landscape and seashores with lighthouses — many of them made at Dungeness and Littlehampton — were favourite subjects. By the early 'thirties he had become, however, increasingly identified with the abstract movement of which Ben Nicholson and Barbara Hepworth were the leading English exponents. In 1933, in the course of a visit to Paris, he met Hélion, Braque, Léger and Brancusi, which decisively confirmed his disposition towards abstraction. But his approach to abstraction differed from that of many of his associates. For them it was an art, dependent exclusively upon form and colour and entirely disassociated from theme — an autonomous art. For Piper it meant something different, namely the 'abstraction' of natural forms from what seemed accidental or superfluous; their stripping down to their basic elements. So it comes about that a number of his paintings of the middle 'thirties (several titled 'Abstract Painting'), which at first glance appear to be strictly orthodox abstracts, in fact include such features as the surface of the sea or an expanse of sky. In any case he continued to paint landscape — coasts, chapels in their settings and other favourite subjects — although in a formalized manner. (At least one of these, 'Newhaven 1936', clearly shows the influence — though this was transitory and slight — of the Cornish 'primitive' Alfred Wallis, no doubt transmitted through Ben Nicholson, who, with Christopher Wood — whose own work Piper particularly admired — was responsible for his discovery. In short Piper's abstracts, like Picasso's, have their point of departure in nature, from which he 'abstracted' but did not exclude.

Absorbed though he was for several years from 1933 by abstraction, he found it, as he said to me, 'interesting but not ultimate; for me not possibly the end'. His allegiance to the movement, however, was both strengthened and prolonged by his friendship with Myfanwy Evans (whom he married in 1935), the founder and editor of *Axis*, the pioneering quarterly review of abstract painting and sculpture — in fact the axis of English abstraction. (Assuming that its title referred to the German-Italian alliance, the Italian Embassy sent for a copy in 1939.)

There are people who have the gift of winning and for a time retaining high reputations while possessing minimal gifts of any other kind. Myfanwy Piper has, on the contrary, preferred privacy, and with such consistency that her various achievements remain relatively little known. After going down from Oxford — she was at St Hugh's — she went, in 1934, to Paris, and met Brancusi, Kandinsky, Giacometti — and even danced with Mondrian. And this at a time when these men were almost unknown in London and when they were known they were apt to be suspect. Before long she was persuaded to found *Axis*, which quickly established itself as an invaluable point of contact between the emerging English abstract movement and its continental pioneers. She proved an invigorating influence as a person as well as an editor. In 1938, the year after *Axis* ceased publication, she edited *The Painter's Object*, an anthology of contributions by artists to the perennially engaging theme of the content of art. Since then she has written on painting, including a book on Frances Hodgkins, librettos for operas by Benjamin Britten, adapted a play from Kierkegaard's *Diary of a Seducer* and much else besides.

To dine with the Pipers at Fawley and to listen to Myfanwy, standing before her cooking stove, saucepan in hand, discoursing upon the thought of Gissing or Henry James is a memorable experience.

I do not suggest that Piper was unduly affected by his abstractionist friends, but unlike many artists who take up — at least after their first youth — attitudes of marked independence or even of isolation, Piper, on the contrary, has always been disposed to collaborate with others in creative activities: he has illustrated books by other writers, designed eighteen stage sets, including six for operas by Benjamin Britten. Accordingly he entered with particular wholeheartedness into the vigorously emerging abstract movement. (*Axis* was published at Fawley Bottom Farm House, near Henley-on-Thames, Oxfordshire, where he moved in 1935 and has remained ever since.) With such wholeheartedness that he was gently but admiringly admonished by Hugh Gordon Porteus in an article *Piper and Abstract Possibilities* published in *Axis* No. 4, 1935, for being too rigidly abstract. 'Piper has made himself an absolute master of the game he plays', it runs, 'I should like to see him loosen the restrictions he still imposes on himself', and refers to 'his still too purified forms'. Another writer in the same issue, Herta Wescher, refers to his 'straight lines, angles, rectangles, trapezes, semicircles, nothing but mathematical forms . . .' Piper was in fact regarded as both a highly accomplished and conformist member of the English abstract group. Accomplished though his abstract works, whether painting, drawings or collages, certainly are, they do not express his deepest impulses as, for instance, those of Ben Nicholson and Barbara Hepworth — who have both made fine works of an unambiguously representational character — do express theirs. Abstractions by these two (and of course a number of others) are creations in their chosen language and they have accordingly a character of finality about them that Piper's lack. These are statements — lucid, inventive, harmonious and sophisticated — but made, so to say, in a language ably mastered but not innately his own. How little his own is even clearer from his occasional returns to near-abstraction, as for instance in some of his Pembrokeshire and Breton coast scenes of the early 'sixties. These lack both the forthrightness of his abstractions of the 'thirties and, of course, his rare sense of *genius loci*.

As early as 1935 at least, although he was to practise abstraction for some more years, Piper was plainly convinced that a strictly autonomous art subjected those who practised it to crippling limitations. In an interview, 'England's Climate', published in *Axis* No. 7 — surprisingly, considering this periodical's abstract orientation — he declared:

> Any Constable, any Blake, any Turner has something an abstract or a surrealist painting cannot have. Hence, partly, the artist's pique about them now, and his terror of the National Gallery . . . . Read Constable's letters, or a poem of Blake's, or look at an early glass painting. Each 'means' far more than itself alone. It 'means' the life of the artist — but beyond that, the life of his time . . . [his] whole existence and surroundings, and it fixes the whole passion of his age . . . .

Two years later he contributed an article, 'Lost — A Valuable Object', to the anthology *The Painter's Object* edited by Myfanwy Piper, in which he voiced the same opinion at greater length and with sharper emphasis. Here are what seem to me its crucial paragraphs:

> The trouble being that the cubists had smashed the objects into fragments. . . . The abstractionists who followed held their noses in the air, and said they'd never been interested in the object anyway. The dada-ists and later the surrealists, all premeditatedly scatter-brained, looked for it and failed to find it — oblivion being one of the few places they don't visit. And they have been celebrating its death ever since. Surrealists, in fact, produce things they call *objects* — fetish-worship idols, in the image of the vanished god of painting. Abstractionists, of course, forbid themselves such irreligious games.
>
> All the time activities have been going on that both the surrealists and the abstract painters disapprove of and pretend do not exist. These range from the wonderful pattern-making in space of Matisse (who could so easily be ignored except for the misfortune that he is a genius) to the seaside toy-making of Christopher Wood.
>
> Where is the object? One thing is certain . . . artists everywhere have done their best to find something to replace the object that cubism destroyed . . . It all seems to me an attempt to *return* to the object . . . . But the object must grow again; must reappear as the 'country' that inspires painting. It may, at the worst, turn out to be a night-bomber, or reappear as a birth-control poster — but it will grow again, somehow.

(The reference to the night-bomber shows an extraordinary prevision of one of the most impressive 'objects' chosen by his friend Paul Nash in the impending Second World War.)

So much for his convictions about painters' urgent need to recover the 'object' — or the subject as it is more generally called.

The article ends by describing two objects that he finds reappearing in his own art. The second is a beach 'which might be Newhaven, or the Welsh coast, or the Yorkshire coast, or Brittany . . . There is an absence of life, of seagulls even: but a sense that life is ready to break in . . .'

This description also shows an element of prevision; for it is a far closer verbal 'equivalent' of the coast scenes of his maturity than of the relatively tame 'Beach Collage' made the following year (reproduced in the article).

So Piper continued to make abstractions, though with diminishing frequency, after he had become convinced that painting — and not only his own — should have an 'object'.

This dichotomy was resolved decisively by the war, and in particular by the threat of the bomb to the buildings he had loved since childhood, and before long by the devastation of many of them. His love was not confined to ancient cathedrals and village churches; like that of his friend John Betjeman — with whom he produced architectural guides to Buckinghamshire, Berkshire and Shropshire and one, edited by Betjeman, on Oxfordshire — it embraced a wide variety of buildings, many of them not previously considered eligible for inclusion in a tourist guide: Nonconformist chapels, country railway stations, public houses, suburban villas and the like.

Among his wartime subjects, therefore, were villas at Reading and Henley (1940 and 1941, oils), 'Micheldever Railway Station, Hampshire' (1944, oil), 'The Ship Inn, Shoreham-by-Sea' and 'The Royal Adelaide, Windsor' (1943 and 1939, oils), and 'Italian Cheltenham' (1939, oil) — to name a few of his widely varying subjects.

The sharp recoil from abstraction, the value of which he had already called in question, provoked by the war, though it radically affected his choice of subjects, did not at first affect his style. The 'Reading Villa', just referred to, for instance, although it represents quite unambiguously a villa, does so in terms of rectangles, planes parallel with the picture surface and so on, closely resembling those of his abstract works. His return to his boyhood loves and his anxiety to make records of them in case of their destruction was too impulsive and wholehearted to impel him, at first, to trouble himself with the evolution of a style that would enable him to describe them more fully than arrangements of flat patterns would allow.

The war years for Piper were crucial for the development of his art and the establishment of his reputation. Not that he had not won high respect in the London art world during the 'thirties as a painter (his first exhibition was held at the London Gallery in 1938), as a designer for the theatre (the scenery and costumes for Stephen Spender's play *Trial of a Judge* in 1937) and, as already noted, as a critic. But the war enabled him to find the Valuable Object whose loss he had ironically mourned and for whose rediscovery he had expressed his ardent hope.

No events had demonstrated so forcibly the importance of the Valuable Object as the two world wars. In both of them the responsible authorities in Britain showed surprising wisdom in their choice of war artists. The humanly significant themes offered by both wars evoked from several artists, among others Nevinson, Wyndham Lewis and Paul Nash, a number of their finest works.

Piper was appointed, in 1940, War Artist to the Ministry of Information (to specialize in bomb damage) and to the Ministry of War; he was also employed by Recording Britain, a publishing project financed by the Pilgrim Trust. For Piper the opportunities which these assignments offered could not have been more propitious. Here was an artist who from his earliest years had been an impassioned student of architecture, who was horrified by the prospect of the destruction of many of the buildings that had been the objects of his study. An artist who possessed, too, a rare degree of the sense of *place*. A tribute to Piper's acute awareness of *genius loci* came from an unexpected quarter — unexpected for an artist among whose associates were Nicholson, Hepworth, Calder, Hélion, Miró, Léger, and other notable abstract artists. In an introduction to a book by Piper entitled *Brighton Aquatints,* published in 1939, a voice from the remote past, that of Lord Alfred Douglas, declared that from the perusal of them 'I discovered that the Brighton of my youth was still in existence and

that nearly all the old landmarks remain exactly as they were.'
Surely to be able to reveal to a perceptive resident the finest
buildings in his own city shows a sense of place of a quite exceptional acuteness. It was a sense that was to increase in range
and penetration.

In addition, his intimate and bracing association with a number
of the finest artists in Britain and the continent, and preoccupation
with abstraction, which enhanced his awareness of structure, of the
basic forms of things, combined to prepare Piper in a way that
could hardly have been bettered for his intensive work of the years
of war. His reception, and his wife's, into the Church of England
in 1939 served to identify him still more intimately with a wide
range of the buildings threatened with destruction. Like those of
a number of other artists, the country's danger and the severance
of all links with the continent focussed Piper's interests for the
time being predominantly on English art and poetry. He renewed
his study of Turner, of Blake, of Palmer (from reproductions, as
the originals had been sent to places of safety); his 'Hampshire
Cottage', a watercolour of 1941, is very close to Palmer in spirit;
and he read Wordsworth, Coleridge and Hopkins as well as the
writers on the Picturesque. Besides their effect on his painting and
drawing, these studies found expression in a short but informative
and lively book, *British Romantic Artists*, published in 1942 in a
series *Britain in Pictures*, in which he traced the Romantic impulse
in British art from a 'romantic' poem by 'the most august
Augustan Pope' to Paul Nash and Frances Hodgkins and beyond.
He even attempts to indicate, in the first sentence, one element of
that most elusive of concepts: Romanticism.

> Romantic art deals with the particular . . . [It] is the result of a vision that
> can see in things something significant beyond ordinary significance:
> something that for a moment seems to contain the whole world; and, when
> the moment is past, carries over some comment on life or experience besides
> the comment on appearances.

By implication — for no theories are developed — Piper's own
attitude to the arts is more clearly manifest in this essay than in
any of his other writings. A friend pleased him by saying, 'I know
it by heart.'

The admiration his work evoked during the war had an effect
upon his method. Although as a person he seems self-confident,

and he easily wins the trust and friendship of those with whom and for whom he works, as well as many others, he was, before the war, diffident about his painting. Admiration gave him confidence to evolve, gradually, the more fluent and 'freer' brush-stroke natural to him and which became, eventually, so conspicuous a feature of his work. Many will remember the praise of his paintings and watercolours of bomb devastation: 'House of Commons, Aye Lobby' (1941, oil, Imperial War Museum) and a watercolour of the same date; those of Bath; 'Interior of Coventry Cathedral' (1940, oil, City Art Gallery, Coventry); the eerie desertion of 'Dead Resort: Kemp Town' (1939, oil, Temple Newsam, Leeds); and the three belonging to the Tate. These are 'St Mary le Port, Bristol' (1940, oil), 'All Saints Chapel, Bath' (1942, watercolour) and 'Somerset Place, Bath' (1942, watercolour). St Mary le Port was destroyed in a great raid on the night of 24 November 1940; according to a letter which he wrote to the Gallery in 1958 'when he went there he found the ruins of two churches still smoking'. In the same letter he describes, with reference to the two Bath pictures, arriving four days after what used to be called a 'Baedeker raid', that is to say particularly devised for the destruction of historic buildings, how 'the ruins were still smouldering and bodies were being dug out'.

Knowledge of architecture and of the early English topographers gave Piper so firm a grasp of his subjects that, moved though he was by the poignant spectacles he chose to represent — there was no time for recollection in tranquillity — his pictures of architectural catastrophe are painted with a sure touch. They are, in effect, a series of grand and elaborate sketches, their absence of traditional 'finish' conveying a moving sense of their having been made on the spot 'when the ruins were still smouldering and the bodies were being dug out.'

Some of them, the more elaborate, were in fact made from studies made on the spot, and he is unable to work from photographs, or from subjects that do not engage his utmost interest. During the war, for instance, he was asked to make a drawing of an Air Raid Precaution Post, and he was unable to do it.

Preoccupation with architecture, threatened or destroyed, led him naturally, as a man with a strong historical sense, to the representation of architecture for its own sake.

In 1941 he received from Queen Elizabeth, now the Queen Mother, a commission to make two series of watercolours of Windsor Castle. This, and the commission during the same year from the late Sir Osbert Sitwell to make a longer series of paintings and watercolours of Renishaw Hall, his house in Derbyshire (and after the war of Montegufoni, his house near Florence), gave his particular gifts the widest scope.

Piper's work as a war artist and the fulfilment of these two inspiring commissions enhanced still further his understanding of architecture, of which he took the utmost advantage, making over the ensuing years paintings and watercolours of a wide variety of buildings. The result has been the most various and by far the most extensive record of the buildings of Britain by any artist of this century.

With the passage of years Piper's style has undergone little basic change. It has indeed become freer, swifter and lighter in colour, but the aura of romance with which he often suffuses his buildings involves no distortion of their structure. He regards even his most highly romanticized representations of buildings as essentially accurate. One day at Fawley he left me for a few minutes in his studio and on his return found me examining a watercolour of the château of Chambord in which the centre of the façade was hidden by a circular blaze, almost an explosion, of white light. 'Perhaps you think that light was invented,' he said, 'but look at this!' And he showed me a photograph he had taken after making the watercolour, which showed the light as no less intense.

Allusion has been made so far — the reference to Chambord apart — only to Piper's pictures of architecture in Britain, but he and his wife make regular continental tours by car, and he has painted buildings in France and Italy; Rome and Venice offer themes which have for him a particularly strong appeal, 'St. Agnese and the Bernini Fountain of the Four Rivers' (1962, watercolour) and 'The Salute' (1960, watercolour) being characteristic examples. Piper spends more time on the continent than most artists resident in Britain. There are some who do so still for the purpose of identifying their work with that of the 'continental mainstream' though, on account of the diminished importance of Paris, far fewer than was once the case. Piper, however, belongs so integrally to the English Romantic tradition

ALBERT HOUTHUESEN. Plate 8 (top): *Rocks and Sea-spray II* (1960), oil on
canvas, 28 × 36 in. Plate 9 (above): *À tout à l'heure* (1961), oil and collage,
48 × 60 in.

Plate 10: JOHN PIPER: *Castle Howard* (1943), oil on board, 25 × 30 in.

Plate 11: JOHN PIPER: *Monument, Waldershare* (1947), oil on board, 24 × 18 in.

Plate 12: EDWARD BURRA: *John Deth* (1932), watercolour, 22 × 30 in.

Plate 13: EDWARD BURRA: *It's All Boiling Up* (1948), watercolour,
23 × 31 in.

that his work is not remotely affected by his continental friendships or subjects. (This was, of course, not the case in the 'thirties when abstract art had already been established for more than two decades and was far more highly evolved than that of its English pioneers, and he learnt much from Hélion, as well as Braque, Léger and others.) Besides buildings he also, though very much less often, makes watercolours and oils of pure landscape. On account of their conspicuously structural conformation the subjects best suited to him are mountains, the 'natural architecture' of Yorkshire and North Wales. I am thinking of 'Gordale Scar' (1943, oil) and 'Rocky Outcrop, Snowdonia' (1948, watercolour), for example.

In a note on her husband in the catalogue of his first exhibition at the Marlborough New London Gallery in 1963, Myfanwy referred to one of his 'preoccupations' during the years 1930-9 as 'an empty stage'. This 'preoccupation' of his seems to me to have far wider implications than she intended. A singular feature of the art of Piper is that in almost the whole of his formidably large production the stage is empty: there are no human figures. Occasionally he makes a portrait drawing or a nude from life but these are relatively few in number and seem to have been done without the intense scrutiny and the technical insight that marks even the slightest of his landscapes with or without buildings. This absence of human figures is singular in view of Piper's exceptionally lively interest in his fellow men, both as individuals and collectively, as is apparent from his readiness to undertake many exacting official duties. But except for his mountain scenes of Snowdonia, Yorkshire and elsewhere, all his landscapes, by the introduction, almost invariably as the commanding feature, of a cathedral or a village church or chapel, a castle, a country house, a Venetian palace, a lighthouse, or the prospect of a town, all indicate the presence in them of man their creator. The stage is empty but, as Robert Melville, in the introduction to the catalogue of a retrospective exhibition at the Marlborough in 1964 perceptively observed, Piper has 'salvaged the Humanist scale and undepicted man remains in his work the measure of all things'. This aversion to representing the human figure in its environment is the more singular in view of the readiness with which he represents representations of it, of the statue, for instance, in 'Juno in the

Grotto, Montegufoni' (1948, ink and pastel), to mention one of his many figures made from sculpture and stained glass.

Whatever merits posterity will attribute to his workmanlike and attractive abstractions of the 'thirties, there can be no doubt that the concentration upon pure form which the making of them required did much to prepare him for the formidable achievements of the next decade. There can be no comparison, surely, between the empty and trivial 'Beach Collage' of 1938 and such works as the best of the Windsor and Renishaw paintings, the bomb-devastated buildings, 'Hovingham Hall' (1944, water-colour), 'Great Coxwell Tithe Barn' (1941, watercolour, the Pilgrim Trust), 'Castle Howard' (1943, oil on board) **(PLATE 10)** or 'The Monument, Waldershare' (1947, oil) **(PLATE II).**

The evolution of Piper's vision, like that of many other painters, has been away from precise definition towards breadth and at-mosphere expressed in what someone described as 'marvellous rapid handwriting'. And from a prediction for sombre skies (I was told that King George VI exclaimed, on first seeing the Windsor series, 'I hadn't realized that our weather was so bad') he has become preoccupied with light. If a choice had to be made from the immense production of his recent work, the finest and most characteristic are, I believe, the representations, in oil, watercolour and lithograph, of church towers, of which Redenhall, Norfolk (1963, oil) and several church tower triptychs, for example, 'Lexfield, Lavenham and Darsham' (1965, watercolour), are radiant examples. The special qualities of 'Redenhall' (and of others of similar character) are poetically described by Robert Melville: 'The colour is informed by mild moist English air. The line defines whilst confiding a diffident lyricism, like a song nearly lost as the singer turns away.'

Such works as these I have occasionally heard described with a shade of condescension as mere sketches. They do indeed lack the intensity and the bony structure of those of such topographical predecessors as Girtin or early Cotman, say. But the description, in its implication, is unjust. To 'sketch' — according to a defini-tion in the Oxford English Dictionary — is to give the essential facts without going into details. Give the essential facts he certainly does, but he can do more than this at his best: namely, in his representations of buildings he endows sculpture and other features with exhilarating life. Often with audacity, sometimes with careless-seeming strokes and dashes of brush, pen or pencil, but with an effectiveness far beyond the powers of an artist without Piper's intimate knowledge of architecture. Sometimes he completes pictures on the spot, but more often makes small studies which, sooner or later, as he has said, have 'roused lively thoughts of further development as drawings or paintings'.[1]

Nobody — least of all Piper himself — would contend that all these many works are of anything approaching equal value, but as a whole they present a panoramic view of Western, in particular British, architecture. The best among them — and they are not few — represent an exhilarating combination of the romantic and the particular searchingly understood. No painter of his generation — and few, surely, of any — has studied and portrayed in England, Italy and France, so wide a range of architecture with such sympathetic understanding.

Piper remains first and foremost the most versatile visual man of his generation — what, from stained-glass windows to pleasure gardens, from designs for the theatre to firework displays, from book illustration to pottery, has he *not* made? — and his versatility has at moments inclined many (not excluding myself) to underrate his finest work.

[1] Studies from Sketchbooks 1940-60 (1967).

EDWARD BURRA
born 1905

In his fourteenth year Burra's prospects for the successful pursuit of any vocation must have seemed negligible; even, indeed, his fitness for any vocation at all could readily have been called in question. Never robust, he was subject to a combined attack of anaemia and rheumatic fever of such severity that he has never fully recovered from its consequences. At the age of thirteen his constitution was gravely impaired and he was compelled to leave school with minimal education. (I once referred to his uncertain health, and he replied 'Nonsense: I have the constitution of a mule; otherwise how could I have made it for so *long?*')

These seemingly catastrophic circumstances combined, however, to enable him to become an artist. Unfit to prepare for a regular profession, he became free to devote his acute and original mind, his prematurely penetrating observation, and his entire time, to his chosen vocation. He was spared the accumulation of knowledge irrelevant to an artist; and moreover his parents, and not only on account of their anxiety about his health, welcomed an interest in the arts and fostered his adoption of the vocation of his choice, however uncertain the prospects it offered.

The artists of the past owed much of their technical resource to prolonged apprenticeship. At the age when the students of today begin their education, their early predecessors had at least mastered the elements of their art and often considerably more. In this respect Burra resembled them, for from the age of fourteen he was able to draw, paint, observe and enlarge his imaginative experience without opposition or distraction. The continuing precariousness of his health has required him to dedicate all his energies to the pursuit of his art; he has little superabundance for conventional pleasures and none for the politics of art. Even his personal relations are of a special kind: he feels, I believe, particular affection for and even dependence on his small circle of old friends, but it is almost invariably they who must take the initiative when meetings are concerned. Were they to fail to do so, friendship would languish. But they do not fail, and he is warmly responsive. 'I have been meaning to write but never have of course' is a sentence that recurs in his letters. When he writes he writes very fluently, though the premature ending of his formal education is evident in the casualness of his spelling: Herbert Read is 'Herbert Reed', foreigners are 'foriegners' and so on, and his handwriting, although not as childlike as Lucian Freud's, can have developed little since his schooldays. His letters reveal at times the same characteristics as his paintings, a preoccupation with the macabre and, particularly in the earlier, with the shoddy.

As a man he seems to suffer from a languor, even an exhaustion, so acute as to suggest that he is incapable of action of any kind. Incapable in fact of standing for long periods, he said to me 'I must sit down most of the time; if I could work lying down I'd do so.' Even in his student days he put me in mind of an inactive, almost run-down being, so near to exhaustion did his reserves of energy seem. There was little about Burra's presence to suggest that he was shortly to show himself to be an artist of astonishing originality, and to be the creator, over some fifty years, of a long series of highly finished paintings.

Edward John Burra is the eldest child but one (who died young) of Henry Curteis Burra JP, active in the public life of Rye, Sussex, living at nearby Springfield, and his wife Ermentrude Anne, born Robertson Luxford. Edward has a sister Anne, with whom his relations have remained very close, who is married to the Hon. Colin Ritchie and lives near Rye. He was born on 29 March 1905 at his grandmother's town house, 31 Elvaston Place, South Kensington. The school which he had to leave prematurely on account of the collapse of his health was Northaw Place, Potters Bar. 'There were a great many strange scholars there,' he said, describing the school, and manifesting his preoccupation, even as a boy, with the quality of strangeness of which he was later to give such masterly expression.

After leaving Northaw Place he drew and painted at home in Rye until 1921, when he spent two years at the Chelsea Polytechnic.

At Chelsea he became friends with the future theatrical director, William Chappell; the fact that they were younger than most of the other students first brought them together, but this friendship — as with others formed in his early years — has flourished until today. Chappell remembers Burra's addiction to squalid subjects with sinister overtones. Looking at some of his drawings of hags screaming at each other in Casey's Court, a slum street, one of the masters asked him why, for a change, he didn't draw some smart people. He did so, and the smart people looked more frightful than the hags. In 1923 he transferred to the Royal College of Art, remaining there for a year.

At the College, where I first became acquainted with him, he was regarded as something of a strange scholar himself, partly on account of occasional eccentricities, but far more for his extraordinary sophistication. The life drawings he made there show that he was already an extremely accomplished draughtsman. During years when his fellow students had been applying their attention listlessly to the Tudors or the binomial theorem — subjects with little relevance or none at all to the nourishment of artistic talent — Burra had been charging his imagination with precisely the ideas and the imagery that it most required. With the literature, for instance, of the cosmopolitan world centred in Montparnasse, Blaise Cendrars, Francis Carco, Pierre Macorlan and Daniel Fuchs. But he was also widely read in earlier writers, in particular the Elizabethans Tourneur and Marston, whose *Scourge of Villainie* was a favourite, as well as Walpole's *Castle of Otranto* and Harrison Ainsworth's *Tower of London*. With *Oliver Twist*, too, he was familiar. Although such works treat of a wide variety of subjects, they do offer an indication of the two that obsessively preoccupied him and accordingly contributed to the enhancement of his creative energy and to the sense of purpose which young artists are often slow to discover.

These two subjects were the Latin South, especially its underworld, and the sinister and menacing aspects of life in general. 'I've never been even faintly curious about any northern country, but I've wanted, for as long as I can remember, to go to Mexico and Venice,' I heard him declare. In later life, however, he has become attracted by the north of England, especially Yorkshire, also by Ireland. About his representation of evil there is a quality that distinguishes him from the satirist, from, for example, George Grosz, whose work he particularly admires. Grosz exposes, with grim ridicule, the brutish callousness and greed, the arrogance and capacity for hatred of his early German profiteer type of subject. Burra creates manifestations of evil of various kinds, but without ridicule or censure. Burra's evil is shown simply as evil, without comment. Since the artist will be personally unknown to the large majority of readers of this description of him, it is only just to make clear that his depiction of evil is not in any way an expression of his own character — far from it. It is simply that evil — which he regards with an obsessive horror tinged with amusement — happens to be the particular aspect of life to which his attention is habitually drawn.

It was characteristic of Burra that he did not wait until he visited the continent to portray with a profusion of detail the various aspects of its low-life that was to be his chosen theme for some fifteen years.

By the time of his arrival at the Royal College of Art Burra's knowledge of paintings was as wide as it was of literature. Caran d'Ache and Doré were early favourites, but El Greco, Zurbaran, and in particular Goya were more enduring influences. From Signorelli he learnt the effectiveness of hard, simple modelling and of the taut pose for conveying suggestions of restrained violence. Among other contemporaries and near-contemporaries those he studied to most purpose were, besides Grosz, Beardsley, Dulac, Walter Crane, Chirico, Wyndham Lewis, Dali and the now all but forgotten Covarrubias. As the number and variousness of the artists suggest, Burra was the disciple of none, but like a magpie picked up what he fancied. But what he took he assimilated into an art that had become, by his mid-twenties, one not remotely resembling that of anyone else: lucid, audacious, fantastic, and conveying often overtones of menace and corruption.

There was something bizarre in the contrast between the delicate young man who, though at times 'a strange scholar', was homeloving, and the products of his imagination: nocturnal encounters in the red-light districts of continental cities, scenes set in the waterside cafés and sailors' brothels of Mediterranean ports. These places were represented with meticulous correctness, for Burra was not only acquainted with picaresque literature in more than one language but, like Utrillo, he made extensive use of picture postcards.

From the middle 'twenties, when he made fairly frequent visits to the continent, his use of postcards diminished, and he came to rely increasingly on his extraordinary memory — a memory so precisely retentive that he has no need even to make sketches and he returns from tours or expeditions to possible subjects with his mind charged with a wide range of images exactly envisaged. When he is driven in a car he appears to look at nothing in particular; just to stare straight ahead.

Not long after leaving the College, he and Chappell, 'chaperoned' by the Henry Rushburys, visited Paris. A year or so later the two of them spent some time in Cassis, a town that delighted him; also, with several other friends, in Toulon. One of them, Beatrice Dawson, remembers that when the others enjoyed themselves on the beach (where he was never seen) he sat in a back room of the hotel, painting and eating ice-cream. A fountain in Toulon he later adapted for the drop-curtain in his setting for the ballet *Rio Grande.* He was seen off by another group of his friends, who noticed that his luggage consisted of no more than one small suitcase containing some papers and a spare pair of trousers.

Allusion has been made to his friends. Between him and them a very special relationship subsists. Burra is a friendly person, ready for instance to strike up an acquaintance with someone met by chance in, say, a pub, but his intimates are mostly among those who were fellow students at the Chelsea Polytechnic or the Royal College of Art (and in one or two instances, both). These are William Chappell, Beatrice Dawson, Barbara Ker-Seymer and Frederick Ashton. Three others, now dead, were John Banting, Basil Taylor and Georgiana Hodgkins. They were drawn together by a common interest in films and ballet, as well as painting. Unlike so many student friendships, they have not only survived but grown closer. The chief friend of a later date is Gerald Corcoran (formerly married to Beatrice Dawson), director of the Lefevre Gallery, where he has shown for many years. On his fortnightly visits to London he stays with one or other of them, and their spare bedroom is often alluded to as 'Edward's room'.

In 1930 he made a journey through France under the guidance of Paul Nash which took him again to visit a number of his favourite subjects, sailors' bars and the like.

Apart from his three student years he has lived all his life in Rye, which provides a small, although of late years a slightly increasing, proportion of his repertory of subjects. Travel, however, is a necessity to him, both as a spur to his imagination and as a means of extending his repertory. Besides the continent he has visited the United States and Mexico, where he became seriously ill, and going to Boston, spent weeks recovering in a basement room. Although his health requires that he preserve almost all his energies for his art, in life he occasionally behaves like one of his own creations 'Which reminds me somehow,' Paul Nash wrote to a friend in the summer of 1934

'of a lovely story [Conrad Aiken] told me of Ed's arrival in New York. Conrad met him at the Customs displaying the most awful mess of Woolworth underwear mixed up with paints and French and Spanish novelettes which was passed by the customs officer, an enormous Irish Yank. But as Ed stooped to close up his bag a large bulge in his hip pocket betrayed a considerable bottle of whisky. The officer leaned over and without a word tapped the bottle with a pencil. Conrad began to feel anxious and I'm sure did a lot of scratching behind his ear. But Ed didn't even straighten up, he leered round at the cop and said in that withering voice of his *"it's a growth."* Conrad said the chap was completely broken, he just got very red and wandered away looking at other things.' [1]

In any case Burra did not allow his precarious health to inhibit entirely his innate disposition to pursue, although fitfully, an independent way of life. There was a story current among his friends that one afternoon he walked out without a word. When night fell he had not come in, nor was there any sign of him for some three months. One evening he strolled back casually, though thin as a skeleton. It appeared that he had been to Mexico and lived in New York, making drawings and watercolours of Negro life in Harlem. When I questioned him he admitted that the story was not entirely apocryphal. It related, probably, to the expedition of 1933-4. One of these watercolours dated 1934 and entitled 'Harlem' was bought five years later by the Tate.

Unlike that of most artists of the present century, Burra's style has changed little: the clearly outlined, suavely modelled forms, usually near the paper's surface, the minutely observed detail, the absence of atmosphere ('I don't believe I *see* atmosphere,' he said to me) have all remained virtually unchanged. Later in his life,

[1] Anthony Bertram, *Paul Nash* 1955, p.221

when he painted landscape observed rather than imagined, English and Irish weather being what it is, he had to 'see' atmosphere, but even in such an outstanding example as 'Low Tide, Rye', of 1963, although mist-covered mud flats are represented, the artist's primary interest was focused on the eerie formation of the trees in the foreground, leafless, almost twigless, and the way they relate to the chilly unruffled surface of the sea. The atmosphere is scarcely more than a backdrop, rather than something to be represented more, as it would have been by Turner, Constable or an impressionist, for its own sake. 'Indistinctness is my forte,' as Turner is supposed to have said: Burra's forte is the near, the sharply defined, the minutely observed yet represented in terms of large, audacious and unexpected form. But if his style has evolved little, the informing spirit has undergone two changes, one of them radical.

From his student years until the middle 'thirties his principal preoccupation remained the low-life of the Mediterranean port, the sailors' café or brothel, exemplified by such works as 'Rossi' of 1930, showing a French sailor eating by himself in a café with eight white, red pom-pommed caps disposed upon a hat-rack like strange, delicate insects, contrasting with the huge Rossi bottle in the foreground, or 'The Café' of 1932, in which a young man sits in slyly smiling meditation upon some unlawful pleasure or nefarious plot, the foreground dominated not by a bottle, but by his companion's huge cloth cap. One feature of his art of those years was preoccupation with the cheap. What other artist has caught so inexorably the exuberant cut and the fibrous texture of cheap clothes? In rather the same way as Francis Bacon, a member of an 'old' family, is disposed to magnify the good qualities of proletarians, Burra, brought up in prosperous upper middle class surroundings, was fascinated by the meretricious. Although he looks occasionally through *The Times*, the 'popular' newspapers are his preferred reading, from which, however, he manages to be extremely well informed about the major issues confronting the world, as well as many comic and bizarre happenings that would elude an exclusive reader of *The Times*. I refer to this fascination in the past tense because it diminished as a consequence of the radical change that affected his art from the middle 'thirties — a change reflected in a gravity of outlook rarely perceptible before. The change was, however, not instantaneous. It is anticipated for instance in the sinister and enigmatic 'John Deth' of 1932, surely among his finest pictures **(PLATE 12)**. In it is portrayed the scythe-bearing figure of death intruding upon a party of dancers, striking the guests with terror, which sometimes expresses itself with tragic absurdity, as in the expression of the coarse-featured man wearing a paper hat who, in the act of embracing a woman, suddenly perceives Death kissing another woman paralysed by fear.

'Original' is a term apt to be too comprehensively applied, but it perfectly fits 'John Deth'. However the radical change, in part temperamental and in part, perhaps predominantly, due to the ubiquitous signs of imminent catastrophe, came a few years later. The assumption of power by the nazis warned the world — although many were long reluctant to face the issue — that people must submit to a slavery of the most degraded character and to arbitrary massacre or else must fight for their liberty, or even their survival. The issue was brought into sharper focus by the Civil War in Spain. This terrible event seized the imagination of a world unable to foresee the far greater catastrophes immediately ahead. Just before the beginning of the Spanish War Burra happened to be in Madrid. 'One day when I was lunching with some Spanish friends,' he told me, 'smoke kept blowing by the restaurant window. I asked where it came from. "Oh, it's nothing," someone answered with a gesture of impatience, "it's only a church being burnt." That made me feel sick. It was terrifying: constant strikes, churches on fire, and pent-up hatred everywhere. Everybody knew that something appalling was about to happen.'

Burra has spoken to me on several occasions of the Spanish Civil War, but he has given little indication of partisanship. To him the all-pervasive element of tragedy seems to preclude it: he was overwhelmed by the cruelty, destruction, hatred and death. It was a tragedy in which all concerned, however culpable, were in the last analysis victims. I say little indication of partisanship rather than none at all because horror at the burning of churches inclined him to identify the Franco party with civic stability, but I never heard him express even the most oblique approval of fascist ideas.

The war had for Burra a special significance as an artist as well as a man. For several years earlier he had been under the spell of Spanish civilization and had studied, with intense excitement, the great Spanish painters, as well as the luxuriantly dramatic (and in England then little known) architecture and sculpture of the Jesuit-commissioned baroque churches of Mexico. He could also be stirred to enthusiasm by lesser artists. 'Have you heard of a Spanish painter Gutierrez-Solana?" he asked me in a letter of 11 October 1942; 'they are very remarkable, but not "well known" as Spaniards are not so good at advertising themselves as the French.' He taught himself Spanish (by the Hugo method), which he reads with ease, also French, though he is reluctant to speak it.

No artist personally known to me has led a more sequestered life. Although he has held one-man exhibitions fairly regularly, he finds them an ordeal: 'they make me quite ill,' he wrote to me. On six occasions, however, work in a different medium brought him before a larger public than was aware of his paintings, namely designs for five ballets and an opera. These were 'Rio Grande' (originally entitled 'A Day in a Southern Port'), the music by Constant Lambert and choreography by Frederick Ashton, in which Markova and Lopokova performed, produced by the Carmargo Society in 1931; 'Barabau' (originally produced by Diaghilef with settings by Utrillo and choreography by Balanchine), produced by Ninette de Valois and performed by the Sadler's Wells Company in 1936; 'Miracle in the Gorbals' performed by the same company in 1944; 'Carmen' in 1947; the following year 'Don Juan', the music by Richard Strauss and the choreography by Ashton; and, in 1950, 'Don Quixote', with music by Roberto Gerhard and choreography by Ninette de Valois. The last three were performed at Covent Garden.

I myself saw none of these and know only of a few of their settings from photographs, and designs, but in the issue of *Ballet and Opera* for January 1949 Richard Buckle, under the pseudonym 'Dorothy Crossley', paid him his tribute.

'In our century it was Diaghilev who first persuaded "easel painters" to work for the stage. He employed the greatest artists of the School of Paris. In England the Sadler's Wells Ballet and now Covent Garden Opera have wisely enlisted artists outside the ranks of the small band of the accepted theatrical decorators. Of these perhaps Burra has been the most successful and shown most feeling for the stage.'

In the same article he wrote of his front curtain for 'Miracle in the Gorbals' that 'the prow of a great half-built liner in the Dockyards was grandly conceived', and of his costumes as 'cunning simplifications of contemporary cheap clothes to be seen in the backstreets of any industrial town.'

These performances brought him into favourable public notice, but after each one he disappeared from view.

In spite of his dislike for showing his work, it has been exhibited regularly, at the Leicester Galleries in 1929, 1932, 1947, 1949, at the Redfern in 1942, at the Hamet Gallery in 1970 and 1971, at the Postan Gallery in 1972, at the Lefevre in 1952, and there from 1955 biennially. 'I am a biennial,' said Ivy Compton-Burnett of her production of books, and Burra might say the same with reference to his exhibitions over the past eighteen years. These were received with respect and on occasion with wholehearted admiration, but until quite recently Burra has not been favoured by the establishment, never accorded, for instance, an officially sponsored exhibition, by the Arts Council, the British Council, even the Whitechapel, whose former director, Bryan Robertson, is an ardent admirer, or, until 1973, the Tate (although the Trustees did purchase seven of the eight examples of his work the Gallery possesses). Not that he has ever lacked admirers: PMAUL Nash — a close friend — and Wyndham Lewis both totd me that they considered him to be one of the finest living painters. And his work sells sufficiently well to enable him to live in modest comfort.

I do not know whether others share my sense of shame at the discovery of their ignorance about aspects of the lives of friends whom they suppose they know well, and of acquaintances when significant circumstances about them — tragedies, interests, achievements and other crucial matters — are revealed in their obituaries, or in tributes when they are the recipients of honours or other distinctions — or most acutely when one has occasion to write about them.

This I felt when Kenneth Clark, aware of my particular admiration for Burra, invited me, in 1942, to contribute the small volume on his work in the *Penguin Modern Painters* series of which he was editor. This undertaking involved a closer association with

Burra, bringing a wider knowledge of his art and character.

My first visit to Springfield, the Burra house in Rye, was an occasion I shall not forget. The house itself is wide-eaved, William IV or early Victorian. Its four-square solidity, the tweed coats and caps hanging in the hall, fishing tackle, shot-guns and the like, reflected a certain conventionality, no less than that of Edward's father, a widely read and cultivated man who encouraged his young children to look at Caran d'Ache and Doré. He greeted me in formal but friendly fashion, and took me for a stroll round the garden. When I had climbed the stairs, adorned mostly by Victorian watercolours, to Edward's studio the contrast was startling — a contrast resoundingly proclaimed by a framed close-up photograph of a face far gone in leprosy. In a book devoted to Unit One, the distinguished but shortlived association of artists gathered in 1933 by Paul Nash (the only group, I believe, that Burra has ever belonged to), there are photographs of the studios of its members. That of Burra's suggests that it was tidy and bare. The book was published the following year but I do not know when the photograph was taken. No room could have been more unlike it than the studio I visited eight years later.

Photographs were pinned up covering the walls almost completely, of paintings by Tiepolo (one of the artists he most admires, but of whom I see no reflection in his work), Signorelli, Magnasco, a wide variety of Spanish masters, pictures clipped from popular newspapers and periodicals, mostly representing dramatic incidents, often with figures in violent motion. Covering his gramophone, wireless, chairs and areas of the floor, were hundreds of books, newspapers and periodicals, novels in English, Spanish, French and Italian, glossy South American picture magazines, Victorian scrapbooks. And scattered among them scores of gramophone records, for he listens to music while he works, Berlioz being his favourite composer. (Beneath a similar profusion in nearby Springfield Cottage to which he eventually moved were discovered, in 1971, five wood-blocks, engraved in 1928-9, but never pulled and long forgotten by him and unknown to his friends. Their discoverer was the journalist, Barrie Penrose; the blocks themselves now belong to the Tate.) Constituting a top layer above this profusion were scattered long, white paper cylinders: his own drawings and watercolours, curled up (owing to his feeble health he prefers watercolour, as exacting less physical effort, to oil paint, which he has rarely used since the 'twenties). None of his own works were hung, but a few, returned from exhibition, leaned framed against the walls. A small work table stood close to a window, the light falling from the left. 'There never seems to be light enough,' he complained, 'and I can't work by electric light.' Since the installation of a 'daylight strip' at Springfield Cottage some years ago he has been able to work at any time of night. I recall this complaint because another visitor described a sheet hung from a corner of the window frame to protect him from the afternoon sun and to shut out the view of Rye. I saw none but ordinary curtains but whether the observation about the sheet is accurate or not the reference to shutting out the view of Rye has relevance. Burra has spent almost all his life there (in three different houses) and lives there to this day, but it has never engaged his affection; indeed indifference has sharpened into positive dislike for what he sometimes calls 'Tinkerbell Town'. It is curious, considering he could afford to live elsewhere, that he should not have left it. Lowry has no deep general sentiment for the Salford area, only for certain streets of poor houses, Oldham Road and other areas immediately adjacent to it, from which he draws the essential nourishment for his art, and needs accordingly to remain nearby. Although he has occasionally talked of leaving South Lancashire, I do not believe he ever will, or if by chance he were to do so that his art would not radically suffer. Burra has made a number of landscapes of Rye and the country round about, which not surprisingly reveal a special perceptiveness, but were he to move elsewhere his art would not be in the least degree affected nor I think — apart from the acute discomfort of picking up roots, even from an unloved place — would his way of life.

After I had looked through all his work he suggested we should go into the garden. The gentle movement — we spent several hours perambulating there — seemed to stimulate him. He spoke of the artists he admired, particularly, among the living, of Paul Nash and Wyndham Lewis; of his being haunted by the Spanish Civil War, and obsessed by Spanish civilization.

There was a picture that I especially wished to see again. 'A big picture of conquistadors' was how I described it: Edward looked puzzled and we recovered the painting I had in mind, which represented a group of soldiers of somewhat sixteenth century aspect, wearing scarlet masks appropriate to a Venetian carnival. 'Oh! *That* was the one you wanted, was it?' he said; 'but it's of *this* war: those are *British* soldiers just outside Rye.' Shortly after my visit *The Studio* offered to present a picture to the Tate and the Trustees readily accepted this splendid work, charged with the energy apparently so lacking in the artist himself, and of a sinister strangeness. Concerned, I think, that its subject should not again be mistaken, he changed its title from 'Soldiers' (under which it was first shown at the Redfern Gallery towards the end of the year) to 'Soldiers at Rye'.

Although all his pictures represent specific themes, he does not give them titles until their exhibition is intended. 'Then somebody comes along,' he explained, 'and stamps them with my signature with a rubber stamp, and presses me to invent titles for them.' Indeed there is an element of the unconscious about his procedures. 'Bring in a psychiatrist,' he replied to an enquiry as to the meaning of one of his pictures, 'and we'll find out.'

The character of Burra's evolution is clear; the Second World War intensified the sense of tragedy evoked by the Spanish Civil War. One seemed to him to be the logical culmination of the other. The themes often drawn from the Mediterranean brothel or sailors' bar were no longer adequate to express his agonized awareness of the dark tide of savagery that was transforming the world as he had known it. At a certain level artists must enjoy what they represent. I remember artists in both World Wars being distressed by the dichotomy set up in their minds between their exhilaration by the spectacle of devastation and their utter abhorrence of its cause. The vein of sardonic humour with which Burra viewed the war is implicit in the sentences which follow. 'About 2 days or so after you left,' he wrote in a letter dated 1 October 1942, 'a bomb or so fell round the cinema suddenly turned into one of its own news reels. I came on a very *romantic* scene, "improved" into the loveliest ruin with a crowd of picturesquely dressed figurents poking about in the yellowish dust. Many more bombs and ye antiente towne really won't have a whole window left let alone a ceiling up — a very pretty little late eighteenth or early nineteenth Wesleyan Chappell went as well in the hubbub. I now notice an anti-aircraft gun outside the door.'

(When the family moved from Springfield after the war their new house was built on the site of the ruined chapel, hence its name 'Chapel House'.)

The same spirit animates — more vividly — passages in an undated letter to other friends evidently written about the same time. 'Christmas night, the night before Christmas as a matter of fact the fun was so fast and furious in ye antiente towne that a Canadian was kicked to death and all the dances closed down by the military police on new year the Canadians came back all ripe for a revenge but found the midgets from Rochdale here shut up in their tumble down residences glaring behind broken panes with military police parading up and down. . . the days pass with many a jest and quip. Also as I was about to approach the level crossing I heard what I thought was machine gun practice, but oh dear me, it was nothing of the kind. It was the real thing . . . they did it again last Friday. Always when I'm going down to buy cigarettes. . .' And 'An American citizen now he is — with a special "pardon" for a murder he committed in that state or an attempted one I'm not sure — but of course in a nice way — it was for the party. . .'

The heightened sense of tragedy evoked by the Spanish Civil War was expressed not only in paintings with military themes such as 'Soldiers at Rye', 'Silence', representing a macabre figure smiling at a bomb-devastated street, of 1936, 'War in the Sun' of 1948 or 'Camouflage' of the same year, but in religious pictures such as 'Holy Week, Seville', 'Mexican Church' (at the Tate), 'The Vision of St. Theresa', all, too, of 1938, a particularly productive year. Religious subjects — although he is not a practising member of a Christian church — have continued to preoccupy him from time to time. In his 1952 exhibition at the Lefevre Gallery he showed 'Christ Mocked' (at the National Gallery of Victoria, Melbourne), 'The Expulsion of the Money-Lenders', 'The Entry into Jerusalem' (at the Beaverbrook Gallery, New Brunswick, Canada), 'The Coronation of the Virgin', 'The Pool of Bethesda' (bought by the Methodist Church) and 'Joseph of Arimathea'.

Parallel with the growth of his tragic sense of life has been that of his perception of the elements of strangeness in everyday things. From his earliest days he has been obsessed by the quality of strangeness, but then he expressed it mainly by the depiction of themes strange in themselves, of which 'John Deth', although a conspicuous example, is only one among many. But from the 'fifties his work shows this heightened awareness of the strangeness in everyday things. In, for instance, 'Owl and Quinces' or 'Bottles in a Landscape' (both of 1955) it is as though he had seen, for the very first time, the stuffed owl and the four pieces of fruit at the foot of its mounting and the ten bottles standing on a path with houses and telegraph poles in the distance. The conviction and the skill with which he conveys his astonishment at the sheer strangeness of these objects compel us to share it. We are seeing a stuffed owl and bottles as though we had never suspected that such objects existed. But here again the suddenness of this preoccupation must not be exaggerated: the coffee-machine (and its reflection) in an early work, 'French Sailors', the big bottle in the foreground of 'Rossi' earlier referred to, the buildings in 'Harlem' of 1934 (at the Tate) are examples of it selected at random; while his perception of the various qualities of cheap textiles has always been acute. Earlier, however, owing to the bizarre or nightmare character of his subjects, this strangeness was less conspicuous. Later, enhanced and applied to everyday objects in isolation, it has become one of the most impressive characteristics of his work.

Burra's art has undergone a further change. Until the later 'forties almost all of it represented people in their environment (occasionally strange non-human beings in theirs), but there has been a gradual shift of interest away from man to landscape and to inanimate objects. He confesses, as an artist, to a diminished interest in people, and more in his surroundings. He makes landscapes near his home in Rye and other regions which he visits, occasionally with his sister, in Yorkshire (where they stay with friends in Harrogate) and in Ireland. He makes no sketches on the spot but returns to Rye with his memory charged with subjects remembered selectively but in the utmost detail.

'There is a time-lag between my seeing a landscape,' he explained to me, 'and coming to the boil, so to say, but when I go back there, I'm always puzzled by what I've left out.'

As was inevitable, with the diminution, although far from extinction, of his interest in his fellow-men the satirical tone of his art has undergone a parallel decline. Discussing this development, I recalled that David Low had said to me that something of its former satiric bite had gone out of his caricature, and that the cause was clear, namely that the world had become so horrific a place that much was beyond the reach of satire. 'What,' he had asked me, 'can a satirist do with Auschwitz?' 'I entirely agree with Low,' Burra said; 'so many appalling things happen that eventually one's response diminishes. I didn't *feel*, physically, for instance, the shock of Kennedy's assassination as I would have done before the war.'

If Burra has become less concerned than he was with subjects inherently dramatic and sinister, he is able to imbue a stuffed owl, a few bottles or even a bunch of flowers with a dramatic and sinister ambience. This ability, this compulsion springs not from fancy or transient mood, but from a consistent attitude to life. *'Everything,'* he said to me, *'looks* menacing; I'm *always* expecting something calamitous to happen.'

The diminution of his interest in people and the drama of their situations is reflected by their replacement, frequent by the 'sixties, by sculpture, which enables him to represent the human figure without concerning himself with the human personality. So highly evolved has become his power of endowing inanimate objects with the quality of mysterious threat that human beings have become less and less necessary features of his art.

The imagery of Burra, the solid figures unmoving, unblinking, charged with nameless menace, yet animated by touches, here and there, of schoolboyish humour as, for instance, in 'It's All Boiling Up' of 1948 **(PLATE 13)**; landscapes, motorcars, lorries, excavators, flowers too, with obscure, disturbing overtones, constitutes, in T.S. Eliot's phrase, 'a more significant and disciplined kind of dreaming', though it has often more of the character of a nightmare than a dream.

Edward Burra is an essentially private person — who takes pride in never 'giving anything away' about himself; so I will not intrude much upon his privacy.

He is without ambition of any kind, either professional or personal. John Banting, who was with him when the offer of a CBE arrived, wrote, he told me, the letter of acceptance on his behalf in case Burra should forget to do so. Invited to become an Associate of the Royal Academy, he did not even reply. If his work sells, he is mildly pleased; if it does not, he is indifferent; he requires only sufficient income to keep up Springfield Cottage (where he has lived since 1968), to afford his bi-weekly visits to London and his occasional expeditions with his sister, but it has almost always sold well. He rarely reads newspaper notices of his exhibitions.

The extraordinary strength of his will compensates amply for the weakness of his constitution and it gives him untiring energy. He walks long distances, stays up late, requires no more than five hours' sleep, and works every day from eight or eight-thirty; rests for an hour or so in the afternoon in order to read (he is a voracious reader in Spanish, French, as well as English, of everything from the classics to science fiction) and resumes work later on.

There is one respect in which artists may be divided into two categories: those for whom the creation of a work of art is an extension of themselves to be, if possible, retained or else in some way safeguarded, and those for whom such creation is an act of parturition. Stanley Spencer, to take a conspicuous example, even at times of extreme poverty never parted with his work without reluctance (aside from landscapes, which he painted specifically for sale) and never at all — so far as I am aware — with any of his sketchbooks. It remained intimately, obsessively, a part of himself. Francis Bacon, on the contrary, would not object (though he might be surprised) if the purchaser of one of his paintings promptly destroyed it. Burra in this respect resembles Bacon: he loses his work and often forgets it. If a friend shows him a work lost or forgotten he will look at it with relish or dismissal, just as though it had been made by someone else, in particular laughing at any feature of it that strikes him as comic or absurd.

However indifferent the general public, his work, even routine life drawings made as a student, has always been treasured by his circle of intimates as well as a slowly growing number of others. It is my own long-held conviction that posterity will share the admiration of his friends rather than the indifference of the general public.

TRISTRAM HILLIER
born 1905

Of several of the painters who figure in this book, even perhaps of most, it can be said that their energies were almost exclusively dedicated to their work and that their lives were uneventful. Their vision, its vicissitudes, their attempts to realize it as fully as lay in their power, these things constituted the drama of their lives. I am thinking in particular of Houthuesen, Burra, Collins and Richards. The lives of Bacon, Freud and Colquhoun, on the other hand, could provide, independently of their art, subjects for biography or fiction. Bacon, for one, has long been a legendary figure. But the interest even in them derives from the audacity and intensity with which they have lived lives in outward circumstances not very different from those of their fellow artists.

Hillier, on the other hand, has led a life which, in spite of his dedication to painting of meticulous finish and elaborate composition, has been almost Byronic in its variety and drama.

The circumstances of his birth and upbringing were unusual; still more so those in which he inherited his religion. His father, manager in Peking of the Hong-Kong and Shanghai Bank, went blind at the age of thirty, and planned to shoot himself. When he confided his intention to a friend, he said, 'Why not become a Roman Catholic instead?' This he did, with far-reaching consequences for his second son.

Tristram Paul Hillier was born in Peking, the youngest of the four children of Edward Guy Hillier and his wife, born Ada Everett, on 11 April 1905. The Hilliers were of Huguenot descent, their name being originally St Hillaire, settling in England in the middle of the seventeenth century, shortly before the revocation of the Edict of Nantes. They were always connected with the sea, first as shipbuilders on the Thames and later, for several generations, as officers in the Royal Navy.

The Hilliers lived for a time in Pa-Li-Chuang, a temple in the

117

Western Hills outside Peking, after their town house was burnt in 1900 in the Boxer Rebellion. Journeys in China and across Russia by the Trans-Siberian Railway accustomed Tristram to travel.

Life, however various and interesting, was not happy for Tristram: his father was aloof and usually absent in China and his mother was an invalid dying slowly of cancer, and he felt little affection for her.

Some twenty years after his mother's death in 1917 he suffered a nervous breakdown, which the doctor who was treating him attributed to the insecurity of his early years and the horrifying impression made by his last visit to his mother's deathbed.

In short, his childhood and boyhood were lonely and loveless. He began to draw in the nursery but the Hilliers were a family without the slightest connection with the arts and it did not occur to him until much later to make a profession of a delightful diversion.

At the age of nine he went to Downside, remaining there for eight years. 'Religion was not in any way forced upon one,' he wrote in his autobiography, 'but the Benedictine ritual had become so familiar a part of my life that I absorbed without thought the strong influence that it was bound to exert upon an impressionable youth'.[1]

At first the influence, I suppose, was primarily aesthetic:

> I had begun to serve Masses at the High Altar of the Abbey, elaborate ceremonies which were conducted by priests clothed in vestments of scarlet, azure and cloth of gold, with a score of serving boys in attendance. The pageantry, the colour and the grave rhythm of movement against a background of delicate Gothic pillars affected me profoundly.

But by the age of seventeen, spiritual had reinforced aesthetic influences: he considered whether he had not a vocation for the monastic life, and with this end in view his curriculum was altered to give more time to theology and Latin. His life was to take a very different course, but his sense of religious vocation was so strong that he could write: 'Even after the passage of thirty years I feel today that my youthful intuition may well have been the light I should have followed.'

In his last months at Downside, with the encouragement of the

---

[1] Unless otherwise indicated all quotations in this chapter are taken from the artist's *Leda and the Goose* (1954).

drawing master and the headmaster, he devoted time to drawing as well as theology and Latin.

In order to consult his father about his vocation he revisited Peking. He also went for advice to the Trappist house in the Valley of the Monks in Mongolia, but during the few weeks he spent there, Tristram became, he tells us, 'alarmed beyond measure by the rigours of the Trappist order, which finally extinguished the few poor embers of that spiritual blaze which had been kindled by my Benedictine schooling'.

This circumstance, and the fascination aroused in him by the landscape of China, indicate that aesthetic aspirations had by then far superseded monastic.

Instead of returning to the novitiate he went to Cambridge. The two years he spent there, 1922 until 1924, he described in his autobiography as 'a waste of time' and dismissed them in half a dozen lines, in which he does not even refer to his college (Christ's) by name. In one respect, however, these years were highly important: for it was then that he began seriously to paint. But in spite of his absorption in this pursuit it did not even then occur to him to adopt painting as a profession; he was not yet sufficiently emancipated from the tradition of a family which would have regarded such a choice as morally indecent and materially insane.

The decisive impulse came from the unlikeliest quarter. After a holiday in Turkey and Rumania he joined, as an apprentice, a London firm of chartered accountants. There he did little but 'doodle': every morning a virgin pad of blotting paper would be placed on his desk and by evening it would be covered with drawings.

One day a cashier told him that he had kept all these drawings and that his wife had wrapped them in tissue and placed them in a drawer.

'Now, Mr Hillier', [he continued] 'I'm an old man and you mustn't take offence if I speak my mind. You'll never make a chartered accountant, nor any sort of business man . . . you ain't got no 'eart for it. I says to my Missus last night 'e's an artist, that's what 'e is.' 'Course 'e is', says she, 'and you ought to tell 'im so.' 'It's a wicked waste . . . you go off and have some paintin' lessons . . . and one day you might be paintin' the portrait of the Lord Mayor of London.'

Tristram never saw his unlikely mentor again but he remembers him with gratitude. Taking his advice he relinquished his apprenticeship and found his way to the Slade, where he quickly became aware of the emptiness of his previous existence. Oppressed by the sense of time wasted he found the hours of work at the Slade — ten until five — too short, and he attended evening classes at the Westminster School of Art, under Randolph Schwabe; also Bernard Meninsky who, although a former Slade student, had little respect for the austere academic teaching of Tonks.

The passionate response among the younger generation to the revolutionaries who had rejected the academic tradition — Picasso and Braque (especially their cubist works), Matisse, Wyndham Lewis, as well as certain of their predecessors, Van Gogh, Gauguin and most of all Cézanne — provoked in Tonks, as in many of his generation, a bitter defensiveness. From this, outstandingly effective teacher though he remained, many of his students suffered. 'Obscene nonsense' was how he described cubism to Hillier. Although he took Meninsky's advice to move to Paris after eighteen months at the Slade, Hillier owed much to Tonks's instruction in draughtsmanship in the classical tradition.

By way of Lake Como and Marseilles he went to Paris, working under André Lhote at the Atelier Colarossi and the Grande Chaumière. He met many of the most illustrious painters, including Picasso and Matisse, and new worlds of vision were discovered to him: cubism, fauvism, surrealism and a host of more ephemeral movements.

> Through this tornado of influences [he wrote] I steered an erratic course, veering first this way and then that, but leaving further behind me all the time the classic shores of my early training — to which, many years later, I was nevertheless destined to return.

Such paintings from his early years in France as I have seen fully bear out this account: they are derivative — sometimes feebly — from Cézanne, Picasso, Braque, Chirico and a dozen others, as well as Lhote with whom he studied. None of them, strangely enough, gives any intimation of the extremely personal style he was to evolve not much more than a decade after his arrival in Paris — a style that thenceforward underwent little change.

Within a few months of finding himself in 'this tornado of influences' his outlook was transformed: the sober instruction at the Slade was rejected as a remote irrelevance; he had become hostile to the church to whose service he had so recently determined to devote his life; and as for England, he had decided never to return.

Before he had given himself time to assimilate in a systematic fashion any of these multifarious influences a romance caused him to leave Paris. At the Ritz bar he met a young woman to whom he was violently and instantly attracted; his feelings were reciprocated and they went away together, settling in a cottage at La Gaude, a village near Nice, where they remained for about a year.

The Provençal landscape evoked a passion for Cézanne, but the four surviving canvases from the period suggest that passion was not accompanied by illumination. They are no better than the average Cézannesque school-pieces mass-produced by generations of British artists ever since Fry, with scholarship and sober eloquence, had established him as a 'tribal god'. But the volume of the work Tristram produced testified to his rare powers of concentration, for his relationship with Jill was tempestuous.

One incident will serve to indicate its climate (no less Jill's spontaneity and indifference to convention). Not long after their return to Paris Tristram happened to be stepping into his bath when she appeared, also naked, claiming the right to have her bath first, which he disputed. Their altercation culminated in violence: she struck him with a soap-rack and he fell bleeding to the floor. Horrified, and still naked, she descended in the lift to an apartment in which some Spanish friends were giving a party. A friend present described the entrance of Jill as the most dramatic he had ever seen: the double doors were suddenly pushed open, and there stood a naked Greek goddess announcing, 'I have just killed Tristram.' His injuries, however, were superficial, and they settled once again in Provence, but before long she left him.

On this sojourn expeditions in the sailing-boat of his friend the Greek artist Varda enhanced a passion for the sea and for the shore, the subjects of many of his paintings a few years later. But yet again his concentration on his art was to be similarly tested. Landing from Varda's boat in Toulon harbour after a narrow escape in a storm, dirty, bearded, spraysoaked, barefooted, wearing only patched trousers and a singlet, he and Varda were instantly invited to join a party of friends. There he again fell at sight in love with a beautiful girl. She was engaged to be married but within twenty-four hours he had persuaded her to remain with him. Her philosophic betrothed observed, on returning to London, 'At Victoria I lost my umbrella, at Toulon my fiancée, at Monte Carlo my money and on the return journey my ticket.'

Tristram bought, for the proverbial song, a large almost ruined fourteenth century castle, Mansencome near the Pyrenees. 'Wuthering Heights must have been positively cosy compared with that,' exclaimed the girl on her first sight of it, but shortly decided that it should be their home. At night bats circled and owls flew hooting through its immense vaulted chambers; but in the sunlight, with bees humming among its ruins, it was a place of enchantment. At Mansencome Tristram worked unremittingly and there she gave birth to twin sons, having reluctantly agreed 'to conform to this archaic survival', for such was her opinion of marriage. The ceremony took place in 1931, and the marriage was dissolved four years later.

In 1931 he held his first London exhibition at the Reid and Lefevre gallery (he had earlier held a smaller one in Paris), and this was amiably received. He and his wife remained at Mansencome, where life assumed a peaceful rhythm of painting and, with the help of their Cossack servant Simeonovitch, of gardening and rearing the children.

One August with Roland Penrose and Darsie Japp, another painter, he walked across the Pyrenees into Spain. He was immediately aware, he told me, of his profound affinity with Spain: 'No grass, no trees, but only rock and tawny earth that stretched away to the shimmering horizon like a lion's pelt.' 'A country I came to love above all other countries . . . The translucent light is comparable with that of Greece, which had so fascinated me,' he wrote, 'with the addition of a dramatic quality both noble and cruel, with which the land as well as the people are invested.'

To Spain he returned in 1935, remaining there until the outbreak of the Civil War. During this time he became a close friend of André Masson with whom he lived and worked for weeks at a time and from whom he received much encouragement and help.

Subsequently he travelled in Belgium, Holland, Hungary, Greece, including Crete, and a leper island.

At last by 1936 his all but insatiable need to travel was almost satisfied and, returning to London, he settled in a studio in an alley off World's End in Chelsea. Circumstances were slowly combining to bring — eventually — a stability both to his vision as a painter and to his domestic life. On a holiday in Austria he met Leda Millicent Hardcastle — the 'Leda' of his autobiography — to whom he was married early in 1937 in Vienna. 'Her values were those I had known as a child,' he wrote, 'against a background of country life, and they seemed sane and comforting after the turmoil of my existence since those early days.'

Through events far beyond his control his desire for a settled way of life was frustrated, for the Second World War was casting its dark anticipatory shadow — particularly apparent to Tristram and Leda who left Austria only 'a very few hours before . . . the entry of the *Führer* and his gangsters'. (Tristram's talk is wide-ranging, but his only allusions to politics in my hearing have been expressions of loathing for nazism and fascism.) Although the war delayed their establishing a way of life in harmony, his redis-covered values, his long and various apprenticeship, culminated in the formation of a style precisely suited to convey his vision of chosen aspects of his environment. He himself thus describes this development:

> Here [near Vence] during the next few months I started to paint landscape again, not in my earlier manner *au plein air*, but attempting to construct my pictures, from rough drawings which I would elaborate in the studio, in the style of the Flemish and Italian masters whose work I had recently had so much opportunity of studying. This was the beginning of my ultimate phase in painting, and became the manner in which I have worked ever since. There's a picture of mine, 'La Route des Alpes', dating from this time [1937] which now hangs in the Tate Gallery and illustrates fairly well, although I do not care for it, this period of transition from abstraction and surrealism to representational painting.

Although prior to the middle 'thirties he had indeed tried and discarded various manners, the ideas which were to fructify in his own 'ultimate phase' were taking shape. A paragraph from a brief essay which he contributed to *Unit 1*, the book published in 1934 devoted to the short-lived but highly talented group of that name formed by Paul Nash early in the previous year, indicates Hillier's preoccupation with the problems of composition so precisely solved in the best of his later work:

> For the design of my pictures I rely on my natural sense of balance and not, as has been suggested, upon numerical proportions; for the essence of what we understand as art lies in that order which is the outcome of assymmetry . . . it is only in the free sphere of irregularity that a man can build an homogeneous arrangement of tones, colours and shapes which achieve an equilibrium not of balancing volumes but in their relative intensities and mutual complement.

In the same essay, too, he refers to his 'deliberate distortion of perspective' 'in order to emphasize the rhythm he feels' — a consistent feature of his 'ultimate phase'.

By this time the special qualities that were to distinguish his work were already apparent. In a foreword to his exhibition at Reid and Lefevre held in 1933 his friend Roy Campbell wrote:

> Round all Hillier's work is that linear Pythagorean harmony which appears to be the dress and outline of all ideas, but is really their essence . . . The painter's passion and his lyricism are not less powerful for being like a kite when it is pulling its hardest, almost motionless.

The artist's indifference to 'La Route des Alpes' is understandable, but although this painting does not stand comparison with his best, it does exemplify with particular clarity the combination of qualities that mark the work of his 'ultimate phase': the austere, the static, the precisely calculated image, its cold sparkle and the almost total indifference to atmosphere.

Ever since the late 'twenties he had been susceptible, too, to the dreamlike quality inherent in surrealist art and had made paintings designed to capture this quality by the use of the prevailing formula of juxtaposing incongruous objects. But in the later paintings realistic landscape, architecture and, to a lesser degree still-life, are invested with an aura of strangeness without diminution of their credibility. Surrealism thus transmuted has continued to play a pervasive part in his paintings.

Although 'La Route des Alpes' is a relatively minor performance, when it was first shown at the Arthur Tooth Gallery in 1943 I well remember the clear, decisive, minutely calculated chord it struck, and how pleased I was to be able to buy it for the

Contemporary Art Society, which presented it the following year to the Tate.

Edward Wadsworth, a friend and a visitor in the middle 'thirties to a furnished villa that the Hilliers rented at Etretat on the coast of Normandy, helped him towards the evolution of his final style. The two painters had certain tastes in common: for the sea and the shore; for boats, lighthouses, cranes, for netting, coils of rope and chain and other impedimenta of deck, dock and pebbled beach, and for all these seen in sharpest focus. In one respect, however, they differed. 'I have always used oil paint,' he wrote to me (21 May 1970), 'but I take a deal of trouble preparing my canvas, which accounts for the very smooth quality of the paint. Wadsworth tried for years to persuade me to try tempera — of which he was a master — but I never cared for it.'

But his full employment of the style he had evolved was delayed by the war. Just before its outbreak his father-in-law bought them a stylish eighteenth century house, L'Ormerie, near the village of Criquetot L'Esteval, in Normandy, which they intended to make their home. But they were swept away in the vast and harrowing exodus of the population before the German advance. After an adventurous journey they escaped from St Malo to Southampton. From 1940 until 1944 Tristram served in the Royal Naval Volunteer Reserve, being invalided out with the rank of lieutenant.

After the war had ended they returned to Normandy, but to their sorrow they found L'Ormerie an almost irretrievable wreck, at least for people in their straitened circumstances.

Tristram's pictures, however, were saved, and since they constituted a large proportion of their assets, he applied to the Board of Trade for permission to import them, with farcical consequences that I well remember.

We are facing a period [the lady bureaucrat concerned gently explained to him] which demands from all of us a standard of living if the economic structure of this country is to survive. Sir Stafford Cripps [President of the Board of Trade] has endeavoured constantly to impress upon the people that they must learn for the time being to forego luxuries. If I were to give you permission to import your paintings there would be people, no doubt, who would be tempted to buy them, and Art, after all, is a frivolity which we simply cannot afford just now.

When he told me of this homily, in praise of a policy which excluded national assets from the country (exportable assets incidentally) and which threatened an artist (also an ex-service man) with bankruptcy by denying him effective possession of his own work, I joined several of his other friends in attempting to reverse this decision, as unjust as it was contrary to the national interest, but with no more than partial success. A licence was eventually granted, but to import only pictures painted before the war and excluding any that he might have done since his return to Normandy, and this subject to the condition that he take up permanent residence in Britain.

Tristram and Leda, like almost everybody in France, found living conditions desperate; they also found that the country itself had undergone disillusioning spiritual and intellectual changes, and they no longer wished to live there. In the spring of 1946 they accordingly returned to England and explored the only part of it, aside from London, with which he was in some degree familiar from his years at Downside and a visit towards the end of the war, namely Somerset. Here they eventually settled. 'I have found my happiness and my home at last,' he wrote, 'in Leda and in England.'

The time of his return to England was marked by another return: to the communion of the Catholic Church. This act was marked with the same meticulousness as his painting. Determined to be sure that his decision was not the result of sentimentality he discussed the matter thoroughly with several noted theologians at nearby Downside.

Between 1941 and 1944 he had scarcely been able to paint, but in Somerset during the last months of the war he worked during every daylight hour. (He never paints at night.) Service with the Navy, however, had not entirely prevented him from working. It is strange that the shattering events of the war and almost three years of enforced cessation of painting, far from impairing, conspicuously enhanced his creative powers. This can be seen at a glance by comparing 'La Route des Alpes' of 1937, with 'Harness' (Tate Gallery) **(PLATE 14)** painted in Somerset seven years later which hangs near it at the Tate (or with the slightly earlier companion picture 'The Bridle' at the National Gallery of Canada). The first looks mechanical and contrived and its impact is less forcible than that of either of the others, or of the fine 'Trinity Wharf', in which a rhythmic poetry is extracted from a lighthouse and a dock on which repose anchor, rope, a rowing-boat: all the maritime miscellanea that he and Wadsworth had represented with such zest a few years before. (This painting, made in 1945, is in the National Gallery of New South Wales.)

But of a different order from these are those he painted in Spain and Portugal. There are painters who delight in what is damp, soft, atmospheric, unsusceptible of sharp definition. Such a one, for instance, as Ivon Hitchens, whose 'Damp Autumn' at the Tate and 'Waterfall, Terwick Mill' perfectly exemplify such preferences. There are also painters of precisely opposite preferences, for what is dry, hard, clear and susceptible of the sharpest definition, such, for instance, as Wyndham Lewis and Edward Burra. But not even they showed quite the passion for these qualities as Tristram Hillier. This disposition may have been fostered by the austere landscape of certain parts of China, as was suggested by his fervent response to it when he revisited the country for the first time as an adult; perhaps, too, by his almost exclusive familiarity with Chinese painting in childhood and adolescence. The fact that he has been so long and so intimately identified with the Mediterranean world has led to his intense interest in Van Eyck and other early Netherlandish painters being overlooked. These he has assiduously studied in Dutch and Belgian museums, delighting especially in their lucidity and mastery of detail. Brueghel and Bosch are among the painters whom he most fervently admires.

Precision and clarity — besides its other-worldness and strangeness — were among the qualities of surrealism that held a particular appeal for him. But what decisively confirmed these various preferences was his long and passionate association with the Iberian peninsula. Since 1947 he has spent several months of every year in Spain and Portugal.

There is hardly a corner of Spain that I don't know [he said to me]. I have painted all over the country and in much of Portugal as well. The region of Spain that I most love is Estremadura, which is still little visited by foreigners. Beside my own affinity with Spain when I first went there, I was aware of an affinity between the landscape of Spain and that of China. Sometimes I find Spain so emotionally disturbing that I take refuge in Portugal, that 'paradise

of flowers and gentleness'. Yes, after a week in Spain I can be absolutely
whacked from emotional exhaustion: by its starkness, its cruelty, its nobility.

There is no cruelty in Tristram's painting, beyond an intimation
in some of the black high-prowed Portuguese fishing boats like
fierce primeval monsters stretched out on the beach, but there is
much stark nobility. At first glance his paintings appear to be
literal representations. Further scrutiny reveals in them marked
imaginative, even dramatic elements. The painter was too long
under the spell of surrealism ever to be tempted into supine
acceptance of the scene before him. Or more precisely of what he
sees when making his preparatory pencil studies. All his later
paintings are made in his studio in Somerset. As already indicated,
he distorts perspective, sometimes radically, in the interests of
drama, lucidity or some other quality he is attempting to achieve.
Discussing a painting of a street in a Spanish town, in which the
perspective appears entirely credible, he pointed out that two of
the architectural features depicted could not, in reality, be seen
simultaneously. The subjects, then, are carefully modified or even
rearranged; likewise their illumination and colour — but never to
the extent of impairing, to the least degree, their credibility. In his
pictures the paint scarcely 'tells' as paint at all; its qualities are as
seriously disciplined in the interests of the representation of his
subjects as they are in those of Ingres. No artist of his generation
is more remote — to define the character of his art in negative
terms — from action-painting than Hillier.

Establishment in Somerset faced him with one serious problem,
posed by his preference for what is dry, hard, clear, and susceptible of the sharpest definition. For Somerset has none of these
characteristics. There are occasions when, in his landscapes of his
neighbourhood — he lives at East Pennard, near Shepton Mallet
— he imposes the qualities of his preference on a subject which is
conspicuously characterized by their opposites. There are,
however, other occasions when the very persistence of the struggle
to overcome temperamental preferences in the interests of the most
searching representation of his subject has resulted in high
achievements. I am thinking, for example, of such as 'January
Landscape, Somerset' of 1962, in the Harris Museum and Art
Gallery, Preston, and 'Landscape with a Stream on Godney
Moor' of 1967. But there can, I believe, be no denying that his

Plate 14: TRISTRAM HILLIER: *Harness* (1944), tempera on canvas, 23¾ × 32 in.

Plate 15: TRISTRAM HILLIER: *Viseu* (1947), oil on canvas, 24 × 32 in.

Plate 16: CECIL COLLINS: *The Sleeping Fool* (1943), oil on canvas, 11¾ × 15¾ in.

Plate 17: CECIL COLLINS: *The Wounded Angel* (1967), oil on hardboard, 36 × 30 in.

Plate 18: VICTOR PASMORE: *Chiswick Reach*, also known as *Evening, Hammersmith* (1943), oil on canvas, 34¼ × 47¼ in.

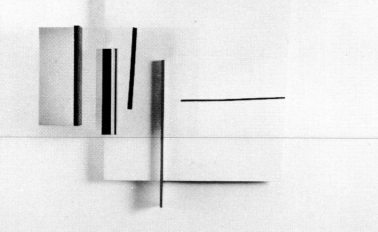

Plate 19: VICTOR PASMORE: *Relief Construction in White, Black and Indian Red* (1965-7), painted wood and plastic, 48 × 48 × 8 in.

Plate 20: FRANCIS BACON: *Figure Study II* (1945-6), oil on canvas, $57\frac{1}{8} \times 50\frac{3}{4}$ in.

highest achievements are reached in response to subjects invested by the qualities which he loves with the austere passion so profoundly appropriate to them; the landscapes of Spain and Portugal. Here the toll of high achievement is far longer. Among what I believe to be his finest paintings are 'Tornada', 'Igredia de Misericordia', and 'Portuguese Fishing Craft' (all of 1947); 'Viseu' **(PLATE 15)**, of 1948; 'Salamanca', of 1961; 'El Convento de San Esteban, Salamanca' of 1963; and 'Cevera, Aragon', of 1964.

'If it were not for Leda's devotion to Somerset,' he told me, 'I'd live in Spain.' When I objected that were he to do so the exhilarating emotional disturbance he experienced on his visits would be likely to diminish, a look of happiness lit up his face; he agreed that the intensity of his response to Iberia could best be preserved by spending most of his time in misty, gentle Somerset.

In the course of our desultory correspondence I asked him whether he thought that what he himself refers to as his 'ultimate style' was in fact ultimate, or whether he was likely to any degree to experience the evolution common to many painters towards a greater freedom and apparent spontaneity of brushstroke.

> I would like to think [he wrote in reply (11 June 1970)] that my present form of painting does not represent my ultimate phase and that I shall eventually be able to express myself with a more free brushstroke and a richer use of paint. But I think this is unlikely for after so many years of working in this meticulous manner, I have become the slave of my own style — which I suppose happens to every painter of my age. In my recent work, however, I have been using a much rougher texture — painting often with a palette knife in my landscapes and skies, and simplifying my architectural forms. It is true that my masters are the Flemish and Dutch painters, but this does not lessen my love for painting of a very different kind. When I look at a Courbet or even a Turner, it is with envy that they can use paint in such a rich and luscious way. It could never be my way, and I learned very many years ago the lesson which every painter has to learn sooner or later — that one must know one's limitations and seek to perfect one's technique within these limitations.

CECIL COLLINS
born 1908

Kathleen Raine wrote of the paintings of Cecil Collins that they 'seem not so much separate wholes as each an aspect of a single world'.[1] This observation seems to me to touch the very essence of his work. His life has been dedicated to the discovery and the depiction of another world — a world governed by many of the same laws as our own, gravity, perspective and the like — yet entirely different. 'The Lost Paradise' is how Kathleen Raine defined it. Later on I will amplify this description by quotations from the artist's own writings. It is a world which — though it took him long to discover, explore and represent — he was aware of even as a child. Awareness of the existence of another world and of his own affinity with it gave him a sense of acute loneliness. Had this world been a child's fairyland it might have served as a refuge from loneliness, but he understood, however vaguely, that it was a real and universal although a hidden world that imposed its own special duties and responsibilities, and that art (he regarded himself as an artist from childhood) was not a private but an essentially communal pursuit. Of course neither the Lost Paradise nor the nature of art were present to his mind in quite such definite terms, but they afford an indication of the direction of his thought and feeling.

Cecil James Henry Collins was born on 23 March 1908 at 2 Bayswater Terrace in Plymouth, son of Henry Collins, an engineer, and his wife Mary, born Bowie. Both his parents were Cornish and of predominantly Celtic blood.

Cecil drew, at least from the age of six, with considerable facility, his earliest enthusiasm being for landscape, but his father opposed his ambition to become an artist, and compelled him to train as an engineer and apprenticed him to a firm in Plymouth. Cecil, at the time aged fourteen, bored by engineering and repelled

[1] Introduction to catalogue of 1965 Exhibition at the Arthur Tooth Gallery.

by the brutality with which the firm was conducted, ran away and refused to return.

His father's opposition, however misplaced, was understandable, for ruined as a consequence of the First World War he was reduced to working as a navvy on roads, and the family lived in one room in a Plymouth slum.

Collins's persistence won him, in 1924, a scholarship at the Plymouth School of Art. Here he received precisely what he required: a rigorous training in realistic draughtmanship. In his determination to be an artist he was encouraged by a local Catholic priest. In 1927 he was awarded a scholarship at the Royal College of Art, where he worked for four years. Recalling many years later his sight there of Albert Houthuesen's 'Supper at Emmaus', he said he felt that the artist 'had touched a mystical stream, a manifestation of a higher form of consciousness'.

Inevitably our talk turned one day on the relation between himself as a student and my father as principal, after he told me that he had been awarded the William Rothenstein Prize for Drawing from Life. 'For me, coming from Plymouth, where I was taught, and well taught, by *teachers*', he said, 'your father's was an exciting presence as the *artist*, a man who was himself part of a magical world. And he put up benevolently with my eccentricities.'

Steadily, in the meanwhile, his ideas clarified and he became ever more aware of the transitoriness of our life and convinced of the existence of another world, which he has many times described, once, in conversation, as 'the continuum of consciousness, which permeates this world as perfume does a fabric'.

In 1931, before taking his diploma, he married Elisabeth Ramsden, a fellow student at the College who worked under Henry Moore when he was an instructor there. Elisabeth is the eldest daughter of Clifford Ramsden, and his American wife Nellie, born Ward, of Hollins, Luddenden, Yorkshire. The family is well known in the West Riding. Their connection with the local newspaper, *The Halifax Courier and Guardian*, has extended over four generations.

Until he came to the College Collins was primarily a draughtsman; but from the late 'twenties he turned to painting, becoming more and more conscious of the evocative power of colour. In the light of his determination to state his often highly complex message with the utmost lucidity, it is to be expected that his art, for all its beauties of colour, should be essentially a draughtsman's. In fact at the very time of his enhanced awareness of the potentialities of colour, familiarity with the drawings of Klee released a vein of fantasy in him that has remained a recurrent element in his work.

It seemed to him, in the middle 'thirties, that surrealism could bring him nearer to that 'other world' by which he was becoming ever more obsessed but which he had not yet 'seen plain'. 'This,' said Herbert Read at the opening of the surrealist exhibition in London in 1936 (in which Cecil was represented), 'is the dawn of a new world.' Collins was present, and, already troubled by doubts about the movement's validity, reflected that 'the occasion was not a dawn but a sunset.'

Collins quickly rejected surrealism and what he called its 'psychic furniture'. 'I do not believe in surrealism,' he wrote in his basic affirmation of faith, *The Vision of the Fool*, published in 1947, 'precisely because I do believe in a surreality, universal and external, above and beyond the world of the intellect and the senses; but not beyond the reach of the humility and hunger of the human heart.'

I do not pretend to be able to trace the precise steps which led from his rejection of surrealism in the late 'thirties to the mature formulation of his philosophy of art and life in the early 'forties. This evolution owed something to Eric Gill, whom he saw often from 1933 until 1936, when they were neighbours in Buckinghamshire. Gill's logical mind, his constant preoccupation with ideas, expressed not only in his art and writings but in his conversation, a bracing blend of the challenging and the humane, no doubt stimulated Collins to clarify his ideas. Far more influential than Gill's own ideas were those of Maritain, to which Gill introduced him. These gave him his first contact with traditional philosophy. Although he owes much to Maritain, he was eventually repelled by his Aristotelian and Thomistic orientation, his own being innately Platonic. It was to Gill, too, that he owed his introduction to David Jones, an artist and writer whom he particularly admires. Perhaps the strongest and most lasting influence was that of Mark Tobey whom he met two years after he moved, in 1936, from Speen in Buckinghamshire to Totnes in

Devon. Tobey, who was teaching at Dartington, evoked his interest in the art and philosophy of the Far East. (More than thirty years later I noticed, on Collins's reading desk in his workroom in Chelsea, prayerbooks and works of meditation of the Ba'hai religion, in which Tobey is a believer. 'I'm studying Ba'hai at the moment,' he said, and opening the book showed me some of the prayers.) Later on, when he himself was working there, another teacher at Dartington, Rudolph Laban, interested him in dance theory, which increased his awareness of the importance of the rhythmic aspects of pictorial composition.

Whatever the influences — and Cecil is widely read, especially in the mystics — Blake became a paramount source of inspiration — it is clear that, by the early 'forties, his philosophy of life and art was fully evolved, and both succinctly and eloquently expressed in *The Vision of the Fool*. In essence it is an elaboration of the injunction in St Paul's First Epistle to the Corinthians: 'If any man among you seemeth to be wise in this world let him become a fool that he may be wise.'

> Modern society has succeeded very well [to quote from some key passages] in rendering poetic imagination, Art and Religion, the three magical representatives of life, an heresy; and the living symbol of that heresy is the Fool. The Fool is the poetic imagination of life . . . . The greatest fool in history was Christ. This Divine Fool, whose immortal compassion and holy folly placed a light in the dark hands of the world [a world in which] Art, Poetry and Religion are not so difficult or important that they can be made mediocre, it only needs education [in which] A great spiritual betrayal is on — it is the betrayal of the love and worship of life by the dominance of the scientific technical view of life in practically all the fields of human experience [and by] the mechanization of contemporary society and by the teaching of the norm of the ordinary man, 'the man in the street' . . . the philosophy of mediocrity, into which, with a sigh of relief, the heavy inert mass of mankind desires to sink.

The concluding sentences are these:

> The Saint, the artist, the poet, and the Fool, are one. They are the eternal virginity of spirit, which, in the dark winter of the world, continually proclaims the existence of a new life, gives faithful promise of the spring of an invisible kingdom, and the coming of light.

At the beginning of the essay he asserts that paintings and drawings cannot be explained, but the concluding sentences at least indicate the subject which his own represent. In the case of a painter for whom subject is integral to his art this indication has high value for the understanding of it. In a later piece of writing, some 'Notes' in the catalogue of the retrospective exhibition of his paintings, drawings and tapestries from 1926 held at the White-chapel Gallery in 1959, he is rather more specific about the nature of his subject.

> Beneath the tyranny and captivity of the mediocre culture of political dictatorships and their mechanical systems, and beneath our commercial traveller's civilizations, there still runs the living river of human consciousness, within which is concentrated in continuity the life of the kingdoms of life, animals, plants, stars, the earth and the sea, and the life of our ancestors, the flowing generations of men and women, as they flower in their brief and tragic beauty. And the artist is the vehicle of the continuity of that life, and its guardian, and his instrument is the myth, and the archetypal image.

To Cecil that 'living river', although perceptible only by the imagination, is also an objective entity, as is suggested by his preoccupation with the angel, the archetypal messenger between our world and another, who figures in many religions. 'We cannot yet bear to come in touch with the external world,' he said to me, 'so the angel is its mediator.' 'With this world,' he added, 'I make contact when I paint. It is a world that Plato mentions, and Dante wrote the *Divine Comedy* in order to raise man from a state of wretchedness to a state of blessedness.'

Collins is well aware, despite such contacts, of the mysterious and elusive nature of this other world. But it does not in the least trouble him. 'I detest ambiguity,' he said, 'ambiguity is something ordinary made obscure. Mystery is the hallmark of all canonical art.'

Both on account of its clarity and of its reflection of a hidden world, Cecil, who as a student admired John and Greco, later Klee and the surrealists, has come to prefer the arts of the ancient world: the best Buddhist sculpture, early Greek sculpture, Byzantine painting, Italian painting before Duccio. His admiration for Picasso is qualified by the melancholy reflection: 'He is a genius born outside a civilized context. Imagine what he would have done in a great culture!' The only modern painter of whom I have heard him express unqualified praise is the Douanier Rousseau.

The being whose paintings, drawings and poems — expressions

of his 'Visions of Eternity' — have most deeply affected Collins is William Blake.

> Shall painting be confined [Blake wrote] to the sordid drudgery of fac-simile representations of merely mortal and perishing substances and not be, as poetry and music are, elevated to its proper sphere of invention and visionary conception? No, it shall not be! Painting, as well as poetry and music, exists and exults in immortal thoughts. [Or again] I assert to myself that I do not behold the outward Creation and that to me it is hindrance and not Action; it is the dirt under my feet, No part of Me. 'What,' it will be questioned, 'When the sun rises, do you not see a round disk of fire somewhat like a guinea?' O no, no, I see an Innumerable company of the Heavenly host crying, 'Holy, Holy, Holy is the Lord God Almighty'.

Collins's paintings and drawings, in a formal sense, his elongated and sometimes skeletonless figures, reveal the influence of Blake, but no more than the most superficial aspects of it. Cecil does not in any specific sense share many of Blake's obscure and in any case changing doctrines, but it is from the example of Blake that he derives the courage to be a visionary painter, to act and act constantly upon the intimations he receives from his other world, or his Lost Paradise. From Blake he does not, however, derive only the conception of the incompatibility between innocence, the visionary sense of the infinite, the religion of the spirit, and materialism, conventional morality, and science. There is much else in *The Vision of the Fool* that echoes Blake. 'The ideal of our education,' for example, 'is the clever scientific technician [which] dominates all other approaches to the mystery of life, including those ancient and eternal ways of perception, Art and Religion.' He even uses the word 'innocence' in the Blakean sense: ' . . . this ancient element of the eternal Adam still exists deep inside a man . . . . That holds converse with the essence of life. Spiritual joy, that is essential joy, arises from innocence . . . ', and this by way of contrast to 'the element of the insect, of the mechanical in man, which degrades man into . . . a sterile state of efficiency.' Although Collins's visionary spirit is akin to Blake's, his painting, in spite of the occasional superficial resemblance, is very different. Blake's forms were largely based upon late renaissance works highly influential during his time, as well as gothic, while Collins's are more hieratic, and influenced by the arts of far earlier civilizations.

On a different level Collins derived something, too, from the lyricism of Samuel Palmer. No one ignorant of his Shoreham landscapes could have made 'The Field of Corn' (a pen and wash of 1944, in the Victoria and Albert Museum), or 'The Invocation', a watercolour of the same date.

Collins's return to his native Devon in 1936 had two other consequences besides his significant association with Mark Tobey. The rounded hills and the forests near Totnes, perhaps because they revived memories of scenes of his childhood, stimulated his imaginative life. And by an accident of war he adopted a new, though secondary profession.

Cecil and Elisabeth attended Mark Tobey's classes at Dartington, but he returned within a few months of their meeting in 1938 to the United States. Just before the Second World War an art school was established at Dartington, staffed mostly by German and Czech teachers, who in the course of it were imprisoned or interned. Unexpectedly Collins was appointed, in 1939, director of studies, and taught painting and drawing at the school's studio workshop. His duties did not seriously interrupt his own painting, and in that same year among other pictures he completed a large oil, of himself and his wife. They are seated at a small dining table, and through the window behind them is a hieratic Byzantinesque landscape with Palmeresque overtones. It is a dignified, serious painting, but it shows little of the imaginative fantasy that was shortly to characterize his work and had already occasionally revealed itself, for instance in 'The Quest', another large painting made the previous year, which represents a king and three others in a small boat skirting a rocky shore of lunar aridity. 'The Artist and his Wife' are ensconced firmly in Totnes, but in 'The Quest' we are shown 'the other world' though hardly a Lost Paradise. The aura of this painting — apart from the fact that the boat is proceeding at a brisk pace without visible means of propulsion — makes it clear that we are remote from even the wilder shores of the terrestrial globe.

Collins enjoyed teaching at Dartington (where he had his own studio) and living in a community, staying there for four years. He resumed teaching in 1956 at the Central School of Arts and Crafts in London. Being something of a prophet, teaching is for him a natural function and, although he evolved a philosophy of art and life relatively early, he finds that discussion with his students further clarifies his own ideas. For him painting and drawing are a form of meditation, but he regards the function of the artist as essentially public. Convinced as he is that art is a form of knowledge, he was delighted when his students, after an interlude during which they demanded entire freedom of action, suddenly asked to have the model back and demanded to be taught. The rejection by many students today of standards of morality of any kind, even though Cecil himself has always been opposed to conformist morals, greatly troubles him. 'Do you realize,' he asked me, 'that owing to the absence of moral standards the student of today can't even *sin*?'

Collins held his first one-man exhibition in 1935 at the Blooms-bury Gallery, and although he contributed to at least three wartime exhibitions: 'New Movements in Art', at the London Museum, 'Imaginative Art since 1939', at the Leicester Galleries, and the British Council's 'Contemporary British Art', shown at the Museum at Toledo, Ohio, and elsewhere in the United States, he nevertheless became averse from the public showing of his work. But in 1943, the year when he returned to London from Devon, he acceded to the urgent advice of a friend and decided to hold an exhibition. For a time he lodged in Carlton Mews off Trafalgar Square. At his invitation I called there to see him and a considerable accumulation of his work. We had known each other when he was a student at the Royal College of Art, but I must confess to my discredit that I had under-rated his work (though there had been few opportunities of seeing it); also the man and his ideas. But my experience at Carlton Mews trans-formed my attitude: I intensely admired the best of his work and formed an enhanced liking and respect for the man. Like his master Blake he is an uneven artist but at his best he has a high place among the small company of imaginative artists active today. Having a wide range of his work to choose from I bought, on behalf of the Contemporary Art Society, the recently completed 'The Sleeping Fool' **(PLATE 16)** (accepted by the Tate in 1951), an unforgettable combination of naivety and sophis-tication, and a painting that has remained as vividly present to me as any picture on our own walls.

This painting is one of a series begun three years before, titled originally 'The Holy Fools' but later, to accord with his essay, altered to 'The Vision of the Fool' — a series he has constantly added to but never shown in its entirety. The essay, although I think even more highly of it now than I did at the time, completed the experience of Carlton Mews: Cecil, Elisabeth, Elizabeth and I became friends, and although for geographical reasons we have not met frequently our friendship has, I believe, flourished.

But it was one thing for a friend to urge Cecil to show his work and very much another to achieve this purpose. Packing as many paintings and drawings as it would hold into a large suitcase he trudged wearily along the streets where the commercial galleries are located, unpacked his work and showed it. It was rejected by all. At the Lefevre McNeill Reid said, after giving one of the paintings a cursory glance, 'It's no good. All this surrealism is *over*.' By this time Cecil was too exhausted to carry the suitcase any further, and he asked whether he might leave it at the gallery. Being a kindly man Mr Reid readily agreed and undertook to look at the work at leisure. Two days later he returned, to be told that 'there has not been time to look at it'. Still exhausted, Cecil asked if he might leave the suitcase for one day more. Next morning he was greeted by Duncan Macdonald, one of the partners in the firm who had just returned from New York, with the words, 'The work you've left here is very important. If you'll allow me I'll visit you in Devon and see more.' The result was Collins's first one-man exhibition for nine years held early in 1944. It was well received and there were a number of sales. In the course of the exhibition Cecil and Elisabeth went to stay with her parents at Luddenden, near Halifax. News reached them there that the Lefevre Gallery had been hit by a bomb. As his exhibition represented some ten years' work Cecil compulsively telephoned to the gallery, though scarcely expecting any response. To his astonishment his call was answered. 'Yes, I'm still here,' a member of the staff said, 'your pictures were all blown off the walls and are among the wreckage on the floor, but I've examined them, and all but two are unharmed.' Among the unharmed was no. 5, 'The Sleeping Fool'. The following year he had another exhibition at the Lefevre Gallery, which was even more successful than its predecessor, and a third in 1948.

Collins has never had a strong constitution, and his happy

married life has not, I believe, been marked by dramatic external events. Like Albert Houthuesen and Edward Burra he has to conserve all his energies for the pursuit of his art. Much of his life, in any case, is passed in his other world, 'in the living river of human consciousness' unseen by the ordinary eye, 'The Lost Paradise'. But until they settled in Selwyn Gardens (number 15, since renumbered 35), Cambridge, in the summer of 1947, and a workroom flat in London, the Collinses were often on the move. Besides the moves already mentioned they spent some time in Oxford in 1946, where he met Paul Nash, who thought so highly of his perceptiveness that he invited him to write a book on his painting, as well as Conrad Senat who sponsored the first book on his work, *Cecil Collins, Paintings and Drawings (1935-45),* produced by Counterpoint Publications, Oxford. (There are times when he regrets not having settled in Oxford. Later, staying with us, he said, 'Cambridge is so *hygienic*; Oxford is redolent of evil. I think I could really *work* here.') After a brief sojourn in Chelsea he returned to Luddenden to live with Elisabeth's parents. Apart from visits during the years 1950 to 1954 to Italy, France, Germany, and one to Greece, he has moved rarely since his establishment on his Cambridge-London axis, though making, eventually, a more permanent home in London, at 47 Paultons Square, Chelsea. The visit to Greece was especially memorable. Seferis, the revered Greek poet-Ambassador in London, suggested to him in 1962 that he hold an exhibition in Athens. 'I found myself en route for Greece with a suitcase full of watercolours,' he told me. The exhibition at the Zyghoe Gallery was welcomed and four works were bought by the Greek National Gallery.

Cecil has held a dozen one-man exhibitions besides receiving the accolade of his retrospective at the Whitechapel Gallery in 1959 which included two hundred and twenty-seven oils, gouaches, watercolours, pen and chalk drawings, lithographs, monotypes and tapestry.

The exhibition was received with marked respect. In the same year he designed a huge curtain with Shakespearian themes for the British Embassy in Washington, made by the Edinburgh Weavers. (He had designed his first tapestry ten years before.) But in spite of the general respect for his work and a circle of ardent admirers he is far from being accorded the place which his talents deserve. Like Roy de Maistre, Edward Burra and Albert Houthuesen, Cecil was never favoured by the establishment. When I brought examples of their work before the Tate Trustees they invariably treated my admiration for it as a symptom of personal idiosyncrasy, to be treated sometimes with tolerance, at others with tight-lipped reserve. Indeed in the Trustees' Report published the year after my retirement friendly reference is made to my sponsorship of 'less popular kinds of painting . . . good examples [were acquired] of the work of .men such as Burra, Houthuesen, Cecil Collins and Roy de Maistre'. Since the Tate was never associated with the acquisition of works which were 'popular' in the sense generally understood, in this particular context the expression 'less popular' is a synonym for 'less popular with "progressive" establishment taste'.

The most singular aspect of such taste is its double standard. It was until quite recently, when there has been a blurring of all criteria, dominated by the abstract idea. Abstract artists of the most modest talent were readily accorded the status of significant figures, and in considerable numbers; their work was selected to represent their countries in international exhibitions and the like. For figurative artists to achieve a comparable status the conditions were far more rigorous. Had he not been the author of *In Parenthesis* and *Anathemata* it is legitimate to doubt whether David Jones would have attained his present eminence; Henry Moore and Francis Bacon are figures whose stature is not easy to ignore, and Henry Moore in any case is the maker of a number of abstract and near-abstract works. But compared with the practitioners of abstraction how few figurative artists were included among the elect! It is as though there had been an unwritten veto on their recognition. Collins, for example, received a number of letters from Herbert Read expressing high admiration for his work, yet in his voluminous writings on his artist contemporaries it is never referred to.

Of the four painters referred to as rated below their merits by the establishment, Cecil Collins has given particular grounds for suspicion. While de Maistre (except as a very young man in Australia), Houthuesen and Burra have not expressed their convictions publicly, Collins has, explicitly and at length. Although written as long ago as 1914 and without specific reference to abstraction, Clive Bell's characteristically uncompromising words remain the clearest statement of the attitude that culminated in abstraction:

> To appreciate a work of art we need bring with us nothing from life, no knowledge of its ideas and affairs, no familiarity with its emotions. Art transports us from the world of man's activity to a world of aesthetic exaltation.

Cecil wrote:

> I am not very interested in what is called 'pure painting' . . . If the subject is unimportant in a picture we may well ask: unimportant to whom? The subject of the Crucifixion unimportant to Grünewald? to Fra Angelico? The themes on the front of Chartres Cathedral unimportant to its builders? The subject unimportant to Rembrandt, to Goya? . . . It is not sufficiently realised how a subject functions in a picture. A subject is thematic energy, the theme in art is a focus or canalisation of visual energy, hence the emotions and associations of the theme are inseparable from the forms and colours in a picture . . . . The terms 'pure painting,' 'pure art' seem to me to be meaningless. All my pictures are based upon a theme, and the theme is the cause of all form and the colour harmonies and no colour or line exists for its own sake.[1]

In this connection he repeated with evident amusement an account given him by Arthur Waley (who was present) of a lecture by Roger Fry in Cambridge, in the course of which, showing a slide of a painting by an old master, he had said, 'I would like to draw your attention to the large mass in the centre of the composition.' 'The large mass' was the crucified Christ, which he did not otherwise describe.

At the Royal College of Art fellow students sometimes ridiculed Collins's ideas — admittedly less lucidly formulated than they since became — and even *The Vision of the Fool* was treated by some of its readers, including a few of his friends, as an extravaganza bearing no relation to the actual condition of society. They were mistaken: this essay, in particular its emphatic and repeated contention that poetic imagination and human liberty are entirely incompatible with our materialistic, technologically orientated civilization, in which the 'plain and ordinary man' has made the philosophy of mediocrity a power, and that this philosophy has an army, armed with guns, bombs, gas, atomic rockets, and other effective instruments for the destruction of the

[1] *Notes by the Artist*, catalogue of his exhibition at the Tooth Gallery, 1965.

human race, clearly predicted certain of the issues that have provoked the almost world-wide revolutionary ferment among recent student generations. Cecil is far from regarding this ferment — however justified — with approval. Discussing this subject he said, 'In the great cultures man's imagination was protected by the idea of the sacred; today his imagination is open to all forces, and often their victim.'

The Vision of the Fool reads in fact as though it had been written in California in the 'sixties rather than in England in the 'forties. It is no accident that it is quoted by students in California and elsewhere in America, and in a book entitled *The Holy Barbarians* by the Californian writer Henry Lipton.

Cecil's writings have been here quoted at some length not because his philosophy is as important as his painting and drawing, or because it explains them, but because it offers so clear a reflection of his outlook on our world and also upon that far less tangible entity, the world of his imaginative apprehension. As he has written, 'Paintings and drawings cannot be explained', but his writings help us to share his own vision of this archetypal world. It is, however, a world which he himself is not always able to keep in focus. At such times he ceases to draw and paint, as in 1959 he ceased for the better part of a year. There are other times when, seeing his subject imperfectly or scarcely at all, he begins simply to apply paint and the process stimulates his creativity, enabling him to give it a clearly defined form. But it is more usual for him to envisage a picture in detail before he puts brush or pen to wood, hardboard or paper. The actual process of applying paint, then, evokes an increasing exhilaration and involvement, but on account of his method the work proceeds slowly. He applies successive layers of transparent glazes, each of which is allowed to dry before another is laid on. This method enables him to give his images the appearance of being at different depths: some submerged deep beneath several subtly toned transparent layers, hovering in mysterious darkness, others floating on the surface. 'The paintings and drawings distil inside me and when they are ready they burst out — complete, for I have long since ceased to make preliminary studies. At the moment,' he told me in 1969, 'I have four visionary pictures in my mind, three clearly but when at peace I can call them all up'

A big painting — often the essence of experience accumulated over years — takes him from three to four months to complete. From the early 'fifties his favoured medium has been oil on wood or hardboard, which has a solid icon-like character that pleases him.

There is something trance-like in his state of mind while he is painting.

> I am not aware [he wrote to me, 30 July 1970] of the qualities of my painting while I am doing it, but I am aware only of the absence of that Reality, that Beauty, so that the process of creating it is for me mostly absence, and the pain of absence, and yet in this process, this state, I am highly critical, my critical faculty is not suspended. Out there is nothingness, and into that nothingness I make an act of faith, and it is only sometime after the painting is done that its Beauty and Reality are revealed to me, so that I can see the qualities that my friends and others find there.
>
> In a word the painting and the vision come to fruition by themselves, but the experience of that fruition is the pain of absence.

It is perhaps inevitable that an artist whose subjects belong to a visionary world, whose eyes are lifted always to the heights of his experience, should be uneven. Failure to attain exalted ideals (likewise failure to realize high ambitions) is always conspicuous in a way that failure to perform some routine undertaking is not. Many artists evolve a series of formulae which they follow with mechanical proficiency throughout their working lives, and the better results are no more successes than the worse are failures, for a failure must bear some relation to a standard, and artists of this sort — and they are legion — have none worth taking account of. An artist with exalted aspirations whose subjects are visionary, Collins is unable, at moments of flagging inspiration, unlike artists whose subject is present before them, to revive it by the contemplation of its form and colour or by an attempt to represent it. The artist dependent on his imagination alone has no such resource: the act of creation is for him a uniquely exacting ordeal, and the results of moments of flagging inspiration, still more of its failure, are conspicuous to a special degree. At such moments, like Blake's, Cecil's work is marred: by want of clarity when paint coagulates awkwardly or by over-simplification or even emptiness of form. But it is by his best — and only by his best — that an artist should be judged. Collins paints pictures in which splendours of form and colour combine to give us an insight into a radiant, unknown world. Such are 'The Voice' of 1938, still (astonishingly) in the artist's possession; 'The Greeting' of 1943; 'Christ before the Judge' of 1954; 'The Sleeping Fool' already mentioned, and the Tate's two other examples, 'Hymn to Death' of 1953 and 'The Golden Wheel' of 1958; 'An Angel' painted in 1969 for a Room of Meditation in the South of France; or 'The Wounded Angel' (1969) **(PLATE 17).** These and a number of other paintings, watercolours and prints, as well as such a tapestry as 'The Fools of Summer' of 1954, all reflect the vision of an artist who has preserved intact a rare originality, and in spite of his highly sophisticated mind and eye, a moving innocence of spirit. Cecil Collins would not himself be an incongruous inhabitant of his own Lost Paradise.

VICTOR PASMORE
born 1908

There is one respect in which Victor Pasmore closely resembles Whistler: both possessed, and sedulously cultivated, a power of achieving the most compelling resemblance to nature while at the same time being deeply convinced that the qualities most worth striving for were the purely formal qualities: form, colour, tone. Whistler's assertion that his celebrated portrait of his mother should be seen as an 'Arrangement in Gray and Black No. I' is well known; perhaps less so are his still more emphatic words about Japanese art, which, he wrote, 'is not merely the incomparable achievement of certain harmonies in colour; *it is* (the italics are his) *the negation, the immolation, the annihilation of everything else*'.[1]   Much of the early work of Pasmore resembles that of Whistler in its delicate romanticism. All the later, however logically it accords with the ideals of Whistler, he would probably have refused to recognize as art at all. Whistler shared with the many advocates of 'significant form' — which include colour — of whom the most influential were Roger Fry and Clive Bell, a curious obliviousness of the logical conclusion to which it would lead, although, unlike these two distinguished critics, he died almost a decade before the emergence of abstract art.

Among its most austerely logical practitioners, as well as teachers, is Victor Pasmore. His work, which at first reflected that of Turner, the impressionists, Vuillard, Bonnard, as well as Whistler, became eventually, by an evolution predominantly intellectual, autonomous form and colour, 'the negation, the immolation, the annihilation of everything else'.

The development of many artists, Henry Moore for instance, and Pasmore's friend and one-time close associate William Coldstream, represents a readily comprehensible, almost, so to say, an organic growth, of course stimulated, diverted, arrested by influences met with on the way, or reactions from influences, and

---

[1] *The Gentle Art of making Enemies:* 1890. 1909 edition, p. 251.

145

the like, and this growth has the quality of naturalness comparable with the growth of a plant. But there are other kinds of development, which, guided by logic, discipleship of a stronger personality, the prevailing artistic or social climate, or ambition, result in radical change. It was primarily ambition, for instance, that transformed Millais from the painter of 'Lorenzo and Isabella', 'Christ in the Carpenter's Shop' and 'The Blind Girl' to the painter of 'Bubbles'. In the case of Pasmore the change in his development — more radical than that of any British painter of the present century — was due to a change of intellectual convictions, the result of tenacious study and prolonged reflection. In his Penguin book on Pasmore Clive Bell describes his artistic temper as

> that of one who paints as a bird sings rather than as an architect builds. So joyfully, so unscientifically, so digressively even does he pursue his theme that he seems never to come up with it till the last moment — and not always then . . . and manifestly his nature rebels against theory and dogma. Essentially that nature is conservative . . .

Pasmore was only thirty-seven when it was published, and on the evidence of his work up to that time it seems a fair description, but it is in fact a description of a temper the precise opposite of Pasmore's.

Edwin John Victor Pasmore was born on 3 December 1908 in Warlingham, Surrey, the eldest of the three children of Dr Edwin S. Pasmore and his wife Gertrude, born Screech. The family was originally West Country on both sides, the Pasmores being from Devon and the Screeches from Somerset. E. S. Pasmore was a respected mental specialist, who at the time of Victor's birth was attached to Chelsham Hospital.

From as early as he can remember Victor wished to be an artist. He went to Summerfield, then to Harrow — where he won drawing prizes — remaining there from 1922 until 1926, and it was assumed that on leaving he would go to an art school. But as the result of the premature death of his father this could not be afforded. The family moved to Hammersmith, living just off Brook Green, and from 1927 until 1938 Victor was a clerk in London County Council's Health Department at County Hall.

Still, determined to be a painter, he attended evening classes under A. S. Hartrick, from 1927 until 1931, whose teaching he found invaluable, at the London County Council's Central School of Arts and Crafts as well as painting whenever opportunity allowed. In 1931 he took a studio in Devonshire Street, off Theobald's Road, Finsbury Park; three years later he joined The London Artists' Association, through which he met William Coldstream and Claude Rogers and which sponsored his first exhibition, at the Cooling Galleries, in 1933.

Although still at County Hall and very much an amateur, he was elected, in 1934, a member of the London Group and contributed to the Objective Abstractions exhibition, at the Zwemmer Gallery, in which several of the exhibits proclaimed the autonomy of paint and brush in a way that anticipated the abstract expressionism of twenty years later. About the same time he also saw abstract paintings at an exhibition of The Seven-and-Five Group.

Like many young painters during the present century Pasmore was confused. I described Bell's statement that he 'paints as a bird sings rather than as an architect builds' as the opposite of the fact, because Pasmore is, more than any painter who is the subject of an essay in this book, a theorist. During his earliest years as a painter, however, he had no intellectual convictions about his art; not only had he never attended an art school full-time, but he had read scarcely any books about painting. So he was susceptible to every wind that blew: the late Turner at the Taten Whistler, the impressionists, Matisse, Picasso, Braque and other cubists, Bonnard, various old masters, including Chardin, Japanese prints; and a number of them he tried to imitate. He also made fauve and abstract paintings. Little of his work, however, before the 'thirties survives. But he was getting nowhere with these imitations, which he was unable even to finish.

It was not that he lacked talent, as his 'Church in Spring', an oil painted in 1926 when he was still at Harrow, clearly shows. Characteristically he adopted a logical point of departure.

Pasmore, although more talented than most of his contemporaries, was less consistently instructed (in spite of his perceptive art masters at Harrow, Maurice Clarke and John Holmes, who interested him in impressionism and encouraged him to read

Leonardo's *Notebooks*, and his fruitful evening classes with Hartrick), less informed and more aimless. This absence of aim, and dissatisfaction with the prevailing geometric style resulted in a development important in both its creative results and as giving Pasmore the point of departure he was looking for. This development was not the work of Pasmore alone, for, as Sickert used to say, 'these things are done by gangs'.

Geometrical abstraction was being pursued from the middle 'thirties with conspicuous success by Ben Nicholson, Barbara Hepworth, John Piper and others whose practice and theory emerged from the pages of *Axis*.

Of the particular 'gang' concerned, the other leading members were William Coldstream and Claude Rogers. All strongly shared, however, a sense of the severe limitations imposed by geometric abstraction, exemplified by the work of some of them shown at the Objective Abstraction exhibition which had led nowhere, and they were deeply attracted by the ideal of a return to nature — 'straight painting' as they called it — yet they were unmoved, in spite of their admiration for Sickert, by the 'straight painting' practised by a number of their seniors. None had anything approaching 'primitive' tendencies and they realized that 'straight painting' must have a point of departure in some tradition. After much reflection and discussion it was accepted that French painting between David and Cézanne had created a tradition which in particular fostered an intimate understanding of natural appearances, a tradition that succeeding generations for some mysterious reason had failed to develop. So they established the School of Drawing and Painting at 12 Fitzroy Street in 1937, and moved later that year to 316 Euston Road, where they were joined by Graham Bell; they were a group of painters who were close friends sharing basic ideas about painting, and also an art school. Both were known as the Euston Road School. (A detailed study of this group-school is long overdue.) It had affiliations with the literary world; Coldstream, for instance, was friendly with Auden and Spender and he painted their portraits.

The rejection of the strongly emerging geometric abstraction called for courage, for young men of such intelligence and talent did not reject the 'progressive' in favour of the 'traditional' without misgivings. Their state of mind was perceptively summed up by Coldstream in an article entitled *How I Paint.*

> I belonged to a set of about a dozen friends, all painters who had just left the
> Slade. We read Clive Bell and Roger Fry, and spent a great deal of time
> discussing aesthetics. All the more intelligent books on art which we read
> taught us to regard subject-matter merely as an excuse for good painting. Our
> discussions were usually on the question of which modern style was best and
> most progressive . . . When we were influenced by Picasso and Braque we
> were troubled by a suspicion that we should be as far in advance of them as
> they were in advance of Cézanne.[1]

Their inability to be 'in advance of Picasso and Braque' and
their preoccupation with natural appearances seemed less perverse
after the economic 'slump' of 1930, which fostered strong left-
wing political attitudes which in turn made abstract art — as
unattuned to 'the people' — appear exotic, 'the people' requiring
an art 'that had to do with life'. The Bloomsbury group, feeling
their neighbours in Euston Road to be their natural successors,
gave them support; they felt the need of successors, as the failure
or defection of many of their protegés left Duncan Grant, their
star, in an isolated position.

I must not dwell at length on the Euston Road School, which
in any case was as promptly extinguished by the Second World
War as Vorticism by the First. Moreover, the theories that pervaded its practice did not affect Pasmore deeply. It was invaluable
to him, as it was to everyone associated with it, as a highly
perceptive introduction to a tradition, but a tradition followed,
however faithfully, with independence. But he was not yet the
theorist he was to become: although an active teacher at the
School, he was primarily an impassioned student. Uninterested in
left-wing politics, the war in Spain or any other public issue, he
studied painting, its techniques, its history, the theories that had
affected it; he read and experimented endlessly.

The late 'thirties and early 'forties were frustrating years for
those artists who were not officially employed as war artists. But
Pasmore was freer than most. Through the generosity of Kenneth
Clark he was able to afford to resign, in 1938, from County Hall,
when he moved from his Howland Mews studio and his quarters
over the then celebrated meeting-place of artists and writers, the
Eiffel Tower restaurant, to the studio at 8 Fitzroy Street, earlier

---

[1] *The Listener,* 15 September 1937.

occupied by Duncan Grant, Sickert and Whistler. In June 1940 he held his first one-man exhibition, married Wendy Blood and settled in Ebury Street. I well remember the terms in which he formulated his attitude towards painting when I spent some time early the following year in the studio there, by then badly bombed. While Wendy, he and I sat on the bed eating a snack lunch Victor emphatically declared: 'Surrealism, abstraction, and the rest of the contemporary movements I look on as aberrations. As *aberrations*, do you see? Now we've got to go back to Degas and the impressionists — they represent the real tradition — as soon as possible. We must begin again at the point where the tradition deviated.' And I remember, as I looked round at his paintings of Wendy, of roses, of bottles, of the sea-shore, all so delicately lovely in colour and tone, I marvelled that this searching mind with its forceful apprehension of the problems of painters of his own generation should be content to tread so well-trodden a path — for I was reminded by his work not only of the impressionists but of Bonnard, Whistler and even of Conder. The path was none the worse for being well-trodden but Pasmore seemed to me an incongruous figure to be treading it.

Over the next decade Pasmore's outlook underwent a change which at its culmination seemed apocalyptic. Seen in retrospect, though it was clearly radical, it was less apocalyptic, less unheralded, than appeared at the time. In the early 'forties he was determined to 'go back to Degas and the impressionists'; to help to reanimate the realistic tradition at the point before which he — and a number of his friends — believed that it had begun to decline. However, by the late 'forties he had decisively rejected that tradition in favour of the abstraction which he had tentatively practised in the middle 'thirties. There was, of course, nothing original about this rejection of tradition: it had been rejected by Kandinsky, Mondrian, and others; the *Realistic Manifesto*, the work mainly of Naum Gabo and issued in Moscow in 1920, had declared: 'The attempts of the cubists and futurists to lift the visual arts from the bogs of the past have led only to new delusions . . . The past we are leaving behind as carrion.'

1947 [he explained to me] was no traumatic experience. It was the logical result of my professional evolution. I had no interest in rebellion; I never tried to do anything new. I learnt from Moore and Nicholson, but I never wanted to be a Mondrian, in fact I don't care a button for him. I explored all possibilities; I'm not interested in my 'style'. I'm not even against subject, but it's not for me: I believe that abstraction is the logical culmination of painting since the Renaissance. No one could follow Picasso, for instance, in his realism. But I was very much moved by his work at the big Picasso-Matisse exhibition held just after the war (even though I didn't like it). I felt that Picasso was the man whom earlier artists, Cézanne and Van Gogh for instance, had been implicitly talking about'

for certain of the ideas they expressed seemed to Pasmore to be far in advance of their own practice.

Pasmore's evolution during the 'forties, though admittedly less 'traumatic' than it once appeared, was nevertheless an extraordinary phenomenon, to which I can recall no parallel. In his Thameside landscapes, such as 'The Quiet River' (1943-44, oil); 'Chiswick Reach' **(PLATE 18)** (1943, oil), in the National Gallery of Canada; 'A Winter Morning' (1944, oil) or 'The Gardens of Hammersmith' (1944, oil), as well as 'The Wave' (1939-44, oil), Pasmore showed a power of evoking a gentle, radiant, misty vision of nature unapproached either for acuteness of perception or for sheer poetry by any of his own gifted generation. They invite comparison with Whistler's Thames paintings of the 1870s. The two painters shared a love for similar aspects of nature and an absorption with the underlying geometry of their compositions. In all the paintings referred to, except 'Chiswick Reach', sharp linear outlines appearing here and there can be perceived — by hindsight — as presaging, however discreetly, the pure abstraction only a few years ahead.

Nevertheless the 'forties for Pasmore were strange years: he was a painter with a rare and growing command of the natural world, especially of its delicately romantic aspects, yet all the while troubled by doubts about the validity of traditional naturalism and by a sense of its impending disintegration. These culminated in a conviction that it had, in fact, disintegrated already. Many years later he described his conclusion.

The solid and spatial world of traditional naturalism, once it was flattened by the fauvists, atomised and disintegrated by the cubists, could no longer serve as an objective foundation. Having reached this point the painter was confronted with an abyss from which he had either to retreat or leap over and start on a new plane. The new plane is 'abstract art'.[1]

1 'What is Abstract Art?' Victor Pasmore, the *Sunday Times*, 5 February 1961.

Characteristically, Victor Pasmore leaped.

The arri al of traditional naturalism at the abyss he regards as no more unheralded than his own, and he has described, in the article quoted, and elsewhere, how it was approached from the later nineteenth century. Turner's 'free development of colour', the Art for Art's Sake movement, Cézanne, Van Gogh, Gauguin played their part and, as already noted, the fauves and cubists. His conception of abstraction, the art on the far side of the abyss, is orthodox: 'an evolution without precedent in the visual arts . . . altogether independent of imitative techniques, literary associations and decorative functions' and manifesting 'complete autonomy of form'.

In 1947 he moved away from the Thameside where he had painted most of his finest landscapes, while living at 2 Riverside, Chiswick Mall, for about a year from 1942 (on his discharge from the Army after a year's service) and at 16 Hammersmith Terrace from about a year later, settling at 12 St Germans Place, a spacious Georgian house in Blackheath. This has remained the family's London base, although in 1970 he bought another house, Dá Gamri, Tá Kaxxina, Gudja, in Malta, where he spends the greater part of the year. From 1947 Pasmore began, systematically, to study abstract art as well as to practise it.

It was characteristic of him that in making his new beginning he should scrutinize the writings of Kandinsky, Mondrian, Arp and other abstract painters, as in 1943-4 he had studied, largely in the excellent library at Biddesden, the house of the Hon. Bryan Guinness (now Lord Moyne), those of Cézanne, Gauguin and Van Gogh before the Picasso-Matisse exhibition had confirmed his determination to explore the implications of their ideas.

Pasmore's decision to become an abstract painter and his wide reading about abstract art did not lead immediately to an evolution of a personal style. For instance, 'Square Motif in Brown, White, Blue and Ochre' (1949-53, oil and collage, Museum of Modern Art, New York) owes much to cubism, and several painted reliefs of the same period are echoes of earlier works by other artists, and less original than those made by Ceri Richards in the same medium in the 'thirties. But this is no cause for surprise: to explore various possibilities was in accord with his character and this innate disposition was stimulated by intensive study of abstract practice and theory of many kinds. (He even compiled an anthology entitled *Abstract Art: Comments by some Artists and Critics*, privately printed in 1949 at the Camberwell School of Art.) The effects of the encouragement he received from Ben Nicholson — who had evolved a highly personal form of abstraction by the middle 'thirties — are apparent in Pasmore's early abstraction. Nicholson and Barbara Hepworth he visited in St Ives in 1950 and exhibited with them at the Penwith Society, which assembled the first exclusively abstract exhibition held in Britain since the war.

For a painter widely honoured as a traditional master, who had developed implications in the work of certain of the impressionists and of Whistler in such a way as to give his own work a strong appeal not only to those with traditional inclinations, but to those sensitive to art of various kinds characteristic of their own day, to transform himself with apparent suddenness into an abstract painter provoked astonished shock. Indeed I cannot recall an effect caused by a change in outlook in a British artist of anything approaching comparable intensity. Its most significant result was to persuade a number of serious artists, particularly his friends and former students, to reconsider their own basic convictions. Among these were Kenneth Martin, Adrian Heath and Terry Frost. The fact that Pasmore's change was seen, even by his friends, as 'apocalyptic' instead of the culmination of a steady evolution over several years is not surprising. I do not believe, however, that this evolution could be traced with any degree of precision, even by his intimates, until his major retrospective exhibition held at the Tate in May-June 1965.

The first abstract paintings quite unmistakably his own were a number of whirling forms made in the early 'fifties, although these are not abstract in the severest, most exclusive sense. Their titles, indeed, show his awareness of their affinities with the world of natural appearances, such, for instance, as 'Spiral Motif: The Wave' (1949-50, oil, National Gallery of Canada) or 'The Snowstorm: Spiral Motif in Black and White' (1950-51, oil, Arts Council). Their allusion is not so much to water and to snow as to the forces by which they are animated. As he stated clearly at the time:

The spiral movement which can be discerned throughout nature, in many different forms, is reduced to its single denomination . . . the act of drawing a spiral in a variety of ways will evoke emotions similar to those associated with the spiral movement of nature.[1]

Pasmore's is a wholeheartedly logical nature, and as could have been predicted he abandoned the spiral motif series because they inevitably evoked images of the natural world. (The last he made was probably 'Spiral Motif in White, Green, Maroon and Indigo', an oil completed in 1952.) The previous year he made several painted reliefs, 'Relief Painting in White, Black and Indian Red' and 'White Relief' being the first.

There were at least three reasons for his preoccupation with reliefs. Admiration for those made by his friend Ben Nicholson, to which his own earliest have some resemblance, though they are less sophisticated and indeed have a 'home-made' look. Increasing recoil from all imitation of nature, however oblique, which disposed him to create, instead of suggesting, form and space. This development was accelerated by reading Charles Biederman's *Art as the Evolution of Visual Knowledge*, which emphasized the significance of relief, and was lent to him in 1951 by Ceri Richards. The two reliefs referred to were tentative beginnings. Characteristically, he carried this development towards a logical conclusion, by boldly projecting form and its accompanying deep space. It was an attempt to create space in front of the picture surface instead of, as in traditional painting, behind. The character of many resulting reliefs is suggested by the title which he gave to several of them, namely, 'Projection Relief'.

Pasmore differs radically in at least two respects from the generality of 'geometric' abstract artists. To them their work constitutes a language more or less private, understood by a perceptive few and these mostly fellow artists, and it is characterized by something less easy to define, a certain impersonality, evident, often, in the look it has of being the product not of the hand but of a machine. (This look is not, of course, the exclusive mark of the work of 'geometric' abstract artists.) Pasmore's contrary 'public' preoccupation found the widest scope through his long association with the small town of Peterlee in Durham, conceived by Mr Peter Lee during the Depression as a

---

[1] *Art News and Review*, 24 February 1951.

'dream town' for miners. Lubetkin was the chief architect but Pasmore was appointed in 1955 as Consulting Architectural Designer for the Peterlee Development Corporation. Here, under the direction of the General Manager, Mr A. V. Williams, and in association with Lubetkin and other architects Pasmore has been concerned with the South West Housing Area. It gave him 'an opportunity,' he said to me, 'to bring abstract art directly to the public — right outside the range of the museum.' (It was not his first opportunity, which was a relief-mural — his first relief — made for the Drivers' and Conductors' canteen at Kingston, Surrey, in 1950, but it was beyond comparison his most far-reaching.) Although not formally trained as an architect he had studied, with his customary diligence and zest, the work of Corbusier, Gropius and others.

The culmination of his work at Peterlee was the design of a Pavilion which serves as an urban centre — as a church would were a new village to be built in Malta. But unlike a church the Pavilion, an integration of architecture and painting, has no function except to give pleasure and a sense of focus, to be, as he put it, 'an emotional centre', an essential urban feature, and one so often lacking in modern urban development. This massive, harmonious, partly painted concrete structure, each aspect of which differs from the others, Pasmore regards as his best work.

The Pavilion is closely related to his linear abstractions in both two and three dimensions. But Pasmore is very much aware of the danger that exclusively 'geometric' art may become mechanical, and he has accordingly practised an art which, though not less abstract, is of a different and even a contrary order. He builds up a composition, at first only vaguely envisaged, from dots and dashes almost arbitrarily applied: in brief he allows the picture to make itself. No artists could differ more from Pasmore (or from each other) than Jack Yeats and Bacon, but all three have this in common: a reliance, at certain times, upon the paint 'to take over' and complete the work. Such a procedure has, of course, a long history in Britain going back at least as far as Alexander Cozens. Even so meticulously precise a draughtsman as Beardsley said to W. B. Yeats, 'I make a blot upon the paper and I begin to shake the ink about and something happens.' One example of many, but perhaps the first, of a painting evolved in this way is 'Black

Abstract' (1963, oil, at the Tate); another is 'Blue Development No. I' (1965-6, ink on plastic). Having explored many of the possibilities offered by the relief he has devoted most of his recent years to two-dimensional painting. His use of the word 'development' in the titles of a number of his works testifies to his continued preoccupation with the possibilities, to use another of his own expressions, 'of the picture making itself'.

No artist of his generation has been so wide-ranging: he has evolved from a painter of delicate poetic landscape to a painter of autonomous forms, who then felt impelled to move from the two-dimensional medium of painting to the actual three-dimensional world of 'construction' 'Relief Construction in White, Black and Indian Red,' 1965-7, painted wood and plastic, **(PLATE 19)**) or pure 'architecture', and returned to painting, every move impelled by a zestful logic largely his own. A writer for whom I have a high respect has maintained that Pasmore's work has an underlying unity. I see him as an adventurous spirit pressing forward, following up the implications of every idea he has realized. His method of evolution indeed has unity, but not, surely, the work. What could be more different than 'The Wave' or 'Chiswick Reach', suffused with a delicate romantic radiance, and the massive concrete Pavilion at Peterlee?

FRANCIS BACON
born 1909

In 1962 the Tate Gallery brought together the first officially sponsored retrospective exhibition of the paintings of Francis Bacon, containing ninety-one examples — nearly half of those that had survived his own self-critical iconoclasm.

It fell to me as director to write the introduction to the catalogue of the work of a painter which I had immensely admired since it was first shown seventeen years before: 'at times it seems to me that I have it all in focus; then suddenly the collective image fades and I have to begin again, and by looking at the paintings, at photographs of them, to recapture what has been lost.'

Ten years have passed and I have, of course, seen much more of his work and read much of what has been written about it, yet its elusiveness has scarcely diminished. This is curious, for the highly informed intelligence of the painter, manifest in all his work, has evoked an extremely perceptive body of criticism. None of his contemporaries, in fact, has been the subject of criticism of so consistently high an order. Writings on Henry Moore, for instance, have often been sheer adulation, while many other artists' outstanding merits have often been ignored or dismissed, at least until late in their working lives. Thérèse Lessore, Robert Melville, John Russell, Lawrence Gowing and David Sylvester (and others, both in Britain and abroad) have contributed substantially to our understanding of Bacon. David Sylvester, moreover, has persuaded him to give a highly illuminating interview in which he talked at length about his complex art with the candour and sophisticated intelligence expected of him. And yet, even with access to so much fact and perceptive interpretation, as well as Bacon's own answers to adroitly devised questions, and my own talks with him, much remains, for me, deeply enigmatic about his art. There is, too, something enigmatic about Bacon himself. He moves freely in several societies, exchanges ideas lucidly and without reserve, yet he is less well known than

Picasso, whose privacy was strictly guarded, who rarely left the house to which few were admitted (and some of these far less frequently than they would have wished) and who expressed himself to all but his few intimates with circumspection.

In earlier centuries artists were often nurtured, for instance, by the practice or patronage of the arts of members of their family. Today this rarely the case. Of the subjects treated in this volume, only one, S.W. Hayter, is an artist's son. In fact many, if not the majority, of the most serious artists of modern times emerge from environments such that it is surprising that they ever became aware of their vocation. One such was Bacon. The only discernible favourable characteristic of his early life was a high degree of mobility that left all options open.

Bacon was born on 28 October 1909, in Dublin at 63 Lower Baggot Street, one of the five children of Edward Anthony Mortimer Bacon, and his wife Christine Winifred, born Firth. His father was a collateral descendant of Francis's illustrious Elizabethan namesake. (Queen Victoria had urged his grandfather to assume the lapsed title of Lord Oxford, which he refused to do, on the grounds that he lacked the means to 'live up to it'.) Edward Bacon also suffered from lack of means and often gambled, and Francis remembers being sent to the post office to place bets by telegram. After serving in the Army he lived by training and breeding race-horses. Bacon's mother, almost twenty years his father's junior, was as lively and sociable as he was censorious and moralistic.

During the First World War Edward Bacon worked in the War Office and the family moved to London, but travelled often between England and Ireland, never establishing a permanent home.

For a short time Francis attended Dean Close School, Cheltenham, from which he ran away.

Long-standing tension between his father and himself culminated in an incident, in itself trivial, which entirely transformed his way of living. He told John Russell that he had tried on his mother's underwear, which seemed to his father a grave breach of   the   rather   puritanical   tone   which   he   set   in   the house.[1] The result was that, in 1926, Francis was sent away from home. Not only with his mother but with her family his relations were happier. Among them the habit prevailed of frequent and lavish entertainment. 'I read almost nothing as a child,' he told me; 'as for pictures I was hardly aware that they existed.' The first he saw in a domestic context were paintings by the preraphaelites and some of their followers at Jesmond Towers, the Northumberland mansion of one of his mother's relatives.

Apart from his uncompleted term at Dean Close and some tutoring by the local parson he received no education at all.

When he left home he was without ambition or objectives of any kind; he wished simply to do nothing, but worked in an office in London, then he spent some time in Berlin and rather longer in Paris. To both the erotic, anarchic society of the one and the perceptive passion for the arts of the other he wholeheartedly responded. In Paris he carried out some commissions for interior decoration and made a number of drawings and watercolours.

The circumstances of Bacon's early life have been briefly recalled because they contributed more to the formation of his outlook and to his way of life than is sometimes supposed; for he is apt to be thought of as a phenomenon quite unrelated to his background. Certainly this extraordinary painter and man seems to owe little to his father, except, perhaps, the vein of austerity which enables him, when working at full stretch, to dispense with the society of his friends and the other pleasures that he so zestfully enjoys, and to sleep and eat little, foregoing alcoholic drink and scarcely leaving his studio. But the freedom of all the societies he had known, in Ireland, Berlin, Paris, their tolerance of individual idiosyncracies, his lack of formal education, of 'formation' of any sort, gave this highly individual boy a prevailing sense of the openness of the choices before him — a sense he has preserved even after making the most crucial choice of all: to become a painter.

The approach to painting of one who was to become so quintessentially a painter was slow, hesitant, for long periods distracted by other preoccupations — gambling for one. (Most painters — Utrillo, encouraged by his mother to paint as a dis-

[1] *Francis Bacon* by John Russell, 1971. p.15.

traction from heavy drinking, is one of the rare exceptions —
certainly nearly all the others who figure in this volume, showed
a consistent determination to adopt their vocation from a very
early age.) Bacon had, however, been fascinated by reproductions
of paintings ever since he left home.

When he settled in London in 1928 in a converted garage at 7
Queensbury Mews he began to paint in a desultory way, trying
out various styles, among them one derived from Lurçat and
Souverbie, portraying dead, pale trees in landscape. But he was
chiefly occupied with designing furniture, rugs and interior
decoration, and it was with these, which he showed in his studio
in 1929, that he began to make a modest reputation. There
appeared in the August 1930 number of *The Studio* an article
entitled 'The 1930 Look in British Decoration' with illustrations of
the furniture and rugs he designed and the interior of his studio
(the first occasion when his work was noticed by the press). The
windows were described as 'curtained with white rubber sheeting
that hangs in sculptural folds'. The general impression the article
conveys is that his work was of a self-conscious modernity. It is
worth noting that the tubular base of one of his glass and metal
tables foreshadowed the railings that sometimes enclosed the
papal, politician-executive figures and the portraits in his paintings
of later decades. The rugs hanging on the facing wall had abstract
designs. Among his occasional commissions was one to design
furnishings for the dining-room in the house in Smith Square,
Westminster, belonging to Mr R. A. (later Lord) Butler; these,
however, were bought by Patrick White, the Australian novelist.

Gradually, however, his concern with decoration — in any case
largely sustained as a means of making a living — dwindled to
extinction, and he determined to paint. But how? He had never
attended an art class, nor even learnt the most elementary drawing
during his single term at school.

Help came to him from the far side of the world, from 'down
under', to be precise. About the same time as Bacon there arrived
in London on a visit Roy de Maistre, a man fifteen years his
senior, who had had a thorough training at two art schools in
Sydney, and won a travelling scholarship which had enabled him
to study in Paris, where he had exhibited at the Salon. The
previous   year   in   Sydney   he   had   held   a   one-man-ex

Plate 21: FRANCIS BACON: *Study for Portrait of Lucian Freud—sideways* (1971), oil on canvas, 78 × 58 in.

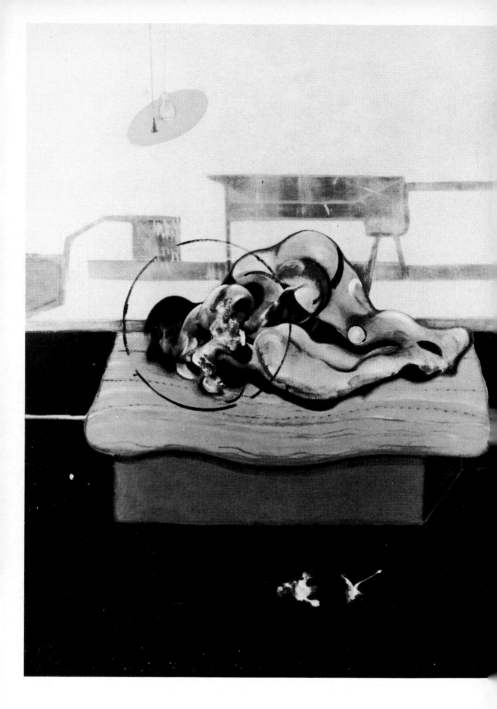

Plate 22 : FRANCIS BACON : *Triptych centre panel. Figures on Beds* (1972), oil and pastel on canvas, 78 × 58 in.

Plate 23: ROBERT COLQUHOUN: *Woman with a Birdcage* (1946), oil on
canvas, 40 × 29¾ in.

Plate 24: LUCIAN FREUD: *Head of a Woman* (1953), oil on canvas, 13 × 9 in.

hibition, and was shortly to hold another in London. De Maistre and Bacon met and immediately a close and lasting friendship grew up between them. Bacon confided to him his ambition to paint and his benevolent friend gave him all the help in his power. Years later de Maistre told me that Bacon, in spite of his perceptive scrutiny of reproductions, knew nothing whatever about the technical side of painting and had scarcely drawn at all. He was amused to hear a man of such rare intelligence, who showed an acute understanding of an exhibition of paintings by Picasso that he had seen in 1927, ask questions that a schoolchild might have answered. Although a man of outstanding determination, to whom few say 'no', Bacon's beginnings as a painter were extremely tentative. The Picasso exhibition, evidently, had a crucial effect; Miss Diana Watson, his second cousin and close friend, told me that before seeing it she had never heard him speak of becoming a painter. For a time he painted diluted Picassos, such, for instance, as that on the left in de Maistre's 'Francis Bacon's Studio' of 1933. The studio was in 71 Royal Hospital Road, Chelsea, one of several he occupied in his earliest years in London; there were others in the Fulham and Cromwell Roads and at 1 Glebe Place, Chelsea. In the first, in Queensbury Mews, he and de Maistre held in the winter of 1929-30 a small exhibition together in which Bacon showed a few watercolours and pieces of furniture. Derivative and tentative as his early work was by comparison with that of his maturity — to judge by the very few examples to survive his consistent iconoclasm — there were about it faint intimations of the qualities which emerged in the middle 'forties with such explosive force, apparent to a few men of particular sensibility. Sir Michael Sadler — the first purchaser of his work who was not a member of his family or a friend — after buying 'The Crucifixion' (1932)[1] sent him a photograph of his skull with a commission to paint his portrait. Another 'Crucifixion', in which Bacon incorporated the skull (painted in 1933), was reproduced as 'Composition' in Herbert Read's *Art Now*, published the same year, when Bacon also showed single works in two exhibitions at the Mayor Gallery.

After these signs of recognition he suffered a setback. In 1934

[1] The medium of the works by Bacon here specifically referred to is always oil, though in a few he has used some pastel and tempera in addition.

he arranged an exhibition of seven of his oils and five or six gouaches in the basement of Sunderland House, Curzon Street, which he called the Transition Gallery. This failed utterly: it was scarcely attended and nothing was sold. Deeply discouraged, he painted little over the next two years, and between 1936 and 1944 scarcely at all. In his despondency he turned to gambling instead. Resumption of painting became the more difficult as a result of the war, during which he served in the Air Raid Precaution Service until discharged on account of the asthma from which he suffers still. However, one painting of these near-barren years, made in 1936 and now destroyed, entitled 'Abstraction', clearly anticipated the central panel of his first major work.

Francis Bacon is surely a phenomenon unique among painters of this century. He had had no instruction at all - apart from some friendly advice from de Maistre; had painted little for two years after a failure; then for eight years had almost ceased to paint at all. And what he had painted, though of sufficient interest to alert a few perceptive connoisseurs, would have been quickly forgotten.

Bacon himself regards his early work with contempt. But it was not destined to stand by itself; suddenly in 1944 he knew that his time had come and concentrated the whole of his formidable powers on painting. These earlier works were the prelude to a long succession of paintings ever more widely acclaimed as the work of a master.

In early April 1945, in an exhibition at the Lefevre Gallery which included works by Moore, Matthew Smith and several others of the most admired British artists, was also hung a painting by Bacon that created a sensation: it was the object of ridicule, astonishment or outright horror — and, by a very few, of cautious admiration. This painting was a large triptych, made the previous year and called 'Three Figures at the Base of a Crucifixion'. Each panel represented a horrific creature, half human and half animal. That on the left hand is tensely bowed as though for beheading; that in the centre, a defeathered ostrich, with a mouth in place of a head, emerging from a bandage; and that on the right, a long-necked creature with a huge open mouth, screaming, with ears but faceless, yet voracious, infinitely malignant. Bacon had long been obsessed by the central figure, which closely resembles the destroyed 'Abstraction' painted some eight years before. 'I began,' he said to me, 'with the "Three Figures at the Base of a Crucifixion".' In the same exhibition was another work by Bacon, painted shortly before its opening, entitled 'Figure in a Landscape', and it differs sharply from the other in both spirit and execution. The 'Three Figures' is frankly horrific and is in essence a vividly coloured drawing. The 'Figure in a Landscape', is the first of his pictures to anticipate the sheer mastery of paint, so integral a feature of the work of his maturity. And as distinct from the character of its companion it suggests the impending calamity that was to characterize many of Bacon's paintings during the next decades. It is also the first of his several portrayals of figures beneath umbrellas. The partially delineated figure is vaguely suggestive of a dead man with a machine-gun, but it was painted from a photograph of a friend asleep in a chair in Hyde Park. The friend was Eric Hall, who presented the 'Three Figures at the Base of a Crucifixion' to the Tate Gallery in 1953.

Less than a year later, in February 1946, again at the Lefevre Gallery, Bacon showed two paintings which confirmed the belief of the few admirers of the 'Three Figures' that it was no accident. These were 'Figure Study II' **(PLATE 20)** (formerly known as 'The Magdalen' but the artist repudiated this title) and 'Study for the Human Figure at the Cross II' (also known as 'Figure Study I'). Both were completed shortly before the exhibition opened, the latter first. This shows a hat and coat which evoke the presence of a mourning figure. 'Figure Study II' shows a similar preoccupation with the expressive possibilities of clothes. This splendid painting — by comparison the 'Three Figures' is the work of an amateur of genius — is pervaded by a sinister ambience not less powerful for being, by comparison, suggested rather than proclaimed. It combines grandeur of design with a subdued resonance of colour. Nothing more clearly indicates the long-persisting caution of Bacon's admirers than the fact that this painting, one of his finest, was bought by the enterprising Contemporary Art Society from the Lefevre exhibition, and was available, and as a gift, to almost any public collection, yet six years passed before it found a home — in the Bagshawe Art Gallery in Batley, Yorkshire, one of the obscurest in Britain. Instead of denigrating his work, as many unfriendly writers had the 'Three Figures', as a grotesque freak, critics saw it must be treated a little more seriously and it was explained as a revival of late eighteenth century gothic 'painting of horror', and he as a latter-day Fuseli. But denigration continued. One critic voiced the opinion of a number of his colleagues when he wrote of Bacon's 'fast-dating Grand Guignol' and his 'creaking melodrama'.

That same year he painted another masterpiece, entitled 'Painting 1946', representing a sinister figure, faintly reminiscent of Mussolini, seated beneath an umbrella with carcases of beef suspended just behind him and enclosed by a fence of metal tubing which, with blinds with swinging cords, were to become recurrent accessories of his backgrounds.

In the course of a discussion about it Bacon said, 'I began that particular figure with the intention of representing a bird of prey alighting on a ploughed field. The carcass? When I was a boy I was fascinated by butchers' shops.'

This painting reflects a procedure the exact contrary of that followed in the 'Three Figures'. The existence of a photograph of the destroyed 'Abstraction 1936', from which the central figure in the 'Three Figures' has clearly derived, shows that this image had been in his mind for at least eight years. In 'Painting 1946' he was clearly working under the effects of chance. It was a procedure that was to dominate his future course. There was an indication of it in 'Figure in a Landscape' in which a seated figure is transformed, but there is nevertheless a relation, however remote, between the photograph which provided its point of departure and the completed picture. In 'Painting 1946' there was no such relation between completed picture and original image. Two years later Alfred Barr bought 'Painting 1946' for the Museum of Modern Art, New York — the first purchase of one of his works by a museum.

It was shortly followed by another painting of somewhat similar character, 'Study of a Man with Microphones' (also representing a figure beneath an umbrella), which the artist destroyed.

On account of the horrific and on occasion sensationally horrific nature of his themes, his reliance on what he calls 'accident', his startling originality, the derivation of much of his work from photographs and film stills, it was not understood that the painting of Bacon is an integral development of the European tradition. Many artists disguise their indebtedness to the example of others. Bacon is candid about his own, whether to Velazquez or Rembrandt or anyone else. Of one of his 'Crucifixions' he said to David Sylvester, 'Without all the paintings that have been done in the past of the Crucifixion I would not have been able to do it.' He studies the old masters not panoramically but intensively, in terms of the works that he admires most deeply. Besides those already mentioned are Cimabue, Grünewald, Poussin, Constable (especially his 'Leaping Horse' at the Victoria and Albert Museum, conveniently near to where he lives), Degas (especially 'Après le bain, femme s'essuyant' at the National Gallery), Van Gogh, and among contemporaries Matthew Smith, Duchamp and Giacometti.

I well remember his visits to exhibitions at the Tate when I was director: he would arrive, usually, in mid-morning, and after a glance round each room he would quickly decide on what he wished to see, then scrutinize a few pictures intently and at length, ignoring the rest. Occasionally he looked at almost everything — in, for one, the Daumier exhibition.

Bacon's relation to traditional painting has been succinctly and precisely summarized by John Russell: his 'ambition is to take "shocking" or "unheard-of" material and deliver it in the European grand manner. People often imagine that any recrudescence of that manner must be accompanied by a certain rigidity, a defensive keeping out of subject matter that is too much of our own time. Bacon's view is the opposite of this. "If only people were free enough to let *everything* in, something extraordinary might come of it".[1]

'The difficult thing,' he says, 'is to keep open the line to ancestral European painting while producing something that comes across as entirely new.'

There is another sense in which he is traditional. Today many painters are experimenting with or adopting new media and often regard oil paint as an anachronism the possibilities of which have long since been exhausted. 'The empty canvas,' announced a prominent constructivist, 'symbolizes the fact that this medium can have no more to offer in our times.'[2] Bacon remains, stead-

---

[1] Op. cit. p.59.
[2] *The New Cézanne*, Charles Biederman, 1958, p.65.

fastly, an oil-painter; in fact much of his power of taking advantage of what he calls 'accident' derives from his understanding of the unique potentialities of oil paint.

Although he belongs integrally to the European tradition, he believes that traditional forms, for the moment, are entirely played out. 'What modern man wants,' he said to me, quoting Valéry, 'is the grin without the cat; that is,' he continued, 'the sensation without the boredom of its conveyance.' By this he means the traditional all-over elaboration, especially of subjects better represented by the camera. This is apparent, for instance, in the way in which, after completing a head which seems to him to be 'illustration', he will sweep away a part of it with a bold, deft stroke of the brush, or even sweater or sock. The likeness remains, but conveyed in terms entirely different from those of a photograph. At the same time he is fascinated by photographs, in particular by the work of one of the most masterly of all photographers, Edward James Muybridge. The principal aim of Muybridge was to show 'actions incidental to everyday life'; human and animal movement as they are in reality and not as derived from tradition and as taught in art schools. Before Muybridge, the precise nature of movement was not known. In order to establish it he took sequential photographs by setting up twenty-four cameras facing a horse's course — the horse was his first subject — and as it passed the cameras it broke a series of threads which set them in action. Each exposure was a two-thousandth of a second. Before he could afford to buy Muybridge's two classic volumes *The Human Figure in Motion* and *Animals in Motion*, Bacon used to study them in the Victoria and Albert Museum's library. These two remarkable books show nude men, women and animals in every conceivable movement; Bacon is able, in an instant, to find any one of the thousands of reproductions of photographs they contain. Fascinated as he is by Muybridge, Bacon was far from being the first painter to learn from his work. Thomas Eakins both learnt from and sponsored him; he also collaborated with him in the invention of a camera — and was photographed running naked. Artists as remote from one another as Meissonier and Seurat benefited from the discoveries of Muybridge. Bacon also studies photographs clipped from popular magazines, of which he has a very large collection, most of them showing figures in motion. The effect upon him of 'Nurse screaming', the celebrated still from the film *Battleship Potemkin*, has long been known. He has never, he told me, taken a photograph himself.

Just as works by the old masters suggest certain of his themes, though they are usually radically, more often wholly, transformed in the process of his own painting, so do photographs. They are not, however, always transformed beyond recognition: Velazquez' 'Innocent X' is the recognizable point of departure for a number of his popes, as are the features of the Nurse for the 1957 'Study for the Nurse in the film *Battleship Potemkin*'.

The photograph has had another effect on the art of Bacon besides providing points of departure for his imagery. In the traditional portrait there is a direct relation between the painter and his subject: sometimes they look at each other; sometimes the subject looks elsewhere, but he or she is aware of the presence of the painter and, however informally, is posing for him. The modern photographer — the earlier worked under the influence of painting — catches people when they are unaware of his presence; off balance, when they are not in the poses which they think most dignified and attractive, nor wearing their 'Sunday best'. Photography of this order has done much to foster in Bacon his predilection for portraying people as though they were alone, unaware of any other presence. To take an extreme example, in 'Three Figures in a Room' (1964, Centre National d'Art Contemporain, on loan to the Musée National d'Art Moderne, Paris), the figure on the left sits naked on a lavatory.

In Bacon's portraits and figure paintings his subjects are in fact not even in his presence; he does not have them in his studio when he paints them. Naturally he is aware of the frequent ferocity of his distortions. 'But who can I tear to pieces,' he asks, 'if not my friends?' 'If I like them I don't want to practise the injury that I do them in my work before them,' he said to David Sylvester. 'I would rather practise the injury in private by which I think I can record the facts of them more clearly.' Accordingly he works mainly from memory but sometimes with the aid of photographs. I asked him why, if he believed he was practising an injury on his friends, he took his friends almost exclusively for his subjects. 'The answer is simple,' he replied. 'It is because I *know* my friends, and

I need that knowledge in order to paint them. You see I know them by heart.' Yet although he is a constant and generous friend, in his portraits of them there are no signs of benevolence.

It is not surprising that Bacon should paint his friends *in absentia,* for no painter of the natural world active today observes it, directly, so little. He prefers to study it in photographs. As it did Blake, nature 'puts him out' and when in earlier days he had to accept an occasional commission for a portrait, he painted laboriously. On one of the rare occasions when he has painted an uncommissioned subject from the life, that of David Sylvester, entitled 'Man Drinking' (of 1954 or '55), the sitter told me that Bacon scarcely looked at him as he sat at a table with a mug before him, which he was not invited to raise to his lips. On another occasion when he sat to him, the portrait became that of a pope and Bacon ignored his model in favour of a big-game photograph because, he said, the animal's texture engaged his interest.

Bacon often carries his preference for indirect vision so far as to prefer, even in cases of the old masters, a reproduction to the original. He has bought many books on Velazquez from which he cuts out and preserves his 'Innocent X', the painting that he perhaps admires the most, yet he told me that when in Rome he has never been to see it.

Bacon's attitude to life has not changed, but in two important respects his art has. The undisguised horrific subjects of many of his earlier paintings, most conspicuous of all in the 'Three Figures', have on the whole been replaced by subjects not intrinsically horrific but imbued with his obsession with human cruelty, vulnerability, loneliness and the pitiful indignity of men, and occasionally women, in solitude, unobserved. There are, however, a number of exceptions: for instance 'Lying Figure with a Hypodermic Syringe' (1963), 'Three Studies for a Crucifixion' (1962, Guggenheim Museum, New York), 'After Muybridge: Woman emptying a Bowl of water and Paralytic Child on all fours' (1965), and 'Triptych: inspired by T. S. Eliot's *Sweeney Agonistes*' (1967, Hirshhorn Foundation, New York).

But far more radical than the modifications of Bacon's subjects has been the evolution of his attitude towards his medium, oil paint, and its potentialities.

The 'Three Figures', however sensational its subject and the treatment of it, from a purely technical point of view is not a revolutionary work. It had been long pondered, as we know from the preliminary study for the central panel made eight years earlier. It is, in fact, a triptych of drawings whose outlines are filled in with more or less uniform areas of colour. In an interview with David Sylvester in 1963 he said:

> You know in my case all painting — and the older I get the more it becomes so — is an accident. I foresee it, yet I hardly ever carry it out as I foresee it. It transforms itself by the actual paint. I don't in fact know very often what the paint will do, and it does many things which are very much better than I could make it do. Perhaps one could say it's not an accident, because it becomes a selective process what part of the accident one chooses to preserve. . . . Can you analyse the difference, in fact, between paint which conveys directly, and paint which conveys through illustration? It's a very close and difficult thing to know why some paint comes across directly on to the nervous system and other paint tells you the story in a long diatribe through the brain.[1]

The interview in which these sentences occur is long and informative, but they seem to me to be crucial, for they illuminate a basic dichotomy in Bacon, but one which does not weaken his art but instead creates a continual and exhilarating tension.

Bacon is a man with intense, wide-ranging interests. The reading and re-reading of classics of many kinds extends the reach and strengthens the grasp of his formidable intelligence. I remember seeing piled high on his bedside table volumes of Aeschylus (in English translation), Pascal, Montaigne, Baudelaire, Nietzsche, and Shakespeare, as well as critical works on several of them. He is fascinated by his fellow human beings and in particular by his friends. 'I have always been more interested in what is called "behaviour" and "life" than in art,' he says, and this from a man with his knowledge of art and reverence for certain works by many old masters is a significant confession. In particular he is obsessed by human cruelty, behaviour to fellow men, to animals. He has studied photographs of animals who know they are about to be slaughtered. His 'Crucifixions' are representations not of a historic event — for he is a non-believer — but 'of an act of man's

[1] The *Sunday Times*, 14 July.

behaviour to another'. Here, then, is a man profoundly and consistently obsessed by great art, great literature, many aspects of human behaviour. How far are these obsessions related to his painting?

In an age less complex than our own, with an authoritative, widely accepted tradition of painting, in an age when the camera had not been invented, many of Bacon's obsessions could have found direct, unequivocal expression in his painting. But this is a highly complex age, with a tradition of painting (like many others) that has withered and in which the camera plays a part which no figurative painter of sensibility can ignore.

Bacon is not a revolutionary, and his belief that traditional forms are for the time being entirely played out does not in the least impair his strong sense of belonging to the tradition of European painting, and he is well aware that the work of those who have done most to revitalize it, such, for instance, as that of Van Gogh, invariably appeared to their contemporaries as destructive of tradition, especially to the self-appointed academic 'guardians' of it. What such men never see is that these 'madmen' rediscover forgotten elements in tradition's infinitely rich and complex legacy. 'I could never disassociate myself,' he says, 'from the great European images of the past.' But just as tradition could not afford to reject the discoveries of the past — perspective, for example, or Turner's or the impressionists' ways of achieving an enhanced brilliance of light — so Bacon is convinced that the eroded tradition of today cannot afford to neglect the most influential discovery of our age: the camera. Upon Bacon its effects are threefold. First he sees, as have many other artists, that the camera has superseded the paintbrush as a medium for recording facts. At the very beginning of the interview with David Sylvester Bacon says:

> One thing that has never been really worked out is how photography has completely altered figurative painting. I think Velazquez believed he was *recording* the court at that time and certain people at that time . . . . But a really good artist today . . . knows that that particular thing could be recorded on film; so this side of his activity has been taken over by something else.

Second, as already mentioned, he knows that the camera has revealed the realities of human and animal movement unknown to, undreamed of even, by painters prior to its invention. Third, he finds in photographs — as in certain paintings by old masters — images 'that breed other images for me'.

The threefold effect is that Bacon rigorously avoids recording what he calls a 'story', which the camera could record better. He takes advantage of the photographs of Muybridge and others with the vastly extended repertory they afford of human beings and animals in motion or unobserved repose; likewise of 'shocking', 'unheard of' material drawn from contemporary life, often suggested by photographs from popular magazines and stills, which he presents in his original projection of the European grand manner. But in one crucially important respect his painting differs from that of any of his predecessors.

Before the invention of the camera painters portrayed definite subjects, the meaning of which could be scrutinized, analysed and enjoyed in detail. Their subjects were integral to their work. But the existence of a machine that can represent subjects more accurately, which has caused innumerable artists to turn to abstraction — which Bacon dismisses as 'decoration' — has affected him in an entirely different way. He is determined to subordinate the subject to the paint, 'to make the paint,' I heard him say, 'speak louder than the story'. It is ironical that this should be the situation of an artist who first made his reputation by the horrific character of his subjects. There has been an inclination among a few recent writers to discount Bacon's preoccupation with the horrific, but his visits to medical bookshops — he was at one time interested in the diseases of the mouth — to butchers' shops and to Scotland Yard's Black Museum surely confirms it; as he says, 'When I was younger, I needed extreme subject matter. Now I don't.' This is not invariably the case, but 'extreme subjects' are far rarer than they were.

The element of violence — 'violence' does not convey my meaning precisely but I can think of no better word — manifests itself in two other ways. One of them, already referred to, 'the tearing of his friends to pieces', is the less important. The other is the element of violence — again not the precise description — so often manifest in his treatment of the paint itself. Just as in the painting of, say, Ingres, the paint, simply applied, plays a minimal part, in that of Bacon it is of its very essence.

Bacon has emphasized many times the crucial part played in his art by accident and the creative effects of the paint itself. In fact no figurative painter has ever gone so far in making an equal, even at times a senior, partner of his medium. Bacon's procedure is complex and ambiguous, but roughly speaking an image lodges in his imagination, is suggested by the memory of an old master or a blurred photograph from some popular magazine; he begins to paint, then, as he says, 'This is the thing that can only probably happen in oil paint, because it is so subtle that one tone, one piece of paint, that moves one thing into another completely changes the implications of the image.'[1] But the image is not allowed to clarify beyond a certain point — that point being when the paint becomes subservient to it. 'What I really love,' he has said 'is the way paint makes things. The way I work now is accidental. The moment the story' — that is to say the subject — 'talks louder than the paint boredom sets in' and 'painting is the pattern of one's own nervous system projected onto canvas . . . an attempt to make a certain type of feeling visual.'[2]

I know no clear statement of his attitude than something he wrote not about his own painting but that of a friend. We brought together at the Tate in 1953 a reprospective exhibition of the work of Matthew Smith, and Bacon accepted our invitation to contribute to the catalogue. It remains his only published writing. Thus runs his 'Painter's Tribute':

> Because I very much admire Matthew Smith, I am delighted to have been asked to write something about him, although I know I will not be able to do him justice. He seems to me to be one of the very few English painters since Constable and Turner to be concerned with painting — that is, with attempting to make idea and technique inseparable. Painting in this sense tends towards a complete interlocking of image and paint, so that the image is the paint and vice versa. Here the brush-stroke creates the form and does not merely fill it in. Consequently, every movement of the brush on the canvas alters the shape and implications of the image. That is why real painting is a mysterious and continuous struggle with chance — mysterious because the very substance of the paint, when used in this way, can make such a direct assault upon the nervous system; continuous because the medium is so fluid and subtle that every change that is made loses what is already there in the hope of making a fresh gain.
>
> I think that painting today is pure intuition and luck and taking advantage

[1] *Ibid.*
[2] *Ibid.*

of what happens when you splash the stuff down, and in this game of chance Matthew Smith seems to have the gods on his side.

Bacon's friends have often heard him define the objective of his painting in these and similar ways; likewise express his repugnance for 'story' — a synonym for 'illustration' — by which I understand him to mean a subject completely and explicitly realized. In fact Bacon is preoccupied, and preoccupied deeply, with his subject. Showing me some of his large collection of photographs, mostly clippings from magazines, and pointing to one of those he values most, a crowd dispersing in panic across a square in St Petersburg during the Revolution, he said something that illuminates the relation between photography and his own art. 'Not one of these hundreds of figures looks remotely like a conventional figure; each one, caught in violent motion, is stranger and at first sight less intelligible than one could have imagined it. Could anything,' he asked, indicating an off-balance L-shaped form in the foreground, 'be more utterly unlike the conventional concept of a man running?' The observation helps us to understand the dichotomy in the art of this man, so deeply interested by many aspects of the physical world — although very little by landscape, sky or water — and by philosophy and literature, besides, of course, painting; why, that is, he is so imperiously determined not to depict any facet of this world so that 'it would speak louder than the paint'. However intense his concern with his subject, his determination to subordinate it to the paint sets up a tension from which he derives his prime motive force.

Wide though his interests are, his subjects have remained similar: mostly single figures, usually male figures, sometimes lying in agony or even dead, crouching or else simply sitting. Even though a number of these are triptychs they still represent, in effect, single figures in that they are mostly oblivious of one another's presence.

There is another dichotomy in the art of Bacon: the 'accidents' to which he often alludes, the 'speaking' of the paint, its 'impact on the nervous system', relate only to his figures; their background and accessories — beds, clothes, curtains, carpets, umbrellas, newspapers and the like — tend to be portrayed with little or no distortion. His interest is focused on the figures, but their environment and accessories also have their part to play, at times by suggesting, by their claustrophobic intimations, the loneliness, though not the privacy, of the figures in their cell-like rooms, at others by directing the spectator's attention upon them.

Portraiture Bacon regards as the most difficult kind of painting. Nor is this surprising, for to subordinate the likeness of a specific individual, one intimately known to him, to 'the paint' must be more difficult than an anonymous figure in which 'accident' is untramelled by the need to approximate, however freely, to the likeness of the subject. In his portraits he plays a particularly complex game with what he has called 'the perilous onset of likeness' without the help from the process integral to his other paintings of 'one image breeding another'. Although in his portraits his freedom of action is not absolute he relies, nevertheless, as in his other paintings, on suggestions produced by the paint itself. 'This head I painted a few days ago,' he said to David Sylvester; 'I was trying to paint a specific person. I used a very big brush and a great deal of paint, and I put it on very freely, and I simply did not know in the end what I was doing, and suddenly the thing clicked, and became exactly the image I was trying to record.'[1]

Inevitably an artist who works in such a way is uneven, but his desire to achieve the perfect image impels him to destroy not so much his outright failures as those which fall just short of his hopes, more especially those which, beginning well, lose their qualities.

'How,' he asks, 'can I recreate an accident?' There is, too, a technical reason for his difficulty in restoring lost qualities: he uses both thick and thin paint on his canvases (working on the reverse, unprimed surfaces) which means that the addition of more paint to thickly worked areas causes clogging difficult to remedy.

Because, then, of his ruthless self-criticism not only his failures, but many paintings which fall just short of success, are destroyed. Most of those permitted to survive reveal the majestic though ambivalent character of his art, in which the paint is not the servant of the subject, but the subject is wrested from the paint and is seen as though he had never seen it before: thus from

[1] *Ibid.*

'Figure Study II' **(PLATE 20)** and 'Painting 1946', through 'Two Figures' (1953) and 'Study after Velazquez' "Portrait of Pope Innocent X" ' (1953), up to 'Portrait of Isabel Rawsthorne' (1966, at the Tate Gallery), 'Study of Isabel Rawsthorne' (1966), 'Portrait of George Dyer, crouching' (1966), 'Three Studies of Lucian Freud' (1969, at the Galleria Galatea, Turin), to 'Triptych' 1970', 'Study for Portrait of Lucian Freud — sideways' (1971, oil) **(PLATE 21)** and 'Figures on Beds' (triptych, centre panel 1972) **(PLATE 22)** — to mention a few among a much larger number.

The compelling power of Bacon's vision, once ridiculed as schoolboy obscenity, derogated as an affront to decent people, and so forth, has imposed itself on the public imagination, not only of Britain but of the western world. In the awkward strangeness of his figures unobserved we recognize ourselves; in his 'affronts to decent people' we recognize understatements about our own age, the age of Auschwitz, Stalin, Hiroshima, Bangladesh, and about much that goes on beneath — though not far beneath — the surface of our own society. So completely, in fact, has it imposed itself that to some among the younger generation it has become almost commonplace. This untaught painter has become by the audacity of his vision, by his dedication, his rare understanding of paint and its mysterious potentialities, a master.

The interview several times quoted here was headed 'The Art of the Impossible'; it is a measure of Bacon's stature that he so often achieves it.

ROBERT COLQUHOUN
1914–62

Colquhoun, a sombre, introspective presence, appeared, except for his dark and piercingly observant eyes, to lack energy. No impression could have been more misleading: he had a rare power of concentration and in a noisy gathering of friends and hangers-on he could work as fast and as surely as if he were alone. It was a power that enabled him to produce — in a short working life — a body of work impressive both in quality and volume: paintings, drawings, prints, as well as designs for the décor and costumes of a ballet and a play, while leading a life which would have frustrated an artist without rare gifts and a rare capacity for giving them full scope in circumstances often highly inauspicious.

Robert Colquhoun was born on 20 December 1914 in Kirktonholm Place, Kilmarnock, Ayrshire, Scotland, the eldest of two sons and a daughter of Robert Colquhoun, an engineering fitter and his wife, born Janet Stewart Candlish. About ten years later the family moved to New Mill Road.

After attending Loanhead School he entered, in 1926, the Kilmarnock Academy where he showed himself proficient in all subjects, but art was his main preoccupation, and from 1929 until 1932 he specialized in drawing and painting under the head art teacher, James Lyle, a man who was to play a crucial part in his becoming an artist. He painted and drew continuously from a very early age, almost everything around him, especially, and in detail, the interiors of the homes of his relations. In 1929 the prevailing economic depression caused Colquhoun, like many others, to leave school or college to help his family to survive. Accordingly he was apprenticed to an engineering concern, but his absence from his class was immediately noticed with consternation by James Lyle, who was convinced that the fifteen-year-old student was the possessor of talent of a rare order. This purposeful man, after obtaining the agreement of his parents, solicited the

176

help, readily forthcoming, of a perceptive local patron of the arts, Sir Alexander Walker, of Piersland, Troon, and of the Rev. James Hamilton, Chairman of the Ayrshire Education Committee and Minister of Henderson Church, Kilmarnock, and thereby made it possible for Colquhoun to resume his studies. This he did to such purpose that in 1932 he won a scholarship at the Glasgow School of Art.

Besides the high quality of the teaching at the School, Colquhoun benefited from Glasgow's fine tradition of painting, its great collections, and in particular from the opportunity of visiting an exhibition which enabled him to study works by Manet, Degas, Cézanne and Picasso.

It was at the Glasgow School that he formed a friendship with a fellow-student of the same year — a friendship so intimate that one of their closest friends said to me, 'they were one person'. Their mutual devotion was to be lifelong. The fellow-student was Robert MacBryde, born MacBride on 5 December 1913, at the Weever Vennel, Maybole, Ayrshire, son of John MacBride, a leather worker, and his wife, born Agnes McKay. MacBryde had a far less auspicious start, having to work for five years in a factory before he was able to go to the Glasgow School, where, like Colquhoun, he studied for five years. Both benefited greatly from the teaching, especially that of Ian Fleming of the Drawing and Painting Department, who was quick to recognize their exceptional talent, though there was no doubt in his mind or in that of others with whom they came in touch that Colquhoun's was the more considerable. Fleming commemorated the intimacy of Colquhoun and MacBryde and his own regard for them in a double portrait. The two students are shown in a corner of one of the School's studios. The relationship between them is perceptively expressed: MacBryde is standing, in the right foreground; Colquhoun on the left, farther back and seated. By his emphasis on MacBryde's face and by bringing him forward towards the spectator the painter suggests his outgoing temperament and his protective attitude towards his friend; his posture is erect, his expression vital. Colquhoun's face, on the other hand, is somewhat veiled, in harmony with his loose, almost slumped posture, in-dicative of its withdrawn, almost passive, relaxation. Fleming, who so clearly shows his insight into their relationship, which never

changed, did much to establish the reputation of 'the Roberts' —
as they were called in Glasgow and in after life. They spoke of him
with respect and affection, as of a man to whom they were
indebted, and when they established themselves in London he used
to stay with them. They owed much, also, to the teaching of Hugh
Crawford.

Colquhoun and MacBryde were happy at the Glasgow School
and believed that their time there was well spent. They kept
themselves somewhat apart from the main body of students,
especially those intending to become teachers, but both, in particular Colquhoun, were much admired. Both won prizes for
drawing and Colquhoun a post-diploma award which enabled him
to spend an extra year there, and both won scholarships which
enabled them to travel widely in Europe together, visiting Rome,
Venice, Florence, Paris, Aix, Avignon, Orange and a number of
other places. At the end of 1939 Colquhoun, with MacBryde,
returned to his native Ayrshire, both working in a studio-hut at his
grandparents' home at Netherton, besides painting and drawing in
various parts of Ayrshire. The following year he was called up,
serving in the Royal Army Medical Corps as an ambulance driver
in Edinburgh — where MacBryde brought him special food —
and Leeds, where in 1941 he was invalided out after collapsing
from cardiac trouble, about which MacBryde was also helpful.
MacBryde himself, being tubercular, was exempt from service.

Later that same year, after a brief visit to Ayrshire, they both
settled in London and their lives underwent radical changes of
several kinds. They stayed first with the enlightened patron of art
and literature, and publisher of *Horizon*, Peter Watson, in his flat
in Prince's Gate, later taking a small studio behind Barker's shop
in Kensington High Street. During the day Colquhoun drove an
ambulance as a member of the Civil Defence Corps, and often
painted at night.

Colquhoun's earliest paintings were mostly landscapes, lucid in
design, solid in construction and reflecting the strong colours of
parts of his native county. Gradually his sympathetic obsession
with his fellow-men and even more with his fellow-women came
to dominate his art. But frequent travel and war service had
discouraged continuous work.

In London his qualities as a painter were recognized, and his presence, magnetic in spite of his sombre silences and proneness to aggressive behaviour (which increased with the years), quickly won him a special place — both as a painter and as a man — in a circle of artists and writers of exceptional talent, and the attention of several perceptive collectors.

The time of his arrival was propitious. The response of British artists to the shock of war and the resulting isolation from the continent was to focus their attention on their own predecessors such as Blake and Palmer, rather than on their most creative contemporaries. Colquhoun, who had little interest in earlier English painting and had so recently spent much time travelling abroad, appeared a conspicuously attractive cosmopolitan figure. (Colquhoun was not entirely immune from the prevailing influence of Palmer, which is clearly apparent in his 'Marrowfield, Worcestershire', an oil of 1941 in the Glasgow City Art Gallery, but paintings in this spirit were not many.) Not that he regarded himself as 'progressive', but rather, like Kokoschka, as someone who hoped to help revivify the great European tradition which he revered. There was, however, one British painter by whom he was radically affected. This was Wyndham Lewis, whose writings he read and reread and the clarity and logic of whose paintings he admired and kept in mind while at work. As a student he had studied his portrait of Mrs Lewis in the Glasgow Art Gallery. Colquhoun's admiration was reciprocated. In a letter to Keidrych Rhys (9 October 1948) Lewis refers to Ceri Richards as 'far and away the best of the younger painters — with, perhaps, Colquhoun'. The year before, but writing with more deliberation and at greater length (in *The Listener* of 13 February), he expressed the opinion that Colquhoun 'is generally recognized as one of the best — perhaps the best — of the young artists. That opinion I cordially endorse.'

Colquhoun settled, late in 1941, in a spacious studio shared with MacBryde, and for a short time with John Minton, at 77 Bedford Gardens, Campden Hill. At a time when the traditional social structure of London was disrupted by the war — even 'bohemia' had had such a structure even though of a more transient kind — this studio became for a time a unique meeting place for artists and writers of the emerging generation. Michael Ayrton, Keith Vaughan, Dylan Thomas, Benny Creme, Prunella

Clough and John Craxton were frequent visitors and Francis Bacon called from time to time. They occasionally met Wyndham Lewis, a near neighbour. Two years later Jankel Adler — whom they particularly admired — arrived from Glasgow (where he had come after service with the Polish Army and where they had known him) and settled in the studio immediately above. The work of Adler, though it had little in common with that of Lewis, did share its deliberation and clarity and this, especially after they became friends and neighbours, impressed Colquhoun.

Adler was not the only link 'the Roberts' maintained with Glasgow. There had been founded not long before, by David Archer, an informal centre where artists met and worked called Sandiford Place (just off Sauchiehall Street) which contained seven or eight rooms that he gave rent-free as studios. Besides Adler, Sandiford Place was frequented by Helen Biggar, sculptor and stage-designer, the poets W.S. Graham and Ian Hamilton Finlay, and the painter Robert Frame. All became friendly with 'the Roberts'. Finlay and Frame hitch-hiked to London and became still closer friends. All these were visitors, some regular and others occasional, at Bedford Gardens. One evening in the same year Colquhoun and MacBryde walked into a Soho pub where they met another friend, the writer Paul Potts who, handing his companion a Pimm's No. 1, said to him, 'I want you to meet two remarkable men.' The companion was George Barker the poet. They became friends immediately (even though MacBryde crushed a small wineglass in his right hand which cut Barker's as they shook hands). The friendship formed that evening between 'the Roberts' and Barker was the closest of their lives and ended only with the artists' deaths.

Colquhoun's relatively wide travels and his acutely perceptive eye enabled him to learn from many painters, and it is not difficult to identify features in his work drawn from artists as remote from one another as Picasso and Palmer, Wyndham Lewis, Assyrian sculptors, Celtic carvers and illuminators and many others besides. But all these borrowings effected very minor contributions to a vision of the rarest originality. In the appreciation of Colquhoun by Lewis in *The Listener* already quoted he continued, 'Perhaps I should have said Colquhoun and MacBryde, for they work

together, and they can be regarded almost as one artistic organism. Usually we say "Colquhoun" when we speak of it.'
Because Colquhoun was the more imaginative, the finer
draughtsman, their work, though it had at times close similarities,
was in fact scarcely 'one artistic organism' and the recognition of
Colquhoun's superiority — which MacBryde himself consistently
proclaimed — has led to MacBryde's unjust neglect.

The two were so close that it is impossible, even for those who
knew them best, to envisage the art of MacBryde if he had never
known his friend's, whereas Colquhoun's, it is not unreasonable to
assume, would not have been very different. But MacBryde often
showed a more resonant sense of colour. Colquhoun's figures at
first superficial glance appear grotesques. It is part of the
mysterious character of his art that on closer scrutiny these figures,
in particular the faces, represent so movingly the artist's preoccupation with certain of the tragic aspects of the human lot. In his
preface to the splendid retrospective, consisting of two-
hundred and fifty-one paintings and prints which he brought
together at the Whitechapel Gallery in 1958, Bryan Robertson
contends that Colquhoun's vision 'was in no way pessimistic'.
Wyndham Lewis (to quote him again) was surely nearer the truth
when he said, 'There is a grave dug behind all his canvases of a
certain kind', namely behind those canvases in which he conveys
most explicitly his tragic vision of life: mostly in terms of old or
elderly women, poor, bloodless, grieving and without purpose.
They are perhaps in part expressions of memories of his own
childhood. Certainly they are emanations of the Celtic world, of
his native Scotland and of Ireland where he spent two months in
1946 in Cork and Crosshaven. (As a rule he worked from
imagination or memory, but in Ireland direct from his subjects.)

An intimate of 'the Roberts' gave me a hint of an interpretation
of the paintings and monotypes in which these women, who
appear together, are also obscure personifications of Colquhoun
and MacBryde themselves and allusions to the situations precipitated by their complex intimacy.

It was in the middle 'forties that Colquhoun reached the height
of his creative power. Comparison between two paintings, made
only two years apart, reveals the difference between high promise
and sure achievement: 'The Two Sisters' and 'The Fortune Teller',

earlier titled 'Women Talking'. The first, made in 1944, is loose and summary, weak in construction: the sister on the far side of the table, for instance, scarcely holds together. These are matters of means only; there are many paintings in which the means, viewed in isolation, are unimpressive and the finished work the very reverse (such as a number of Lowry's, for example). But 'The Two Sisters', whatever its intimations of interest, falls, so to say, with a dull thud. 'The Fortune Teller', made in 1946, grips, and retains, the viewer's interest (mine at any rate. How, in the writing of the work of contemporaries, can one speak for anyone but oneself, when all judgements, even those which seem most secure, are liable to radical modification or else outright reversal?) The painting has so humane, so elegiac a poetry, that one thinks only about the effect, but the means will withstand severe critical examination. A few of the substantial number of paintings of comparable quality are 'Seated Woman with Cat' (1946, oil) belonging to the Arts Council; 'Woman with a Birdcage' (1946, oil), Bradford City Art Gallery (PLATE 23) and, although not of quite the same sureness, the Tate's 'Woman with Leaping Cat' (1945–6, oil).

These paintings and a number of monotypes of similar character, such as 'Women Talking' (1945–6), represent his *annus mirabilis*, the high point of his achievement. His reputation appeared to be firmly established; he had won the respect and admiration of fellow artists, of a number of collectors, and held exhibitions, well received, at the Lefevre Gallery in 1943, 1944 and 1947. In 1948 he and MacBryde were approached by Leonide Massine with a view to their designing costumes and décor for a Scottish ballet. The year following they and George Barker went to Italy with two purposes in view: to see the puppet-plays at Modena and the Palio at Siena, which Colquhoun used later in a series of paintings and prints (and perhaps to attune himself to theatrical design), and to illustrate a book on Italy that Barker was projecting, but neither text nor illustrations were completed. They also visited Rome, Venice, Florence, Verona and Settignano. Being interested in the extent to which painters study their predecessors, I asked Barker how much time Colquhoun spent in museums. 'About one day a fortnight', was the answer.

The new Scottish ballet for which Colquhoun and MacBryde

had designed costumes and décor, entitled *Donald of the Burthens*, was produced in 1951 at Covent Garden; Beryl Grey and Alexander Grant danced the principal roles, the music was by Ian White and the choreography by Massine. I saw neither this ballet nor *King Lear* produced at Stratford two years later by George Devine (Michael Redgrave played Lear, Marius Goring the Fool and Yvonne Mitchell Cordelia, with music by John Gardiner) but experienced judges who did regard the first as amateurish and the second as impressive.

Colquhoun continued to make paintings, drawings and prints of a high order until near the end of his life, and even those of lesser merit are almost always marked by a dignified humanity — a humanity not confined to human beings. Many of his drawings and prints of animals, especially of horses, are masterly in the understanding they show of both movement and repose, expressed with the utmost economy.

In spite, however, of his continued, if less consistent, command of exceptional powers, his close friends were increasingly distressed by signs of decline in both the man and the artist — a decline no less evident in MacBryde. It was the subject of frequent discussion between them, but there was no consensus about the causes of the gradual but, to intimates, painfully apparent symptoms of disintegration. Although its basic cause eluded them they were agreed that it was accelerated by three events, which exacerbated some deeper malaise.

By the middle 'forties Colquhoun and MacBryde were the focus of an admiring and congenial group of friends, and 77 Bedford Gardens had become their home. From this studio they were ejected in 1947 by the landlord, who said that it was intended for working. in by day, not for 'drunken orgies' by night. After their ejection their lives, one of their closest friends said to me, 'began to fall apart'.

When they first came from Glasgow the two young artists did not touch alcoholic drink, or scarcely at all, but in the paradoxically exhilarating atmosphere of wartime London, finding themselves at the centre of a circle of high-spirited young artists and writers, they began to drink heavily, almost nightly frequenting for long hours such Soho resorts as The Black Horse,

'The French Pub', the Caves de France and the Gargoyle Club, often meeting Dylan Thomas, Roderigo Moynihan, John Craxton, Keith Vaughan, John Minton, George Barker and others. Being hospitable when they had the means, they also accumulated numerous 'hangers-on'. But excessively as they drank, it did not appear to affect them until they lost the studio where they had won their reputations, made lifelong friends and formed the habit of regular work. Regular, indeed, in a special sense: both required the incentive of an impending exhibition or of a probable sale to impel them to work at full stretch. Both, especially Colquhoun, could paint and draw at exceptionally high speed; he could complete three prints in a morning, not in the least degree deterred by a noisy talk in their studio, in conditions in which most artists could hardly even think. With MacBryde it was otherwise: he needed quiet and very few ever saw him at work.

Bedford Gardens was their home and they suffered permanent distress from their expulsion from it, even though two sisters, Frances Byng Stamper and Caroline Lucas, who lived at Lewes, Sussex, lent them a studio where they lived for nearly two years, and commissioned Colquhoun to make many lithographs and drawings for Miller's Press, which the sisters owned and ran. Here he also made colour lithographs for *Poems of Sleep and Dream* edited by W.J. Turner and Sheila Shannon and selected by Carol Stewart.

It was after their return from their Italian journey with George Barker in 1949 that they suffered a further blow to their confidence. Duncan Macdonald, a director of the Lefevre Gallery, died. He had long been a friend and an ardent supporter of their work. The Lefevre Gallery had not only given Colquhoun three exhibitions but acted as a sort of banker for him and MacBryde. It in fact gave him a fourth exhibition in 1951, but with Macdonald's death the intimate link between the artists and the gallery was broken. This was a shock to Colquhoun's dignity: he never troubled to find another dealer.

George Barker, the most devoted and loyal of their friends, and his wife, invited them to live at their home, Tilty Mill near Dunmow in Essex, which, like Bedford Gardens, was a resort of writers and artists. Here 'the Roberts' remained for four years. Elizabeth Barker, quite simply, kept them. In return they looked after the children when she was away working in London. But eventually serious and continuous tension prevailed at Tilty, which led, in 1954, to their return to London. Shortly afterwards Tilty was sold.

Whatever the cause for the progressive disintegration of 'the Roberts' its results increasingly alarmed their friends. Of these the most obvious was their increased addiction to drink. At Tilty they went to the local pub as soon as it opened in the morning and remained until it closed. They drank on credit and when they left Elizabeth Barker settled their enormous bill.

In spite of these tensions and their results George Barker remained as devoted a friend as ever: 'I have never known more fascinating men,' he said to me, 'and this was true of many besides myself.'

In most respects 'the Roberts' could not have been more different beings. They had indeed a few qualities in common besides their extreme addiction to alcohol. Both were deeply conscious of their Scottish heritage. They could sing: MacBryde had the better voice and a wide repertory of Scottish songs which was a joy to their friends to listen to. In spite of their liability to use such expressions as 'the English Occupation of Scotland', these were no more than weapons of aggression. None of their friends who has spoken about them to me remember their advocating the separation of their country from England; indeed they seemed to have few if any serious political preoccupations. Colquhoun had a romanticized vision of the artist as an anti-social being derived originally, perhaps, from Rimbaud.

Colquhoun's professed Scottish nationalism is indicative of an ambivalence in his character, for after 1946 he never visited Scotland, and never again saw his parents. Apart, in fact, from a very occasional letter or telephone call he deliberately severed all links with Kilmarnock. This ambivalence was not confined to his native city to which he owed so such. Devoted though he was to his friends, after leaving the Kilmarnock Academy in 1932 he never visited — or I believe communicated with — James Lyle, to whose confidence in his powers and persistent and effective help he owed the opportunity to become an artist.

They shared a self-respect with regard to their appearance, in the case of MacBryde amounting to vanity, on Colquhoun's behalf as well as his own. One evening Colquhoun, whose sight troubled him at times, put on a pair of spectacles. MacBryde snatched them off his face and crushed them angrily under his heel. Before going out for a night MacBryde would iron their trousers with the utmost care. (He anticipated the narrow trousers which became fashionable decades later. Colquhoun was too vain to bathe in public owing to the thinness of his legs.) Lucian Freud saw him ironing a shirt of Colquhoun's with a teaspoon.

They also shared a sensitiveness which, especially under the effects of alcohol, took the form of deliberate, aggressive rudeness towards those whom they met for the first time, as a test. If the victim responded with good nature, after ten minutes or so, they might become friendly. It was a test which I unhappily failed to pass. One night, as a guest of Francis Bacon, at a late dinner at the Gargoyle Club, I was accosted by two men unknown to me (fellow-guests, it shortly appeared) with truculent demands for whisky, addressed to me and other members of the party as they assembled and took their places at the table. My response — to my regret — was curt, and I accordingly never came to know these two remarkable men.

In other respects they might be regarded as opposites, or else as contrary but complementary aspects of the single person they almost were. Colquhoun was inward-turning, withdrawn, prone to long periods of silence, when he could sit, hour after hour, staring. He read widely but without discrimination; anything at hand, whether a classic, a detective story, or even lists of racehorses or of objects for sale. The sight of this immensely creative man just reading, for days on end, simply to pass the time, continually surprised his friends, even though they knew that when he worked he worked surely and fast. Colquhoun was, strangely, at once the dominant yet in several respects the passive member of the couple. When he talked — he rarely mentioned painters or painting — he showed, according to George Barker, 'a natural, a beautiful intelligence'.

MacBryde was extrovert, expressing himself freely and with ease, though reticent and modest about himself. He looked after all the practical aspects of their life: he did the cooking, the shopping, maintained contacts with dealers and replied to most of their letters. He used to declare his pride in being 'the servant of

the great master' and in having sacrificed his own career to further
that of Colquhoun. Without Colquhoun's inhibitions and reserve,
he made friends easily. But in spite of his aloofness Colquhoun
was liable, towards men, to an emotional susceptibility that could
stir jealousy in MacBryde.

The relation between them was so strange that I doubt whether
it was fully understood even by their closest friends. Its strangeness
has never been more evocatively described to me than by George
Barker's son Sebastian. When 'the Roberts' were living at Tilty
Mill he was a boy — eight when they left. They were delightful
companions to the children, he said, entering wholeheartedly into
whatever they were doing, gentle, humorous and sympathetic,
incredibly dexterous manually, making bows and arrows and
inventing original games. When the children became too
demanding they had ingenious — and sometimes macabre —
ways of getting rid of them, by sending them, for instance, in
search of an allegedly crashed aeroplane. The evenings were
idyllic: amusing talk, sitting round the dinner table, varied by the
beautiful singing of Scottish songs. The idyllic evening ended and,
when all had retired to their bedrooms, from that occupied by 'the
Roberts' would suddenly be heard a variety of sounds: of fist-
fights, of crashes, of screams. On one occasion their double-bed
was set on fire, but the flames were promptly put out.

Next morning, although black eyes and cuts were evidence that
these sounds were not emanations of nightmare, 'the Roberts'
were as gentle and sympathetic as before and any damage to
furniture or anything else had been skilfully repaired.

The failure of the Barkers' attempt to provide peaceful working
conditions for 'the Roberts' at Tilty Mill aggravated the susceptibility to despair that their expulsion from Bedford Gardens and
the death of Duncan Macdonald had exacerbated. The result was
the decline of all their faculties. But such was Colquhoun's talent
and such his resilience that he was still able to work well, although
less impressively and consistently than before. Even so intense and
monumental a painting as 'Woman Ironing' (one of five
completed at high speed specially for his Whitechapel retrospective
in 1958) has passages in which a summary breadth of form is the
result of loss of the application so evident in the best of his earlier
works. (Francis Bacon, always conscious of the crucial part played

by impulse generated by the actual process of applying paint and also by sheer chance, deplored Colquhoun's 'destruction of his art by his gradual enslavement to a constrictive style'.) But whatever the shortcomings of his later work, it shows, almost invariably, strains of nobility.

There was something about the character of 'the Roberts' that survived the general decline of their faculties; nothing showed this more clearly than the undiminished affection and loyalty of their friends.

I had met them only rarely but on every occasion they had been . extremely drunk and behaved unpleasantly to all within earshot. Early in April 1958, the 9th to be precise, I went to the Colquhoun retrospective at the Whitechapel. Although I had long admired his work — we had bought 'The Woman with the Leaping Cat' for the Tate four years before — I realized that I had not recognized his full stature. There I met Colquhoun and MacBryde, for the first time sober. When I spoke to Colquhoun of the deep impression made on me by his assembled work, he made no reply but simply looked at me gravely and I could see tears in his eyes which said as clearly as any words that if he and circumstances had been different he might have achieved infinitely more. A moment later he seemed serene and happy; we had a long talk and I formed an immediate liking for him and also for MacBryde; they spoke with enthusiasm of plans for starting a new life in Sudbury in Suffolk. Of all Bryan Robertson's notable achievements at Whitechapel, none was finer than this great tribute to a noble but now wasting talent.

In spite of the obvious delight that the exhibition gave Colquhoun, his last years were bleak and restless. After returning from Spain — where 'the Roberts' went on the proceeds of the exhibition — they were without a home, living in rooms in 47 Gibson Square, Islington, 9 Westbourne Terrace, 8 Norland Square and elsewhere, declining in health and confidence — but according to their friends never in courage. 'I never knew men more courageous, less afraid', I heard one of them declare.

On 20 September 1962 Colquhoun died of heart disease, while at work on a drawing of a man in space, dying — a drawing, in effect, of his own death. George Barker travelled to Kilmarnock for his funeral and wrote this poem:

FUNERAL EULOGY FOR ROBERT COLQUHOUN
inscribed to Robert MacBryde

It was at four in the morning at work on his sketch of Death
He felt on his shoulder the tip of that twisting wraith,
He had at least etched on the negative of his life.

As the flying Scotsman to the landscapes of the Pennine Chain
Or the Flying Dutchman to all illusions of the Ocean
So was Colquhoun to those through whom his devotion drove him.

What we saw was a winged engine illuminated with flame
Or the skeletal hull loom through the fog of our time
As he dominated and dogged the heart marked X.

I shall know him again by the self-graven epitaph in his face
When, as he may, he chooses to revisit this place
That gave him, as haven, little more than a grave.

Tenderest of men in the morning before the ravening ghouls
Swept out of his holyrood conscience like lost souls,
In the evening we heard him howling in their chains.

All things were, to this man, a sort of structural
Crucifixion, like the god of the straining pectoral
Brought down to the flayed stoat nailed to a tree.

II

By moonlight I see a stallion of Stubbs-Uccello
Gaunt, long-barrelled, yellow, lifting its head
Proudly out of a bunch of fallow thistle

Which is the Knoxian conception of Scottish
responsibility. And now this proud man is dead.
This Highlander, this skinny Aryan, this, yes, British

Mountaineer of spiritual violence
This draftsman who was not so much a painter
As the graphologist of our dying conscience,

Elected to go home to cold Kilmarnock
And render those he left behind a mere remainder,
For what he wanted lay north of Cape Wrath and the rock.

In the ferocious exhibition bout he conducted
With himself both Jacob and the Angel, we, the audience,
Had at last become superfluous. We were subtracted.

I have to believe that, having contested the issue
With his own passion, he now resumes it in regions
To which neither our love nor our grief shall ever have ingress.

Intensity of spirit, that energy with which
Energy creates itself, is indestructible.
Now where is the wrestler Jacob meeting his match?

And supernaturally, why? To that rigorous
Calvinist of the Image, canvassing the invisible
Icon in colours seemed at heart futile and frivolous.

What, I think, broke this horsebreaker of a man
Was the knowledge that not in things but in their distances —
Yes, there the love that kills them always began.

Such a hero — and by this I mean
A heart that acknowledges the glory of consequences —
Foresees that the love that generates between

All things must in its own turn destroy them
Like rubbing hands of wood. What possible pretences
Existed for such a man? How could he employ them

In the already burning theatre of his spirit?
The consolation that pacifies those ashes
Is his. It is not ours. We cannot share it.

So let him lie now near the rock and the cold loch
Not to awaken again till Cape Wrath one day dashes
The last wave over that long grave in Kilmarnock.

The other Robert could not long survive. He lived in what was
scarcely more than a cupboard, declining quickly from cleanliness
to abject filth. Then in Dublin, on 15 May 1966 after a night's
drinking, he was run over by a car and killed — Robert
MacBryde, who had said to George Barker, 'We must be certain
to create our legends before we die.' That legend he failed to
create, but George Barker, also wrote:

IN MEMORY OF ROBERT MACBRYDE

It is midnight. The moon is high
and staring down with a white eye

on Dublin where she saw you die
knows how black her magic was

when you met Nothing face to face.
How can I think, dear Robert dead,

you are not here, but lie instead
under every stone I tread?

How can a shovelful of dirt
lie so heavy on your heart

that I too feel some living part
of me lies there, and always will?

When that huge room at Notting Hill
on Sunday nights began to fill

with those whom you loved all too well,
then I and each one was the most

devoted, O intemperate ghost,
of all the lovers you have lost.

And bluer days in Italy
when, footloose around Fiesole,

Colquhoun and you, and she and I
wove like a tartan or like dances

Love into all circumstances
not caring that the grave advances

and that of our four, too soon, three
would sleep so far from Italy

and further from what used to be.
My memory is that pearled room

high over Florence in the gloom
of a March evening. There you, whom

too often I waited for, you three
return, and perhaps smiling, we

rise and take hands silently
as the sun through the French window

turns on Florence far below,
leaving us in a great shadow.

Or I hear, now growing softer
the mocking birds of your laughter

I follow, a sleepwalker, after;
as, fitfully, from the town below

those sleepers of so long ago
rise from the bed of the Arno.

And once again, well-washed, we are
standing against that little bar

in the Piazza Signoria,
happy, silly, a bit mellow,

joking with a cyclist fellow
named — you remember? — Donatello.

Now even that March sun is gone.
The night divides, for everyone

Sleeps, dear Robert, like you, alone.

LUCIAN FREUD
born 1922

Three at least of the painters discussed in this volume, Burra, Houthuesen and Collins, have been accorded by the establishment far less recognition than their achievements merit. All three, although still subject to official neglect, have sufficient recognition from private collectors to live in modest comfort; Houthuesen, indeed, over the past decade would be unable (were he disposed to attempt it) to meet the ever-growing demand for his work.

The case of Freud is different: the establishment, owing to the fact that he has many highly influential friends (Francis Bacon is an intimate and an ardent supporter), has always been aware of his existence and, particularly when he was in his twenties, of his precocious talent. A few members of the establishment have bought an occasional example of his work, but in the main its attitude has been one of lack of interest and he is meagrely represented in British public collections; but it is only fair to recall the smallness of his production. Lucian reciprocates this lack of interest. When it was one of my duties to attend official receptions and the like he was never present. It would be untrue to suggest that official indifference towards him is complete: he was awarded an Arts Council Prize in the 1951 Festival of Britain Exhibition and three years later a group of his works was shown in the British Pavilion at the Venice Biennale. The Tate Trustees responded warmly to my proposals for the purchase in 1952 of 'Girl with a White Dog', a painting completed the previous year, and 'Portrait of Francis Bacon' (on the jacket of this book), and in 1964 they even exercised their prerogative of taking over any work falling within the scope of the collection bought by a member of the staff at the price paid for it, claiming his 'Self-Portrait', a painting of 1946, which my daughter bought at Sotheby's on my behalf for £120. He is also represented in the Museum of Modern Art, New York.

Lucian holds himself aloof not only from official life but from

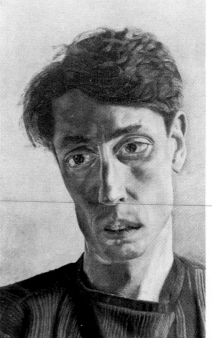

Plates 25 and 26: LUCIAN FREUD: *Mike
[Michael] Andrews and June* (1965-6), oil,
23¾ × 27¾ in. and (right) *John Minton*
(1932), oil, 16 × 10 in.

MICHAEL ANDREWS. Plate 27 (opposite, top): *All Night Long* (1963-4) oil
on hardboard, 3 panels, each 72 × 48⅛ in. Plate 28 (above): *Good and Bad at
Games II* (1968), oil on canvas, 60 × 80 in. Plate 29 (opposite, below): *Lights III:
the Black Balloon* (1973), acrylic on canvas, 51 × 63 in.

BRIDGET RILEY. Plate 30 (above): *Movement in Squares* (1961), tempera on board, 48 × 48 in. Plate 31 (below): *Fall* (1963), emulsion on board, 55½ × 55½ in.

conventional social life as well. This is due largely to his determination to preserve the utmost possible independence, but even
more because he needs an exceptional measure of freedom from
distraction in order to work. His talk is an easy and wide-ranging
expression of a sophisticated and well-stocked mind and I, and no
doubt other friends, on first coming to know him was surprised at
the intense difficulty he finds in drawing and painting. This
difficulty in expressing himself otherwise than by the spoken word
is also apparent in his handwriting, which is almost childlike. This
was in part due to his having to learn roman script when he had
been brought up to use gothic and in part to his being badly
taught at his English school, but had this difficulty not been
innate a man of Lucian's talent would easily have overcome it.
Spontaneous expression comes to him unsought, but deliberate
expression is a different matter. He has disciplined himself in the
effective use of brush, pen or pencil, but as he has no aspirations
after writing, except as a means of ordinary communication, he
has barely troubled to master its elements.

Lucian is, in fact, an anomalous figure, a socially sought-after
solitary with a seemingly facile mind to whom the pursuit of his
vocation is a sombre ordeal daily renewed, a seemingly material
temperament, who, like Francis Bacon, beyond needing ready cash
in his pocket, is without the acquisitive urge and whose successive
studios would be rejected as unfit to live in by the student of
today.

Lucian Michael Freud was born on 8 December 1922 in Berlin,
the second of the three sons of Ernst Freud, the architect and
younger son of Sigmund Freud, and his wife Lucie Brasch. At the
age of nine he was brought to England by his parents, where he
has lived ever since. In 1939 he became a naturalized British
subject. He often saw his illustrious grandfather, Sigmund Freud,
who lived at Maresfield Gardens, Hampstead, and he enjoyed his
jokes and his prevailing good humour — and the gifts of money
he used to send him when he was at school.

For as long as he can remember Lucian has drawn and painted;
it had always been assumed by himself and his family that he
would be an artist. In the middle 'thirties he spent three years at
school at Dartington, where his predilection for drawing and

painting was frustrated by the artiness of the art master (he was accordingly tempted to become a jockey instead of an artist), followed by a few terms at Bryanston, where for a time he took up sculpture and sometimes considers making more. After leaving school in 1939 he studied at the Central School of Arts and Crafts, with Cedric Morris at his school at Dedham, and in 1942 he drew part-time at Goldsmiths' College. In the meanwhile, by visits to art galleries and the study of reproductions, he gained a wide knowledge of European painting, of that of the present century in particular. One of the most ambitious of his early paintings, 'The Refugees' of 1941, shows, for instance, familiarity with the work of the Germans Grosz and Dix. The satiric spirit of the former was a source of lively pleasure to him, but his form seemed to him superficial; he was more deeply impressed by Chinese art, the engravings of Dürer and the paintings of Van Gogh.

In December 1939 he and a friend, David Kentish, rented a miner's cottage at Capel Curig at the foot of Snowdon. They were joined by Stephen Spender, who had become a friend of Lucian's the previous year: here he wrote *The Backward Son*, and stirred by Lucian's example briefly tried his hand at painting. Together they compiled *The Freud-Schuster Book* (Spender's mother was a Schuster). The illustrations are by Lucian and both contributed some lively but disconnected text, abounding, like the illustrations, in esoteric allusions and jokes. The themes of the drawings, many of them in indian ink and wash, some in watercolour, are extremely various. There are portraits (several of them of Spender, Kentish and the artist himself); horses (Lucian, having learnt to ride at Dartington, has had a particular affection for horses ever since); Welsh landscapes and interiors, and many expressions of fantasy, recollections of dreams, of paintings, surrealist concepts and other ideas. A few of them were made after Lucian had left Wales.

The book took over two months to finish, though finish is a term not strictly applicable to a work which, though replete with wit, acute observation and vision, is without coherent form. Had circumstances been favourable it might have been in progress for two years as readily as two months.

To those familiar with the paintings of Lucian the illustrations in *The Freud-Schuster Book* (never published or exhibited and not even seen by many of the artist's friends) offer a surprise due to the contrast between them. The paintings, especially the early ones, are marked by extreme deliberation and precision; the drawings by a playful spontaneity. Lucian gave the book to Sir Colin Anderson, a helpful friend and supporter, who, in 1968, returned it to him, inscribed with an amusing poem of his own composition.

At Capel Curig Lucian worked almost continuously, all day and far into the night, though little of what he did survives. (He still works as well by electric as by sunlight — and almost always on several paintings at the same time.) The war, however, interrupted the work of all British artists except those employed by the War Artists' Advisory Committee and others advanced in years, and Lucian served for six months in 1941 in the Merchant Marine. (My own first meeting with him was at the Café Royal just after he had been invalided out; he was still wearing a striped sailor's jersey and was suffering from an injury inflicted in the course of a fight with a fellow-member of the crew.)

Lucian began to paint shortly after his discharge, producing 'The Refugees' already referred to; 'Man with a Feather' (1942, oil); 'Still Life with Chelsea Buns' (1942-3, oil), and 'Quince on a Blue Plate' (1944, oil).

By the middle 'forties, able to dispense with anything approaching the degree of reliance on other artists apparent in 'The Refugees', Lucian Freud entered upon the first phase of his creativity as a mature artist, when he made a number of paintings and drawings that won him a place among the foremost artists of his generation. These works are surrealist in spirit but entirely independent of such surrealist devices as torpedo-like clouds, drawers projecting from torsos, liquified watches and the like. They are suffused with the dream-world strangeness of the best surrealist art, yet their subjects are entirely credible and belong unambiguously to the world of natural appearances. Among such works was 'Dead Heron' (1946, oil), which is worthy of comparison with the superb painting of the same subject made by G.F. Watts at the age of twenty.

He was amazed, he told me, by its resemblance to Watts's painting when he saw it, nineteen years later, reproduced on the cover of the issue of *The Masters* (of which I was editor) devoted to the Victorian master. There followed 'Still Life with Aloe Plant' (1948, oil) and 'Dead Monkey' (1950, pastel, now at the Museum of Modern Art, New York.)

The time when he entered upon his maturity may be dated fairly precisely as about 1946. 'The Woman with a Daffodil', an oil at the Museum of Modern Art, New York, painted in 1945, is a naive, almost primitive work in comparison with 'Dead Heron' and 'John Craxton' (a pastel), both made the following year.

The fascinated unblinking stare with which Lucian Freud fixed his subjects enabled him to represent them in a manner that makes it impossible for the spectator (for this spectator at least) ever to look at them casually: the eye is compelled to see them, down to the smallest detail, with something of the intensity with which he saw them himself. When the history of art in Britain in the middle of the twentieth century comes to be written, I believe that these quasi-surrealist paintings and drawings will be found deserving of posterity's interest and respect.

This first phase of maturity lasted but a few years, and by the early 'fifties his work showed intimations of a change that was, in less than a decade, virtually to transform it.

In this early work, original, poetic, lucid, in which sophistication is tempered by a strain of naivety, certain of Lucian's friends supposed him to have evolved a language that would serve him for many years, and they were critical of his modification and eventual abandonment of it. Of course it must be a matter for regret that a phase in an artist's development, when he made works of such unusual beauty, should be of brief duration, but a harder look than those friends gave at the nature of the work and the temperament of the artist would have warned them it was a phase unlikely to be prolonged. For these paintings and drawings are the visual equivalents of lyric poetry and of a poetry of youth, and Freud is the last person to prolong any phase of his art beyond its natural term. Increasing skill and sophistication in any case inevitably excluded their strain of naivety. But a far more decisive factor was making itself ever more imperatively felt. This was the conviction that his was a painter's rather than a draughtsman's temperament, which could not find lasting satisfaction in a language that was predominantly linear. A tendency to abandon detailed in favour of broader treatment is a phenomenon often observable, as was noted in relation to a comparable change in the work of Houthuesen.

It was perhaps a tendency innate also in Freud, a predestined feature of his evolution. However that may be, it was fostered by at least one outside circumstance. Francis Bacon had been a close friend since 1945 and Lucian's admiration for him was intense. Lucian was one of the smallish number of Francis's friends privileged to watch him at work. So doing in the early 'fifties, he marvelled at the evocative power of his friend's handling of paint. Until then he himself had drawn constantly, confident that the pen or pencil could fully express his ideas. But this experience made him aware, as never before, of his need to represent *volume*, more naturally fulfilled by the brush than the pencil. In order to stimulate his urge to paint, he told me, he denied himself the delight of drawing. His paintings of the early 'fifties show a delicate balance between the linear and the painterly, inclining gradually yet perceptibly towards the latter. This progressive change is charted in the following portraits: 'John Craxton' (1946, oil), and the Tate's 'Self-Portrait', an oil of the same year; 'Girl with Roses' (1947-8, oil); 'Girl with White Dog', oil of 1950-51, at the Tate; 'Francis Bacon' (1952, oil), also at the Tate; 'John Minton' **(PLATE 24)**, an oil of the same year, at the Royal College of Art; 'Head of a Woman' (1953, oil), belonging to the British Council **(PLATE 25)**, and 'Woman Smiling' (1958-60, oil). During the twelve to fourteen years after 1946 the evolution from the linear to the painterly, from emphasis on one-dimensional pattern to emphasis on volume, seemed virtually complete. In the following years, however, all trace of the linear was lost through preoccupation with volume and, increasingly, with paint as a medium, exemplified by such a portrait as 'John Deakin', an oil of 1965 or 'Mike Andrews and June' **(PLATE 26)** (1965-6, oil). At first glance the first and last of these portraits might be attributed to two hands as unrelated as those of Ingres and Courbet.

The earlier and the later work of Freud, however widely different in both vision and technical procedures, are linked by a highly significant attribute of his character: his intense preoccupation with the familiar and the near. Many artists are drawn to depict the exotic, the remote, the imagined, the out of focus. Not Freud: he is obsessed by his friends and other familiars, by his immediate environment, a shabby and untidy workroom flat, and its neighbourhood. It is significant of this love of the familiar that since settling in Paddington in 1941 he has never moved away and even his moves within its boundaries — from 20 to 4 Delano Terrace, and thence to 124 Clarendon Crescent and again to 227 Gloucester Terrace — have been dictated rather by circumstance than preference. His devotion to this district has grown stronger with the years, and one of the most impressive of his recent paintings is 'Waste Ground with Houses, Paddington' (1971-2), which expresses a perception of the particular character of the place in which he lives which puts one in mind of that of Lowry or even of Constable.

Attachment to familiar surroundings does not preclude occasional expeditions abroad. He has made two expeditions to Greece, in 1946 and 1967, and I met him by chance in Paris (which he has frequently visited) in 1953 when he was at work on 'The Hotel Room' (oil, at the Beaverbrook Gallery, Fredericton, Canada). This has an element of drama usually absent from his painting, representing the artist standing in near silhouette against the window and his golden-haired companion lying in bed.

All his subjects, human and environmental, he observes minutely and at close range. Yet his vision has nothing of the warmth, the affection, that we usually associate with *intimistes*. On the contrary, it is cold, and with the years has grown as responsive to blemishes as to beauties. On several occasions, when studying nudes as coldly seen as they are intimately depicted, I have recognized them with a start of surprise as friends for whom he entertains a particular affection.

The prime focus of Freud's ceaselessly probing mind is aspects of human personality. When he depicts a cactus, a window, a mattress, his purpose is to provide a setting for the man, woman or child under his unblinking scrutiny — which has issued in portraits (those earlier mentioned prominent among them) which bear comparison with the best portraits of the time. The 'Francis Bacon' for its psychological insight, its formal perfection and its aura of a magical strangeness, is a masterpiece.

It was logical that Freud's absorption in quintessential personality should have led him frequently to represent his subjects without clothes. For most painters the unclothed body is a 'nude' — a more or less impersonal figure. Freud's nudes are all portraits, in the widest sense, the absence of clothes affording the fullest opportunity for achieving the likeness of a total personality. The naked body, represented with searching detached candour, is surmounted by a highly characterized head. The impact of a nude by Freud is sometimes startling, for the spectator may find himself unprepared for confrontation not with a 'nude' in the traditional sense but with a naked individual. Although the face is, beyond comparison, a person's most expressive feature, a naked portrait by Freud reminds the spectator that all a body's features contribute, some to a greater, others to a lesser degree, to our understanding of a person. Such a portrait prompts the realization that the 'face-painting' of tradition can offer only a partial view. This realization, of course, serves little practical purpose, for those willing to be portrayed stripped of all protective disguise (especially by a brush at the service of a remorseless eye) are very few and are unlikely, even in our 'permissive' society, to become appreciably more numerous. We should be grateful to Freud (and his models) for combining to give us such impressive examples of a very rare kind of portraiture. The most characteristic as well as the most impressive of the group is 'Nude' (1965, oil).

It is a sad reflection on the present state of patronage that this impassioned portrait painter has been compelled to accept, in the entire course of his life, commissions far fewer than one would have thought conceivable — those referred to in these pages are of wives (he has been married to Kathleen, daughter of Sir Jacob Epstein, and to Lady Caroline Temple Blackwood) or of friends — and this at a time when serious portrait painters have never been so few. But then, as T.S. Eliot said, human beings can't stand much reality.

Lucian Freud is not a man to develop a style not subject to evolution; his mind is too exploratory and too probing to make permanence likely. His earliest mature style was largely innate: he always worked hard, but it was as though, at first, he was reaping a harvest, gathering something already sown. That severely linear style, suffused with a naive, sometimes surrealist poetry, he determinedly abandoned in favour of a painterly style, adapted to the portrayal of his subjects in terms of volume, which was accompanied by and perhaps even fostered a down-to-earth, prose attitude towards them. Nothing could be more different — apart from the informing purpose, the intense probing of a human personality — than the 'Craxton' or the 'Bacon' portraits on the one hand, and the 'John Deakin', 'Mike Andrews and June', 'Head of a Man' (1968, oil) on the other; than the hieratic idealization of the first two and the focusing upon the 'earthiest' aspects of the subjects of the others.

The change in his vision of his subjects has been accompanied by a change of method. In his earlier work he made no preliminary studies; his paintings and drawings — to quote his own words to me — 'often surprised me by the way they developed'. In his later years he draws in charcoal on the canvas, sometimes for hours, to prove to himself 'that the picture could be done'; this does not preclude his making changes in his designs, however elaborately worked out beforehand. I mention this paradoxical circumstance because it is the earlier work that looks precisely calculated and the later spontaneous.

It is as though, the challenge of paint and volume and the quality of the down-to-earth having at last been successfully met, there has been some easing of his determination to exclude every vestige of the poetry of his earlier work. When I visited his studio in 1969 he had just completed 'Large Interior, Paddington' which — for me at least — held intimations that the element of poetic strangeness, still an integral part of his vision, is once more, though within severe limitations, beginning to reassert itself.

MICHAEL ANDREWS
born 1928

Somebody once wrote of Michael Andrews that he was in danger of being taken for a rumour rather than a person. Several of the painters who are the subjects of this book are not widely known to the public at large but none is so elusive a figure as he, however ardently admired by several of his most illustrious fellow painters or perceptively praised by several critics on the rare occasions when he exhibits.

Only two years after he had left the Slade, for instance, he was described in *The Times* as 'perhaps the most imaginative and serious young painter we have' (14 October 1955) — yet he remains elusive and paradoxically little-known as both painter and man. This is due partly to his being something of a recluse, spending his leisure with his wife and child, shunning public occasions and meeting even his friends comparatively rarely. One of them, of several years' standing and a particularly ardent admirer, told me that he had never seen his studio. His telephone is ex-directory. But his relative obscurity as a painter is due to a greater degree to the paucity and character of his art. Although a hard and able worker, his production is very small indeed, owing to the degree to which each painting is the expression of some deeply felt experience. For him aims are more important than means. This is an over-simplification, and I will try to clarify their relation later on, but because every painting represents some unique experience Andrews has not, so far, evolved a consistent or a readily recognizable style. If someone were to come upon a Christopher Wood, a Piper, a Bacon or a Hockney, for example, in an environment entirely improbable, they would nevertheless be able to identify it instantly. With Andrews it is otherwise: I believe that if on the far side of a crowded and noisy nightclub one saw even his most celebrated painting, one would be unlikely immediately to exclaim, 'A Michael Andrews *here*; how strange!' Closer examination would of course evoke a clear recognition —

201

but that is a different matter.

Michael James Andrews was born on 30 October 1928 at
Brunswick Road Hospital, Norwich, the second of the three
children of Thomas Victor Andrews, who worked in Norwich for
the Norwich Union Life Insurance Society, and his wife Gertrude
Emma, born Green. Their home was at 142 Glebe Road. Thomas
Andrews's family were East Anglian, though his maternal
grandmother was Dutch. The Greens were from Derbyshire. The
Andrews family had only one artistic connection and that remote:
Thomas Breeze, the watercolourist, was a second cousin of
Michael's father.

While at the City of Norwich School, which he attended from
1940 until 1947, he worked during his last year at the Norwich
School of Art. Michael, who felt the artistic impulse for as long as
he could remember, told me that he 'was quite good at art at
school, though more imaginative than skilful'. He was fortunate in
the encouragement his parents gave to his ambition to be an artist
and in the proximity of the Castle Museum, with its splendid
collection of works of the East Anglian school; those of Crome
and Cotman particularly compelled his attention.

Michael's parents were devout Methodists whose lives revolved
round their church, but early in life, 'kicking against it', he became
an agnostic, which he has since remained.

After leaving school he served for two years in the Royal Army
Ordnance Corps, nineteen months of it in the vast camp at
Tel-el-Kebir. Discipline was strict, and he was able to see little of
Egypt, but it was there that he made a number of watercolours
that he regards as his first adult works.

In the meanwhile Randolph Schwabe, the Slade Professor, saw
a few of his sixth-form drawings and, discerning something of his
promise, kept a place for him at the School; William Coldstream,
Schwabe's successor, confirmed his admission, and he studied
there from 1949 until 1953 when he was awarded a Rome
Scholarship, tenable for two years. The award pleased him, but he
accepted it with misgiving because he had become extremely fond
of London, and felt that if he left it he would be renouncing a
necessary, comprehensible and a glamorous way of life. Accordingly he remained in Rome, and briefly in Anticoli, only for five

months. On his return he found London as enjoyable as ever. At the Slade he owed much to the encouragement of Coldstream, the first eminent painter whom he came to know. After his return from Italy he taught for four years at Norwich at various times, at Chelsea from 1962 until 1964, and the Slade from 1963 until 1966.

Andrews also acted in two films, both made by Lorenza Mazzetti, one in 1953 when they were fellow-students at the Slade called *Metamorphosis*, based on a story by Kafka, the other, in 1954-5, called *Together*, based on Carson McCullers's *The Heart is a Lonely Hunter*, in which Eduardo Paolozzi had a part.

In the meanwhile he began the slow succession of paintings which won him the whole-hearted admiration of a still small but steadily growing number of collectors and critics, but most conspicuously of fellow painters.

The first of these while the artist was still a student and, so far as I was concerned, not even a 'rumour', was 'The Man who suddenly fell over'. This I happened to see at the Slade while on a visit to Coldstream just after its completion in 1952, described with enthusiasm to my wife — and forgot. Delightedly reminded of it when it was shown at his first one-man exhibition at the Beaux-Arts Gallery in January 1958, we bought it for the Tate. Coldstream, who remains a warm admirer of Andrews and owns a drawing of the woman's head in this particular painting, was at the time one of the Tate's trustees. Although in certain respects, in comparison with his later works, it is technically naive, it clearly exemplifies the intense and complex ideas which almost all his painting expresses. On 16 July 1958 he wrote to the Tate:

> About the picture. I didn't see it happen as far as I can remember though I have seen big people fall down. It's a catastrophe and as stunning and bewildering as the fable of the sky falling always seemed to be. It's about the complete upsetting of someone's apparently secure equilibrium and about their almost immediate efforts at recovery and their attempts to conceal that they *have* perhaps been badly hurt or upset which would only be allowed to show if they were by themselves.

A painting of the following year — the only one he made in Rome while on his scholarship — is 'Lorenza Mazzetti in Italy,' which shows her in in Piazza di Spagna (also included in his first exhibition at the Beaux-Arts Gallery). While it also gives an intimation of his powers, it shows little of the intellectual and emotional impulses by which its predecessor and the more significant of its successors are inspired. Technically it is a tentative work, in which the sober, tonal, painterly handling deriving from the example of Coldstream combines with a clarity of composition indicative of his study of early renaissance Italian masters.

Andrews works very slowly, producing at most two or three big paintings a year — and rather more small ones which he regards not as complete works but as experimental preliminaries. (Until he saw how much faster other Slade students worked he was unaware of his own slowness.) Usually he works only on one painting at a time, but in the process, particularly near its end, he realizes that it has given him ideas for its successor, and that, although this may not be readily apparent, there is accordingly some degree of continuity in his work.

It was not until the middle 'fifties that he began fully to understand the real potentialities of his gifts, as shown, for instance, in a painting such as 'Four People Sunbathing', of 1955, in which one characteristic that was to mark his work is apparent, namely figures informal in posture and disposition but formally related to one another and with the utmost care likewise to their environment. When this painting was shown at the Institute of Contemporary Arts in 1955 (characteristically his was a single contribution to an exhibition 'Eight Painters'; one of the others showed ten) his note on it concluded that the people sunbathing 'were supposed to have plumped themselves down unceremoniously — but formally with respect to their surroundings'. Not all the figures in his future paintings are 'plumped down', though they are often seated or recumbent, but this sentence indicates his preoccupation with representing the casual subject in formal terms. But the representation in formal terms of figures casually posed is in itself, of course, no innovation; this is precisely what Seurat — to cite a conspicuous example — so consistently did.

Andrews is a highly complex painter. He belongs, unequivocally, to the 'modern' movement. In a conversation he referred to some of those by whom he was affected: 'Auerbach, Bacon, Tim Behrens, Harry Cohen, Uglow, Freud . . . Kitaj.'[1]

[1] A Conversation with Victor Willing, *Art and Literature* no 2, 1964

Talking with me about Duchamp and Klee he said 'In the light of Duchamp I can do without Klee.'[1]

Yet in spite of his intimate 'modern' affiliations his subjects are in one important respect traditional: they are often groups of people — sometimes large groups — in landscape or interiors, sometimes a combination of both. One reason why the work of Andrews evokes such intense interest in those — not yet very numerous — who know it is the way in which he uses contemporary means to represent such conventional themes as people sunning themselves in a field, a family sitting in their garden, people in night resorts and the like.

It is clear that he could not represent traditional subjects in a traditional manner without inviting the acute boredom of the spectator. The fact that traditional realism, which reached such inspiring heights in the seventeenth, eighteenth and nineteenth centuries, now appears to have exhausted its potentialities, and that the photograph would in any case have deprived it of the magic it earlier exercised, compels those few painters who still represent complex traditional subjects to evolve entirely new approaches. This, cautiously and at times haltingly, is what Andrews has done, and what he had in mind when in *Notes & Preoccupations* he wrote, by themselves, the two words 'Mysterious conventionality'[2]

More original, though at first sight more conventional — having, for instance, no exaggerated feature such as the elongated leg of the central figure in the early 'Four People Sunbathing' — is the very large 'Family in the Garden' (the Gulbenkian Foundation) of his own family made during the summers of 1961 and 1962. As his family were not easily persuaded to sit for the requisite length of time, he worked closely from studies made while the painting was in progress, which he transferred to the canvas, even using photographs as additional guides. This painting of his family having tea in their garden — it would be difficult to name a more conventionally English subject — nevertheless has overtones of strangeness, persistent if not obvious. But in the year of its completion he painted another which represented a deviation from his belief that, difficult though it is to distinguish them, ends

[1] *X*, a literary and art quarterly of 1959-62, vol. 2, p. 141.
[2] Volume One, 1960-61, p. 141.

are more important than means, namely 'The Colony Room' (in which Francis Bacon and Lucian Freud figure in a group of friends in this celebrated night resort); Andrews has told us quite simply that 'technique had become an aesthetic and this wasn't appropriate to what I wanted to do'. This is more evident in the first of his major works, 'The Deer Park', inspired by Norman Mailer's novel of that name.

Gradually the procedure of making drawings, small studies and of drawing on the canvas came to be supplemented and even superseded by photographs, many clipped from newspapers and magazines of which he has a large number tacked onto the walls of his studio, of works of art, of heads and figures by Giacometti (for whom he has a particular admiration), of historical events (one, for instance, of a group of settlers taken during the Matabele Revolt), others of cities, London and New York by night, with hundreds of lighted windows, of balloons, and scores of other subjects.

The photographs taken for his 'Family in the Garden' were primarily substitutes for drawings, because of his difficulty in persuading his relations to sit, but in 'The Deer Park' it was otherwise. For this he did indeed make a few preliminary drawings but it was photographs that played the integral part in its composition. 'The Deer Park' was immediately followed by 'All Night Long' (PLATE 27), an even larger canvas — the first measures 84 by 96 inches, the second 72 by 144 inches — which is based entirely on photographs, some of which he acquired while working on 'The Deer Park' (one of them, suggesting the central group, played a crucial part).

I shall not forget my own first sight of it. Andrews was personally unknown to me. A considerable time had passed since I had seen any of his work, when Tilly Dower, a painter of talent, the daughter of our next-door neighbour in Oxfordshire and the subject of a portrait by Patrick George at the Tate, who had been a fellow-student of Andrews at the Slade, took me to his studio. At that time — it was 1964 — he was living at 3 Duncan Terrace, Islington. 'All Night Long', almost completed, would have dominated a much larger room. Its huge scale, panoramic character, brilliant colour, and its night-club themes compelled my prolonged attention and seemed an amusingly improbable production for the slight, apparently shy and unworldly young man who welcomed us in so friendly a fashion. The gentleness of his manner does, however, mask a strong will.

It is a painting that exemplifies 'mysterious conventionality'. A panoramic view of numerous figures in a waterside resort on a hot night: a distressed woman trying to support a drunken man, a couple making love, a group of naked intruding bathers going towards a swimming pool or sea inlet, several in bathing clothes lying on chaises longues, people talking and drinking, a man playing a saxophone among others. The setting, like that of 'The Deer Park', is part interior and part landscape. Every group or individual figure, he has told us, was based, directly or with modifications, rarely radical, on a photograph. Again as in 'The Deer Park', the spectator is introduced as though he were a familiar, who feels free to wander about in this exotic panorama. Anything approaching *la belle peinture* is systematically avoided — the brushwork at various points indeed looks deliberately casual, as though this huge painting were a preparatory study, merely, but the composition is highly professional and gives the whole an air of grandeur. It is marked by an astonishing variety: elements of orgy, forced cheerfulness, genuine enjoyment, indifference, boredom, acute loneliness and much else are to be discerned among the figures in their tawdry, pseudo-luxurious setting. Just as Rembrandt could ennoble the head of an ugly old man, so has Andrews given this scene of vulgar pleasure-seeking an aura of dream-like beauty.

Being at the time of this visit director of the Tate, I asked the artist whether I might bring it before our trustees with a view to its purchase. 'I wish you could,' he said, 'but the Felton Bequest have just bought it for Melbourne.' Another of his major paintings, a triptych in oils completed, after three years' intensive work, in 1968, is cryptically titled 'Good and Bad at Games' (**PLATE 28**).

In the conversation with Victor Willing already quoted from, Andrews said, 'I think a painting should be clear. It worries me when I look at other people's paintings if I haven't the slightest idea of what they're about.' However easy it may be to understand the meaning of a number of his earlier paintings — nothing could be more comprehensible than his block of 'Flats' (1959, oil) in his second exhibition — it would be difficult to think of a contemporary painting more difficult to have 'an idea of what it's about' than 'Good and Bad at Games', his series of the large oil paintings just mentioned, of which plate 28 is the central panel. It has nothing whatever to do with games and only peripherally with good and bad. It is set, to use his own words to me, 'in the sort of place parties might be given in'. 'Good' and 'Bad' refer not to athletic skill and very remotely to moral qualities, although it is relevant to recall his statement (in his *Notes* in *X*) that 'Every aesthetic adjustment reflects an ethical preference' (p. 137). It is a painting primarily symbolizing the ascendency of the positive qualities, intelligence, vitality, strength, creativity, over their opposites in terms of social behaviour — a complicated social game in which the success of those possessing some or all of the first qualities is shown by their growing larger as the series progresses, and those who do not diminishing. Alluding to the series in a letter to me (17 February 1973) he wrote:

> I was thinking about the variable effect a number of people (initially a group of ten) had on each other. The chosen conventional occasion was a party at which people noticeably behave in one way or another. — This might range from, or change gradually from, stage fright to indifference or boredom, or someone's composure or agitation might remain almost unchanged. At any rate I was trying for a definition of how these fluctuations of self-consciousness showed.

Both heads and figures reveal Andrews's ardent admiration for Giacometti, and several of them closely resemble certain of those in a photograph of a group of his sculpture on the studio wall. What differentiates 'Good and Bad at Games' from its predecessors is its dream-like, even at certain points nightmarish, quality. In my opinion it is, with 'All Night Long', his finest work.

In the later paintings his use of photographs is far more radical; in the earlier he used photographs as he might have used studies, but in 'Good and Bad at Games' photographs were silk-screened onto the canvas, then worked on, and modified, with oil paint.

Speaking with specific reference to 'Good and Bad at Games' but with much of his work in mind, he said to me: 'My vision is clear when I start, then it becomes obscured, then suddenly something happens to bring it into focus again — but I invariably think I will finish it more quickly than I do.'

Andrews's most recent painting, 'Lights III: the Black Balloon' **(PLATE 29)**, completed in 1973, the last of a series of three of the same subject, was carried out not with a brush and oil paint but with a spray-gun and acrylic (which he had never used before the balloon paintings). It is as suave and highly finished as its predecessors are the opposite: as someone wrote of him, 'his stylelessness is almost doctrinaire'.

'All my paintings have a psychological significance,' he said to me. 'My greatest satisfaction is to have defined something I really mean.'

The balloon paintings — suggested by photographs of balloons which he had clipped from newspapers and tacked to his studio wall — are for him highly symbolic, the balloon being an 'ego symbol', subject, like a person, to inflation, deflation — and accident; '*its* buoyancy or well-being' (to quote from the same letter) 'is affected, or noticably changed, by circumstances.' Discussing his identification of the balloon with a person he showed me the following quotation from Alan Watts: 'the prevalent sensation of oneself as a separate ego enclosed in a bag of skin', which he said precisely expressed the sensation which impelled him to paint his balloon pictures. But about the 'Balloons' I will say no more, as he is still at work on them.

Andrews reads widely and, as he paints, slowly but intensely: Conrad, Proust, detective stories by Ambler and Chandler for preference, but most of all Kierkegaard ('his ideas,' he said to me, 'fall over me like fructifying rain').

To say that an artist's work is an expression of his intimate self is a commonplace. Yet it is also true that the work of some artists is a more intimate, a more personal expression than that of others. Some professional portrait painters, for instance, away from their subjects, and travelling, hunting, fishing or just walking about, may not, for the time being, be deeply involved with their art. But virtually nothing experienced by Michael Andrews is not, directly or by oblique allusion, expressed in his painting. And not only visual experiences. In his *Notes and Preoccupations* he wrote: 'The most vivid visualization [is] sometimes prompted by something written or spoken' (p. 140). And: 'The painting episode is a real situation imagined' (p. 138); and: 'To feel I am placing the brush on the place, on the real thing' (p. 140). I am not an intimate of Michael Andrews's and to pretend to be able to discern all or even many of the experiences expressed in his work would be presumptuous, but I know no artist — in spite of the smallness of his production — who includes in his art so wide a range of deeply felt personal experience, whether of his environment, the companionship of others, of his thoughts, profound or casual, of his reading.

BRIDGET RILEY
born 1931

Since about 1910 the most pervasive idea among artists has been that subject, at least the subject drawn from the external world, should either be strictly subordinated to form or else excluded altogether. In Britain in the 'twenties and 'thirties, for instance, subject for many painters was no more than the occasion for the creation of 'significant form'. Apples, sanctified by their frequent depiction by Cézanne, were favoured, but most other subjects would have served as well. Even before the period of the widespread subordination of subject to the treatment of it, there briefly emerged an abstract movement. In the second number of *Blast* Wyndham Lewis wrote, 'There should be a bill passed in Parliament at once FORBIDDING ANY IMAGE OR RECOGNIZABLE SHAPE TO BE STUCK UP IN ANY PUBLIC PLACE.' Kandinsky exhibited in London in 1911, 1912 and 1913. Vorticism, the term coined by Ezra Pound for the London practitioners of abstraction or near-abstraction (for several of them occasionally allowed machinery as a subject), established in 1913, was virtually brought to an end two years later by the war. Among the small group of young painters associated with the movement were Gaudier-Brzeska, Bomberg, Wadsworth, Roberts, as well as Lewis himself. The outstanding originality and energy of their vorticist works has been, until recently, unjustly neglected and is even now not recognized at its true worth.

A few of those associated with the movement, such as Lawrence Atkinson and Cuthbert Hamilton, continued until around 1920 to pursue its ideas. By then the movement was extinct, and it was not until the middle 'thirties, with Ben Nicholson, Barbara Hepworth and a small group of their friends, that abstraction re-emerged, and although its influence was temporarily circumscribed by the impending war, it reasserted itself with the coming of peace and before long became the most powerful and pervasive force in

British painting and sculpture, as it had been in that of the continent for several decades.

Abstract art exercises its powerful hold, partly because it is in close accord with the high degree of specialization, with the division of labour, by which industrial societies function. The artist accordingly attempts to do what he believes cannot be better done by the camera or any other means, namely the creation of autonomous form and colour. Nothing better illustrates the pervasiveness of abstraction today than the fact that the president of the institution which, far more militantly than any other, has upheld inherited conventional values and opposed innovation, often innovation of a very discreet character, namely the Royal Academy, should at the time when I write these lines be an abstract painter.

The pressure upon artists to practise abstraction is therefore often difficult to withstand. Why, a critical reader may ask, should the withstanding of it be referred to at all? The answer is that only a small minority of abstract artists are fitted by temperament to pursue the kind of art they practise. Most born in Victorian times would doubtless have painted puppies in baskets and the like. To practise abstraction by spraying a board with a uniform colour, for instance, or by ordering a metal cube from a foundry over the telephone, is one of the most facile pursuits an artist can engage in – painting puppies in baskets well is far more exacting. The serious practice of abstraction, however, can be infinitely exacting. A portrait or a landscape painter, when feeling dull, may easily find stimulus in the subject before him or memories of it in the contemplation of preliminary studies, but an abstract artist has no comparable resources: he must rely wholly on his imagination. It is a practice so exacting that the innately abstract artist, the artist whose essential self is expressed in the language of abstraction, is a very rare person indeed. Of course such an artist may portray subjects from the world of appearances, as Ben Nicholson for instance does, but the results, however admirable, are peripheral to his major preoccupation.

One of these rare persons is Bridget Riley. Although no work could be more radically exclusive of the world of appearances than that of Victor Pasmore since the late 'forties, after his brilliant maturity with his romantic paintings of riverside landscapes and figures, he revolutionized his art only when convinced that he had been working in a tradition in which everything significant that could be said had been said already. With Riley it was otherwise. Although her early drawings and paintings give indications of her talent, she could not express her essential self until she discovered that abstraction was her language – her only language. The process of discovery was long and at times painful; how long and painful would surprise anyone who met for the first time, after the completion of the process, the extremely assured and successful Riley of the last decade.

Bridget Louise Riley was born on 25 April 1931 in South London, the elder of the two daughters of John Fisher Riley, a commercial printer, and his wife Bessie Louise, born Gladstone, whose father, a distant relative of the prime minister, worked with Edison on the discovery of the electric light bulb. His brother was a founder-member of the Fabian Society. Bridget's mother had an aunt, Ruth, who had been a governess at the Russian Imperial Court and, incidentally, served as a model for the heroine of James Hilton's *Goodbye Mr Chips*. Bridget Riley spent part of her childhood in Lincolnshire but the war years near Padstow in Cornwall with her mother, sister and an aunt, Bertha Joyce, who had studied art at Goldsmiths' College, and who first aroused her interest in the arts. In the meanwhile her father, who served in the Royal Artillery, was taken prisoner in the battle of Singapore and forced to work on 'the railway of death'.

Riley spent from 1944 until 1946 at St Stephen's Convent at Taplow, and then she entered Cheltenham Ladies' College, where her growing interest in the arts was fostered by the art master Colin Hayes, the former Euston Road painter, who made her aware of the history of his subject and encouraged her to draw from life at the local art school. In 1949 a copy of Van Eyck's 'The Man in a Red Turban' in the National Gallery, made from a reproduction, gained her admission to Goldsmiths' College, where she remained for four years, concentrating exclusively on drawing, encouraged by Sam Rabin, who held life-classes both in the day and in the evening. She owed much to Rabin, for his perceptive teaching of drawing and for directing her interest to the drawings of Ingres. Their precise, linear, almost impersonal quality may well have evoked her first faint recognition of a quality that she herself wished to characterize as her own art. But the attainment of anything that might be truly described as 'her own art' was still a very long way off. The years at Goldsmiths', spent exclusively in drawing, were put to excellent use, but eventually, for two reasons, she wished to learn to paint, and in spite of the intelligence and sympathy of Rabin she was oppressed by a sense of remoteness from the centre of things, of ignorance of what the liveliest members of her own generation were doing and thinking. In 1952 she accordingly transferred to the Royal College of Art, remaining there for three years. Although she learnt there the elements of painting and met several painters, including Frank Auerbach, Peter Blake and Richard Smith (all shortly to win high reputations), she made no constructive friendships such as that with Rabin at Goldsmiths', and left feeling directionless and frustrated. Partly on account of her state of mind and partly through devoting much time to nursing her father, in Lincolnshire and Cornwall, after a serious car accident, she suffered a nervous breakdown and for more than two years she scarcely drew or painted. When she returned to London in 1956 she was an out- and in-patient at Middlesex Hospital, where she was allowed to sell glass at an antique shop. In 1957-8 she taught art at the Convent of the Sacred Heart in Harrow and in 1958-9 she was employed by the J. Walter Thompson advertising agency, where she was engaged in photo-realist illustration of a kind entirely unrelated to her interests as a painter.

Her obsession with her art, however little she was able to paint or draw, was undiminished; indeed it was further stimulated by the exhibition 'Modern Art in the United States: a Selection from the Collections of the Museum of Modern Art, New York' held at the Tate Gallery at the beginning of 1956, and by the ideas of Victor Pasmore and Harry Thubron, exemplified in 'The Developing Process', an exhibition held at the Institute of Contemporary Art two years later. Slowly she began to renew her contacts with the art world and in 1959 she resigned from her post at J. Walter Thompson and attended Thubron's Summer School in Norfolk. Here she formed a close and constructive friendship with Thubron's principal assistant Maurice de Sausmarez, a painter, historian and educationalist – a friendship that lasted until his death eleven years later, shortly after finishing his informed and perceptive monograph on her work.[1] In 1959 she painted in France and Spain and initiated the Basic Art Course at the Loughborough College of Art.

By 1960 Riley had begun to find her way. In the summer she visited, with de Sausmarez, many galleries and churches in Italy, and painted, studying not only masters such as Piero della Francesca but the futurists, in particular Boccioni and Balla. She was deeply impressed by the black and white architecture in Pisa. The futurists – of whose work they saw the comprehensive exhibition at the Venice Biennale – helped her to clarify the preoccupation with movement – however differently interpreted – of the work of her maturity and the Pisan architecture helped to give her the sense, for a time, of the sufficiency of black and white.

For the impact of the futurists she was already well prepared. Earlier that year she had collaborated with de Sausmarez in the preparation of three lectures he gave at the Royal College of Art to mark the fiftieth anniversary of the publication of the Futurist Manifesto. About the same time she made a full-size copy of 'Le pont de Courbevoie' by Seurat at the Courtauld Institute Gallery, whose uncompromising logic affected her deeply. A big reproduction of his 'Grande Jatte' hung in her flat. The most substantial picture she made after their Italian journey was 'Pink Landscape', painted, de Sausmarez has told us, 'from the experience of a stretch of landscape in the hills south of Siena, drenched in a blinding shimmering heat-haze that ended in one of the fiercest storms of that summer', and he quotes David Thompson as saying that it 'is already concerned with a kind of optical situation which constantly recurs in her later work – that of a dominant formal pattern under pressure of disintegration'.

'I talked endlessly with Maurice de Sausmarez,' she said to me, 'and gradually the gap between what I was doing and what I hoped to do narrowed, and eventually there was a breakthrough.'

Early in 1961, in the year following that of so much intensive thought and wide-ranging study, Riley made a painting which anticipates that of her maturity — 'Kiss' (tempera) — in which one massive black rectangle with a curving base descends upon and almost touches an almost equally massive black rectangle. It is a not unimpressive work, but did it not mark the beginning of her style it would be rather less highly regarded than it is, for it

[1] *Bridget Riley*, 1970.

affords only the faintest indication of the qualities that identify the best of the works that followed – and followed quickly. The first unmistakably her own, painted later in the same year, was 'Movement in Squares' **(PLATE 30)** (1961, tempera on board, Arts Council), which clearly expresses one of the principal subjects of her art, namely the interaction of opposing elements: stability and movement, discord and harmony, constancy and change, passivity and energy, light and darkness, advance and recession, ease and tension, repose and disturbance. 'Movement in Squares' shows the gradual compression of the central squares into rectangles by those to the left and right, and the resulting contrast between the solid, regular and the compressed squares. The visual experience thus generated is one of dynamic contrasts. 'Fission' (1962-3, tempera, Museum of Modern Art, New York) is identical in theme but the compressing units are black circles and the compressed black ovals.

One of the finest of her works in black and white is 'Fall' **(PLATE 31)** (1963, emulsion, Tate Gallery) included in her second exhibition at Gallery One in 1963, to which Anton Ehrenzweig thus described his response:

> We are faced with an inexorable yet almost imperceptible variation of linear elements and units. So smooth is the change that it does not allow the eye to organize the series of units into stable, larger entities on which it might linger and rest. There is a constant tug-of-war between shifting and crumbling patterns, but at a certain point this relentless attack on our lazy viewing habits peels our eyes into a new and crystal clear sensibility.[1]

The first exhibited works were all in black and white, though she made studio experiments with colour. Then in 1965 a variety of greys were cautiously introduced and finally pure colour, as in 'Late Morning' (1968, emulsion, Tate Gallery). Movement, which figures constantly in her art, is entirely different from that of the futurists whom she so diligently studied, for in their work it is a series of successive images; in hers it is a single one.

One of the original qualities in Riley's work is, in fact, a consequence of her subjects. Many artists, whose finished work is abstract, take as their subjects suggestions from nature which they reduce to purely formal terms; others, notably a number of the abstract expressionists, apply their medium arbitrarily and take

[1] Introduction to the catalogue.

advantage of what happens when the paint is dripped or splashed on to the surface. Riley's subjects, opposing or contrasting elements of many kinds, although not unique, are rare; for her the subject is not a material object itself but its animating force or its contrasting stability: she is an abstract artist, therefore, on a deeper level than many others. But strangely enough her art, which has so decisive a look – an article on it by Robert Melville was headed 'An Art Without Accidents' – is far more intuitive and experimental than is apparent in the finished work. She once said:

> I felt that this thing, the medium, was so strong and rich, that I was just the agent who caught these various inflections . . . when these elements are not asked to do something which is against their nature – not asked to serve concepts or to represent — then I think that they are allowed to 'play freely' – to show their vitality. But there are hazards. For instance, of merely recording automatically in a random kind of way. These energies are in a proper sense 'wild'. One can easily be overwhelmed, carried away. This results in images which are virtually inaccessible, beyond perception in fact. And yet this is the core of the medium and it is in this area that fruitful dialogue takes place. It is not only the one-way relationship of taming the wild, but can also be the reverse. I am supported by the medium but at the risk of being overwhelmed by it. The medium both carries you and threatens to carry you away.[1]

These words could have been spoken by Francis Bacon, an artist as different from Riley as could well be imagined in every other way. Although both regard their medium as an active partner, their 'dialogue' with it is quite different: Bacon makes no drawings or preliminary studies and relies on taking advantage of fortunate 'accidents' in the behaviour of the paint; Riley makes many and detailed studies, and when the final version is made – usually not even by herself but by assistants – the struggle with the paint is resolved so completely that, although she often alludes to it, no trace of it remains on the canvas.

Critics have remarked on the affinity of Riley's work with that of Victor Vasarely. To see how clear this affinity is one need only observe the close resemblance between her 'Blaze I' (1962, emulsion) and his 'Mach-C', a tempera made some eight years earlier. But Bryan Robertson in his catalogue for Riley's retrospective exhibition at the Hayward Gallery, 1971, has pointed out with

[1] Conversation with Robert Kadielka Catalogue, Arts Council Touring Exhibition, 1973.

accuracy a crucial difference between the two artists.

> Vasarely confines his use of space to the picture plane: whatever obtrudes from that plane or recedes into it is implied by *perspective within that picture plane* . . . Riley's true space is not confined to the picture plane: it is the *distance between the spectator and the canvas.*

Both artists, of course, practise what is generally known as op or optical art, that is to say an art whose primary and sometimes sole object is the retinal response of the viewer. In this, as in the two earlier volumes, I have, so far as is reasonable, avoided collective terms, groups, movements and the like, as tending to obscure the artists' individual characters. But it is relevant to observe that the object of optical art – though the term was not used until the middle 'sixties – was to use optical laws not, as was the case in earlier times, to serve some aesthetic purpose, enhancing brilliance of colour, for instance, or likeness to the subject, but as visual stimuli. Op painters have not only derived much from predecessors, Seurat notable among them, but from scientists' studies of the functioning of visual perception. Optical effects characterize much, perhaps most, of the work of Riley, but she does not introduce them – like some other op artists – with aggressive or startling intention but as enhancing the exhilaration – or the electric shock, to use an expression of her own – that it is her purpose that the viewer should experience through her resolution of tension between active and static and other conflicting forces already referred to. These forces as well as equivalents of various states of mind (as indicated by such titles as 'Remember', 'Hesitate', 'Pause', 'Search', 'Shiver' or 'Deny'), although expressed by forms of such extraordinary precision that at a first glance they might seem to be products of a computer, are in fact extremely subjective. In his introduction Bryan Robertson wrote that 'although Riley is patchily aware of the history of colour theory from Newton to Chevreul, and Seurat's contribution to colour analysis, her grasp of theory, of any sort, is elementary'. She herself has stated:

> I have never studied 'optics' and my use of mathematics is rudimentary, confined to such things as equalising, halving, quartering and simple progressions. My work has developed on the basis of empirical analyses, and I have always believed that perception is the medium through which states of being are directly experienced . . . The basis of my paintings is this: that in

each of them a particular situation is stated. Certain elements within that situation remain constant. Others precipitate the destruction of themselves by themselves. Recurrently, as a result of the cyclic movement of repose, disturbance and repose, the original situation is restated.[1]

The development of her work and of her maturity has been impressively logical. In the earliest she used straight lines and black and white. A little later she introduced sharp angles, then narrow, curved lines, having the effect of rhythmic waves of water, in some of which, in recent years, she has used colour. Of the relation of form and colour in her work she said:

> In my recent work I have been using stripes of colour, either parallel or twisting round each other. Form and colour seem to be fundamentally incompatible . . . in my earlier work, when I was developing complex forms, the energies of the medium could only be fully released by simplifying colour to a black and white constant (with occasional grey sequences). Conversely colour energies need a virtually neutral vehicle if they are to develop uninhibited. Their repeated stripe seems to meet these conditions.[2]

The final versions of this art of the expression of deeply felt conflicts between opposing forces and their resolution and of varied states of mind are carried out by studio-assistants. The artist herself makes many preparatory studies on plain or graph paper in pencil and gouache, with elaborate notations, detailed instructions with regard to scale – sometimes to one-sixteenth of an inch – coloured pieces of cardboard to be placed one beside the other to try out harmonies and contrasts. Finally skilled assistants are called in (as they are by Vasarely) who carry out, under Riley's critical eye, the final versions. When asked why she did not make the final versions herself, she said, 'I need assistants for speed's sake: before one painting is done I have ideas for others (in any case I work on several at once). Without help I'd be frustratingly held up.'

The result is Riley's immaculate and logical 'art without accidents' – serene yet revealing visual energy emanating from basic forms. In spite of its deceptive simplicity – deceptive because, for instance, bands of colour and other forms that at first glance seem uniform often in fact differ minutely from one another – Riley's

---

[1] *Art News*, October 1965.
[2] In conversation with Robert Kadielka. Catalogue Arts Council Touring Exhibition 1973.

art has made an impression on a steadily growing public ever since she evolved her own lucid and concentrated formal language, and not only in her own country. One of her paintings was reproduced on the cover of the catalogue of 'The Responsive Eye' exhibition of op art at the Museum of Modern Art, New York, in 1964, and her first one-man exhibition in the U.S.A., at the Richard Feigen Gallery, was sold out before it opened. Her work has been included in important exhibitions in several other countries, in Paris, at the Venice Biennale, where she won a prize, and in Germany, Switzerland and Japan, as well, of course, as in Britain. Few painters of her generation have attracted more perceptive criticism, among others by David Thompson (who also made, in 1969, a film of her work), Anton Ehrenzweig, Bryan Robertson, in the retrospective exhibition which he selected at the Hayward Gallery in 1971, and the tribute, already referred to, by her friend and mentor Maurice de Sausmarez. Few of her British contemporaries, especially those whose work requires experienced eyes to understand, have at the age of forty won such international acclaim – acclaim which I believe is amply merited.

DAVID HOCKNEY
born 1937

In one respect it is a curious experience for someone of my generation to write about Hockney, because he has enjoyed an immediate, international success that began when he was still a student – something achieved by no serious painter within my earlier personal experience.

All through my own childhood and boyhood, indeed throughout the greater part of my life, 'instant success' was regarded as synonymous with the superficial. Every serious artist I had known had endured a long and often bitter struggle to achieve recognition – if he had achieved it at all. The story has often been told how fellow students at the Slade so greatly admired the drawings of Augustus John that they used to collect and paste together even those he had torn up and thrown away; but he, nevertheless, had a struggle before him. Henry Moore was approaching his middle forties and had had no officially sponsored exhibition when we bought his first watercolours for the Tate for £5 or £6 each. From his first exhibition Francis Bacon sold nothing at all and was so discouraged – as was related earlier in these pages – that for a time he entirely ceased to paint.

There are indeed serious living painters whose work commands considerably higher prices than Hockney's, but no British artist except Henry Moore is more persistently sought after for interviews, articles and the like, and few are more widely admired. When I first visited his luxurious studio flat in Powis Terrace, Notting Hill, he had recently changed his 'ex-directory' telephone number, and yet it rang about every fifteen minutes. In order that we might talk without interruption, a friend answered the calls on his behalf. I mention these circumstances to show how rare it is that a painter as young as Hockney should have become so notable a figure by the age of thirty-five; also by way of confessing that a lifelong experience of the struggles, frustrations, failures, self-doubts of all other serious artists had made me suspicious of 'instant success'.

I first saw, quite by chance, his 'Rake's Progress' series in 1963 at the Alecto Gallery; they had been mostly made while he was still a student at the Royal College of Art. They impressed me as showing talent of a quite exceptional order. In the same year, impressed though not fully convinced by a painting made the previous year, 'The First Marriage', I persuaded the Friends of the Tate to buy it, through whom it passed into the Gallery's possession. The circumstances of my first encounters with the art of Hockney are mentioned here, not to show my own early recognition of its qualities, but the reverse: how unjustifiably mistrustful 'instant success' can make people of my generation. Although, when I happened to see his work, I scrutinized it with care, it was not until his Whitechapel retrospective held in 1970 that I recognized him at what I now believe to be something of his true worth. Nor was it until later that I learned from him how intensely he suffers, and always has, from self-doubt and worry about his work, though he has become resigned to it as the inevitable consequence of the serious practice of any art.

David Hockney was born on 9 July 1937 at St Luke's Hospital, Bradford, Yorkshire, the youngest but one of a family of three brothers and a sister, the children of Kenneth Hockney and his wife Laura, born Thompson. David attended Wellington Road Primary School and, from 1948 until 1953, Bradford Grammar School. Already determined to be an artist, he went straight from there to the Bradford College of Art where he remained for four years, working two days a week from the life and two on figure composition, concentrating on academic drawing. The degree of interest in contemporary art at the College was shown by the fact that Sickert was regarded as its culmination and Braque, Hockney recalls, 'as a freak'. A fellow student at Bradford, Norman Stevens – woodcarver, close friend and frequent model – told me

> David was an incredible worker. When he was not at the College he'd walk about the little streets with a pram to carry his paints, like Stanley Spencer, whom he admired, and made fine little street scenes. I remember David's laughing when another student said he wanted to learn to draw and that the masters were no good, and he replied 'Then draw hard for three years' and the student said *'I haven't time'.*

After leaving the College, being a conscientious objector, instead of doing National Service he worked as a ward orderly at St Luke's Hospital, Bradford, and St Helen's at Hastings. (He is also an impassioned vegetarian.) Two years later his application to enter the Royal College of Art was successful. There he studied from 1959 until 1962, benefiting from the teaching and from the freedom given him to spend much time in drawing. At the College, R.B. Kitaj, his dynamic American fellow-student, widely extended his hitherto extremely limited knowledge of contemporary painting, helped him towards the recognition of the nature of his own talent and encouraged him to portray whatever most deeply stirred his interest. To Kitaj his debt was considerable indeed. Another fellow-student told me how intensively Hockney worked there also, especially at drawing. To what purpose is evident in 'A Rake's Progress'. As happens often in the lives of artists, talent is revealed or stimulated by external circumstance. In Hockney's case the circumstance was commonplace: total lack of money. He was living in a shed in Kemsford Gardens, Earls Court; the rent was 7s. 6d. a week and to keep on the electric fire cost about that sum. The shed had no water supply, so he used to wash at the College. Professor Carel Weight once found him having a bath in a sink. More distressing was his inability to afford to buy paints. In the Print Department materials were free, so he decided to etch. Julian Trevelyan, the engraving tutor, showed him how to do it (he had not learnt etching in Bradford) with the result that he won the Guinness Award for Etching in 1961 with two prints 'Myself and My Heroes' (Walt Whitman and Gandhi) and 'Three Kings and a Queen' – to the annoyance of several students long dedicated to its practice.

The etchings that, more than any of his student work, made his reputation were 'A Rake's Progress/London/New York'. When they were shown in 1963 at the Alecto Gallery, Hockney wrote:

These etchings were begun in London in September 1961 after a visit to the United States. My intention was to make eight plates, keeping Hogarth's original titles but moving the setting to New York. The Royal College, on seeing me start work, were anxious to extend the series with the idea of incorporating the plates in a book of reproductions to be published by the Lion and Unicorn Press; accordingly I set out to make twenty-four plates, but later reduced the total to sixteen, retaining the numbering from one to eight and most of the titles in the original state. Altogether I made about thirty-five plates of which nineteen were abandoned, so leaving these sixteen in the published set. Numbers 7 and 7A were etched at the Pratt Graphic Institute in New York in May of this year, the others at the Royal College of Art from 1961-63. But I always remained reluctant to make more than the eight originally conceived.

In 1961 he had raised £105 to enable him to visit New York, and it was the squalor he discovered there – comparable to the squalor of Hogarth's London – that inspired the series.

Rarely, aside from the gambling table or the book-maker's, can the expenditure of £105 have paid off so handsomely. 'A Rake's Progress' was published by Editions Alecto, and atl fifty sets were sold within a year, making the penniless Bradford student £5,000.

Such sudden wealth would have meant much to any poor student, for most, perhaps, security to pursue a vocation. To Hockney it meant this and something besides. The distinction has been drawn earlier in these pages between artists whose vision is raised to its utmost intensity by the familiar and those who respond in the same way to the unfamiliar. It is to the second category that Hockney belongs: he is exhilarated by the unfamiliar, the unexpected. 'This sum,' he told me, 'gave me freedom to live for two years without worrying about teaching or selling my work. So I was able to go to California.' He enjoys his luxurious London studio flat, but has only to think about the attractions of some city, or some region, however remote, and off he flies there. (Just as, although he has close friends, he is generally accessible to anyone likely to offer information or good companionship.) This open-minded attitude towards places and people is clearly reflected in his art.

'A Rake's Progress' was not the proverbial 'flash in the pan'; other prints, paintings and drawings, made while still a student or shortly afterwards, brought continuing success. He not only won further official recognition in the form of the Royal College of Art Gold Medal, the Guinness Award, the First Prize at The Graven Image Exhibition and the Junior Section Prize at the John Moores Exhibition, Liverpool, but the ardent admiration of a number of his contemporaries. The playwright Christopher Taylor bought a painting from The Young Contemporaries Exhibition in 1961 and not long afterwards a dozen others besides a number of

DAVID HOCKNEY. Plate 32 (above): *The Second Marriage* (1963), oil on
canvas, 77¾ × 90 in. Plate 33 (below): *Henry Geldzahler and Christopher Scott*
(1968-9), acrylic on canvas, 84 × 120 in.

Plate 34: DAVID HOCKNEY: *Still life with TV* (1968-9), acrylic on canvas, 48 × 60 in.

drawings and etchings. These, he complains, are constantly away
on exhibition. 'It's just like having a beautiful debutante daughter;
she's almost never at home.' A young woman who in 1965 went
to work at the Kasmin Gallery, where he had his first exhibition
in 1963, said in an interview, 'Every time some Hockneys came in
I fell in love with one and just bought it.' She was spurred to make
her first purchase when a client asked to buy a drawing, 'Pacific
Mutual Trust', which she had admired for weeks. She said, 'I'm
afraid you can't. It's reserved.' 'Who by?' Mr Kasmin asked.
'Me,' she said. What, then, was the character of the work that
evoked this widespread enthusiasm?

An artist's virtues (like those of others) are often complemented
by weaknesses. Hockney, naturally talented, had, by hard work,
made himself an accomplished draughtsman. This, accompanied
by a rapidly increasing knowledge of contemporary art, and a
nature highly responsive to stimuli of many kinds, often led in his
early years to his works being superficial and derivative –
Dubuffet, graffiti and pop being favoured exemplars – yet carried
out with a wit and elegance that made it immediately attractive;
also with an engaging air of simplicity, implying, 'Come on; you
could do it just as well.' Examples of the influences referred to: 'A
Grand Procession of Dignitaries in the Semi-Egyptian Style'
(1961, oil) of Dubuffet; 'We Two Boys Clinging Together' (1961,
oil, Arts Council) of graffiti; 'Tea Painting in an Illusionistic Style'
(1962, oil) of pop. Certain of his works are marked not so much
by an air of simplicity as by its caricature; to take two examples
from among his lithographs: 'Picture of a Landscape in an
elaborate Gold Frame' or 'Picture of a Simple Framed Traditional
Nude Drawing' (both 1965). Hockney is of course exactly aware
of what they are, yet he allowed them, and others of a like kind,
to be included in his retrospective exhibition at the Whitechapel
Gallery in 1970. This exhibition – admirably arranged – was,
Hockney believes, invaluable to him. The opportunity of being
able to contemplate, for the first time, so substantial a proportion
of his work gave him a clearer understanding of both his shortcomings and potentialities: of the need to concentrate more
intensively on his subjects in their entirety, but also a sense of
gathering momentum and of multiplying images. 'I learnt a great
deal,' he said, 'from studying that exhibition.'

In sharp contrast to such a painter as, say, Rothko, who over a period of years painted variations, and often slight ones, of a single theme, Hockney is responsive to a very wide variety of approaches to many themes; it is therefore hardly surprising that as a student and for some years afterwards his attention should have been too easily attracted by trivia. This partly accounts for his early success: the interesting subject, fashionable or bizarre. What could be more bizarre than 'Teeth Cleaning II' (1962, oil) in which two embryos, depicted with exceptional skill, are locked in erotic embrace? A recipe for success.

But whatever the shortcomings apparent in some of his earliest work, no artist discussed in these pages had to his credit a volume of work as a student so various and accomplished as Hockney. A substantial part of his Whitechapel exhibition was composed of student work. It appears, however, that his qualities were not invariably appreciated. In one of his many interviews he said, 'I was threatened with not gettino a diploma because they said I hadn't done enough life painting. So I copied that muscle man out of a magazine.'[1]

He was in fact bored by the models at the College and used to bring in one of his own, Mo McDermott, who also figures in later paintings, as in 'Domestic Scene, Notting Hill' (1963, oil).

After he left the College, a change, at first barely perceptible but gradually accelerating, came to characterize his work. At the College he responded to innumerable influences, ideas, things seen, situations that took his fancy, personal situations in which he found himself. What he painted, drew and etched, although he early evolved an individual style, was almost infinitely various and often extremely complex. The change was in the direction of greater clarity of both subject and design.

Two paintings in particular which, however tentatively, offer intimations of this change are 'The First Marriage' already referred to, and 'The Second Marriage' **(PLATE 31)** (1963, oil, National Gallery of Victoria, Melbourne). Although he does not discount the play of intuition or even chance in the process of carrying out his ideas, he is perfectly clear about his ideas themselves. In his student days, in order to make his work entirely comprehensible, he used sometimes even to introduce lettering into

[1] *Town*, September 1962.

the composition. For instance, across 'The Cha Cha that was Danced in the Early Hours of 24th March' (1961, oil) the words 'cha cha cha cha' are written in bold characters. He is able to explain – if explanation is necessary – not only the subject of any of his pictures but its genesis and evolution.

The 'Marriage' paintings he has explained in this way.

In August 1962, I visited Berlin with an American friend. Whilst in a museum I wandered off and lost my friend . . . I went to look for him . . . I eventually caught sight of him . . . in profile. To one side of him, also in profile, was a sculpture in wood of a seated woman of a heavily stylized kind (Egyptian, I believe). For a moment they seemed held together – like a couple posing. At first I was amused at the sight of them together; but later I made some drawings incorporating both my friend and the sculpture. When I returned to London I decided to use the drawings to make a painting. The first painting I did from the drawings was very much like the statements I had made in Berlin. I did not alter the position of the figures . . . I had made no notes on the setting there, so I placed them in the painting in a rather ambiguous setting. It looks as though they are standing on a desert island with white sand and a palm tree. But the white at the bottom is only a base for them to stand on and the rest of their setting is intended to be slightly out of focus, apart from the ecclesiastical shape in the bottom left-hand corner (an association with marriage). I called it 'The Marriage' because I regarded it as a sort of marriage of styles. The heavily stylized female figure with the not so stylized 'bridegroom'. On completing this picture I decided to do another version of the same theme . . . Taking the idea of marriage literally I decided to put them in a definite setting – a domestic interior.

The head of the woman in the second painting was made from a photograph of a carved head of an Egyptian princess, which he had seen in a book. Of 'The Second Marriage' he said, 'The theme is the same but the couple are seen in a more complicated setting involving illusionistic and perspective effects'.[1]

Asked in another interview about the most significant changes in his work, Hockney answered in terms which I can imagine no other artist using but which throw light not only on his work but his mode of thought.

Well, actually, I think the most significant change over the past three years – say since 1967 or 1966 – is that it's really got more and more naturalistic or more conventional. You saw that portrait of Henry Geldzahler? It was quite a conventional picture of two figures in a room and the space in it was quite conventional. I wanted the paintings to be clearer, more specific really, as opposed to the painting in the Tate, 'The Marriage', which is not a specific

[1] Catalogue of the Whitechapel Exhibition.

painting. Its subject is vague and there are allusions to all kinds of things. I really don't want that kind of vagueness any more.[1]

The process of which Hockney was speaking began in fact some time earlier than he suggested. It is conspicuous in his treatment of 'The Second Marriage' as distinct from 'The First Marriage', as comparison will instantly show. Indeed in the earlier interview quoted, speaking of his aim of 'taking the idea of marriage literally', he said, 'I decided to put them in a definite setting . . . involving illusionistic and perspective effects'. In the 'First' the pine tree and the gothic window, in the 'Second' the bedroom and the bottle of champagne.

In spite of Hockney's avid responsiveness, tempting him constantly to excessive diversification of interest, the general development of his work has been towards – to repeat his own words – the 'more naturalistic or the more conventional'. He is unjust to himself: the latter word is, I suspect, a synonym for 'realistic'. There is nothing to which he is more responsive than travel. Berlin he first visited in 1962; Egypt the following year, to make illustrations for the *Sunday Times*, and on various occasions France, Italy, Germany, Holland, Ireland, Japan, Mexico and parts of Africa. The country which has most affected his art, however, has been the United States, California in particular.

I had a hunch [he said to me] that California was a place I'd really like and in 1964 I went to Los Angeles – where I did not know a soul – and decided to work in that part of the world. When I flew over San Bernardino and looked down and saw the swimming pools of the houses, I was more thrilled than I've ever been arriving at any other city. I've spent months in California in 1964, '65, '66 and '68. It was in California that I made my first mature paintings. Almost every time I went there it was to a different place. In California I began to try to paint a place as it really looks. I was not only inspired by Californian subjects, the sense of space, the clear light, but I found it a great help living for so long away from England. It gave me a sense of detachment that I'd not had before, a greater interest in the art of other countries and a more direct understanding of where artists' ideas come from, instead of through the watered-down version that one gets staying only in one country.

In California I changed my method of painting, using acrylic instead of oil. Because oil takes time to dry I had to work on several paintings at the same time, but using acrylic, because it dries almost as soon as you've applied it, I could concentrate on one painting, which I prefer. As acrylic doesn't mix easily like oil I sometimes keep the surface wet by spraying it with water but

[1] Interview with J.C. BATTYE, *Arts and Artists*, April 1973.

more often by glazing with successive washes in the traditional way. [When I saw him early in 1973 he was just about to leave for California intending, however, to resume painting in oil.] But I continued to paint, as I always had before, from drawings done from life – I draw a lot from life – from memory or from photographs I take myself – I almost always carry a small camera. [He has many volumes of his photographs, luxuriously bound, in his studio-flat in Notting Hill.] Sometimes I follow my drawings very closely, squaring them up on the canvas, at others to stir my memory. It takes me two weeks or about 278 hours to finish a big painting – occasionally as long as a month. Films play a part in my painting – I think the great tradition of figurative painting has moved into films.

One of the sharpest distinctions between good painters and the rest is that the former make progress, and it is evident that Hockney's later paintings are his best. I am thinking, for instance, of figures in rooms, such as 'Christopher Isherwood and Don Bachardy' (1968, acrylic), or 'Henry Geldzahler and Christopher Scott' **(PLATE 32)** (1968-9, same medium). In both these double portraits he achieves a combination of utter serenity with potentiality for movement. I find myself watching them intently and waiting expectantly for whatever it is that is just about to happen. Modern furniture and men's formal clothes pose particular difficulties for a painter. The rows of men in 'business suits' is a feature that gives an exhibition of portraits its repulsive look. Bachardy wears a white pullover but — though Geldzahler has taken off his coat — his formal waistcoat, trousers, collar, tie, and the raincoat of Scott, appear inevitable constituent parts of still and harmonious compositions, and the ample but ordinary settee in the middle of which the museum official sits forms a noble base for this epitome of expectant stillness.

Hockney shows his ability to achieve something of these qualities even in such a modest work as 'Still Life with TV' **(PLATE 33)** (1968-9, acrylic on canvas), in which the TV serenely waits to be turned on, the pencils to be used. Certain of his later nudes – almost all his nudes are men – for example, 'Man Taking Shower' (1965, acrylic) are elegant combinations of the realism at which he has come to aim and lucid design, shown in this painting by his use of the white spear-shaped shower to lend a touch of mystery to the body while giving a tightly knit unity to the composition. However intense his interest in paint – 'there are people who think painting old hat. But I still think it's still some use myself,' he has said – he remains essentially a draughtsman. Large areas of his pictures are often virtually monochromes. But how fine a draughtsman he is, is clear from his portrait-drawings: the Isherwood, Auden, both I and II, Richard Hamilton (all 1968, ink) and James Kirkman and Celia Birtwell (both 1969, ink) are particularly penetrating examples.

I have, I hope, conveyed in the preceding pages my high regard for Hockney, but his spectacular success is due not only to his exceptional talent and his capacity for work but to the time of his emergence. Most of the painters of the century are not abstract, but the concept of abstraction, involving the elimination of the subject or at least its total subordination, often to the point of unintelligibility, apt, too, to be accompanied by an attitude of denigration towards the explicit portrayal of subjects by contemporaries or near-contemporaries as 'literary' and them as 'academic', has had immense influence. One of the manifestations of this influence is the assumption that art progresses; it has, too, fostered a pervasive atmosphere of constrictive pedantry. The painters who figure in this book are among those unaffected by it, but none so spectacularly successful at so early an age, so 'fashionable', has treated this concept with such total and publicly expressed indifference. He has not only ridiculed art, for instance, by his 'Picture of a Painter's Abstraction Framed Under Glass' (lithograph 1965) – though there is abstract art which he wholeheartedly admires – but has said:

> I have stopped bothering about modern art, in that at one time you would be frightened of doing things in painting because you would consider them almost reactionary. I've stopped believing that it's possible for art to progress only in a stylistic way.[1]

It is characteristic of him that he should have expressed admiration for Dubuffet as a student, later on for Klee and later still for realists such as Balthus, Morandi, Hopper and even for Sargent. 'You see,' he said, 'I admire Sargent enormously.'[2]

No other painter very closely identified with contemporary movements would, I believe, thus proclaim his admiration for Sargent.

I believe that Hockney's openness, his spontaneity, his total

---

[1] *Art and Artists*, April, 1970.
[2] Catalogue of the Whitechapel exhibition, p.10.

freedom from pedantry, his indifference to received dogma, has done much to liberate the opinions of his generation, and his own reputation as an artist has been vastly enhanced by the liberation which, however unconsciously, he has helped, by his work and his public attitudes, to bring about.

BIOGRAPHIES

WOOD, Christopher
1901–30

Painter mainly of landscapes, in particular of coast scenes, and figure compositions. Born 7 April 1901 at Knowsley, Lancashire, son of Dr Lucius Wood and his wife Clara, born Arthur. Met Alphonse Kahn, who encouraged him to come to Paris. Studied, in 1921, at the Académie Julian and the Grande Chaumière. Knew Picasso and Diaghilef and became friendly with Cocteau who wrote the preface to the catalogue of his first exhibition (with Ben Nicholson) at the Beaux-Arts Gallery, London, in 1927. Travelled widely and frequently on the continent and Britain, also visiting Turkey. Member of 7 and 5 Society 1926–30. Worked in Cornwall in 1926 and 1928; the latter year discovered, with Ben Nicholson, the primitive painter Alfred Wallis. His finest work was done towards the end of his life, largely in Britanny. Killed by a train in Salisbury station, 21 August 1930. Retrospective exhibitions at the Wertheim Gallery, in 1931, and a memorial exhibition organized by the Redfern Gallery and shown at the New Burlington Gallery in 1938. The catalogue contains a chronological list of works and brief critical biography by Eric Newton. In 1959 the Redfern Gallery published *Christopher Wood*, prefaced by an abbreviated version of Newton's essay and a souvenir by Max Jacob.

HAYTER, Stanley William
born 1901

Engraver, painter, teacher and writer, born in Hackney, London, son of W.H. Hayter, a painter with a tradition of painting in his family extending over several generations, and his wife Ellen Mercy, born Palmer. Scholar at Whitgift Middle School, Croydon 1913–17; when visited National Gallery with his father became interested in the old masters and made tentative attempts at painting himself. On leaving school worked in research laboratory of Mond Nickel Company. At King's College, London, 1917–22, taking an honours degree in chemistry. First experiments in print-making 1921. The following year worked for Anglo-Iranian Oil Company till 1926, mostly at Abadan in the Persian Gulf, but also in Iraq, Arabia and Egypt. On returning to London showed numerous pencil portraits of fellow-employees (of which he made about a hundred and fifty), land- and seascapes and studies of the oil refinery itself. In April 1926 he left the company's employ and settled in Paris next door to Giacometti in the rue du Moulin Vert, working for three months at the Académie Julian, exhibiting paintings and prints for the first time that year at the Salon d'Automné. The year following he founded Atelier 17 for research into and the teaching of print-making, which before long became the most highly regarded institution of its kind. He also held his first exhibition at the Sacré du Printemps Gallery, and his first in London the following year at the Claridge Gallery. In the meanwhile he had become on familiar terms with most of the leading artists in Paris, and a number of the writers, in particular Eluard, who in 1938 wrote a poem *Facile Proie* based on a series of his engravings. He published, in 1930, a set of fifty-four plates entitled 'Paysages Urbains' and two months later another six, 'Apocalypse', when he held his second exhibition at the Galerie Vignon. In 1933 he exhibited with the surrealist group in Paris and in 1936 helped to organize the Surrealist Exhibition in London and was represented in it. In 1934 work from Atelier 17 was exhibited at the Galerie Pierre and at the Leicester Galleries. From this year until the outbreak of war he was on friendly terms with Picasso, who was one of a number of illustrious artists to whom he gave technical assistance with engraving. In 1939 he married Helen Phillips, the American sculptor, and they left for London settling in 1941 in New York, where, he established Atelier 17. He remained in the U.S.A. until 1950, teaching engraving in a number of other art centres including Brooklyn College and the Art Institute of Chicago. Returning to Paris he re-established Atelier 17, though not closing that in New York, which remained open until 1955.

His work has been widely shown in Europe and America, both

North and South; retrospective exhibitions have been held, at the Whitechapel Gallery in 1957, one of recent paintings at the Musée d'Art Moderne de la Ville de Paris in 1972. His published works include *Jankel Adler,* 1948, *New Ways of Gravure,* 1949, *About Prints,* 1962, *Nature and Art in Motion,* 1964, and numerous articles. Légion d'Honneur in 1951; O.B.E. in 1959, and C.B.E. in 1964.

RICHARDS, Ceri, 1903–71

Painter and maker of reliefs, often inspired by music and poetry. Born at Dunvant, near Swansea, 3 June 1903, the eldest child of Thomas Richards and his wife Sarah, born Jones. Briefly apprenticed as an electrician. Studied at Swansea School of Art 1921–4 and at Royal College of Art 1924–7. After leaving he worked for a year as an illustrator for the London Press Exchange. Made drawings of tin-plate workers for Ministry of Information 1943; designed mural decorations for P. & O. liners 1937 and 1954; décor for 'Homage to Dylan Thomas' (a reading at the Globe Theatre) 1953; décor and costumes for Lennox Berkeley's opera *Ruth* produced by the English Opera Group 1956 and for Britten's *Noyes Fludde* in 1958; in the same year he painted an altarpiece for the chapel of St Edmund Hall, Oxford; designed tabernacle, reredos and windows for Cathedral of Christ the King, Liverpool.

His first exhibition was held at the Glynn Vivian Gallery, Swansea, in 1930 and his first in London two years later at the Leger Gallery. Since then his work has been widely exhibited; twenty-five one-man exhibitions of his work have been held, including a retrospective at the Whitechapel Gallery in 1960. Richards also made illustrations for books, including *Under Milk Wood* (1971). He held a number of teaching posts and served as a trustee of the Tate Gallery, 1958–65. C.B.E. in 1960, and the same year Hon. D.Litt. of the University of Wales. He died in London in 1971, and the following year an exhibition, 'Homage to Ceri Richards 1903–71', was held at the Fischer Fine Art Gallery.

SUTHERLAND, Graham
born 1903

Painter and draughtsman of imaginative landscape, still-life and portraits. Born 24 August 1903 in South London, the younger son of G.H.V. Sutherland and his wife Elsie. After leaving Epsom College was apprenticed as a railway engineer at Derby. Attended Goldsmiths' College School of Art 1921-6, specializing in etching and engraving. In his early years Samuel Palmer was the chief formative example, but he was also affected by Paul Nash, Henry Moore and the late Turner. He began as an engraver and taught engraving at the Chelsea School of Art 1926-35 and composition and book illustration there until 1940. The market in prints — on which he had been principally engaged — collapsed about 1930, and in 1935, having been inspired by the landscape of Pembrokeshire in 1934, he decided to devote himself to painting. He contributed to the Surrealist exhibition in 1936 and two years later his own first exhibition, consisting largely of Pembrokeshire landscapes, was held at the Rosenberg and Helft Gallery. He served as an Official War Artist 1941-44, painting mainly scenes of bomb devastation and work in foundries and mines. In 1945 he painted a 'Crucifixion' for St Matthew's Church, Northampton, designed a large tapestry 'Christ in Glory at the Tetramorph' 1954-7 for the new Coventry Cathedral, and in 1960 he painted a 'Crucifixion' for the Catholic Church of St Aidan, East Acton. In 1940 he designed costumes and décor for the ballet *The Wanderer*; as well as posters, book illustrations and ceramics. Trustee Tate Gallery, 1948-54. His work has been widely exhibited in Europe and America; retrospective exhibitions were held at the Musée d'Art Moderne, Paris, 1952, and at the Tate Gallery the following year. Among many other honours he was awarded the O.M. in 1960. Three books have been devoted to his work, by Edward Sackville-West, 1943, by Robert Melville, 1950, and Douglas Cooper, 1961.

HOUTHUESEN, Albert
born 1903

Painter and draughtsman of landscape, seascape, still-life and religious subjects. Born in Amsterdam on 3 October 1903, the eldest of the four children of Jean Charles Pierre Houthuesen, half Dutch and half French, a pianist who turned to painting. A year after his death in 1911, his widow brought the family to London, where they remained, Albert being naturalized in 1922. For five years after leaving school (at the age of fourteen) he worked as an errand-boy, grocer's assistant, furniture restorer, engraver's assistant and draughtsman in an architect's office, attending the St Martin's School of Art in the evenings.

In 1923 he was awarded a scholarship of £80 a year at the Royal College of Art, remaining there for four years. In 1931 he married the painter Catherine Dean, a fellow-student at the Royal College. From 1927 to 1936 he taught at the Mary Ward Settlement and the Working Men's College. In 1936 he suffered a breakdown in health which lasted for some two years. In 1940 his studio in St John's Wood was damaged by a bomb and much of his work was destroyed. Rejected by the Army as medically unfit, he worked as a tracer in the draughtsmen's office of the London and North Eastern Railway locomotive office at Doncaster from 1941 until 1944. They returned to London in 1945, living near the Elephant and Castle, and after two years at Oxted, Surrey, finally settled in 1952 in Love Walk, Camberwell, where they live still.

Besides misfortune, Albert Houthuesen suffered almost total neglect. It was not until 1961 that he held his first exhibition at the Reid Gallery, followed by another two years later. In 1967, 1969 and 1970 he has held exhibitions at the Mercury Gallery, all of which have been attended by considerable success. A portfolio of lithographs, entitled 'Clowns', was published in 1970 and a book, *Albert Houthuesen, An Appreciation*, with an introduction by John Rothenstein, in 1969.

PIPER, John
born 1903

Painter of architecture, landscape, abstract compositions; book illustrator; designer for the theatre, of stained-glass windows, pottery; poet and writer, on the arts and the countryside. Born 13 December 1903 at Epsom, Surrey, son of C. A. Piper, a solicitor, and his wife Mary Ellen, born Matthews. Worked in his father's office until his death in 1926. He then studied at the Kingston and Richmond Schools of Art, at the Royal College of Art 1928-9. He wrote and illustrated a book of poems, *The Wind in the Trees*, published in 1924. From 1928 he was a regular contributor to *The Nation and Athenaeum* and continued to do so after its amalgamation with *The New Statesman* in 1933, and showed himself a perceptive critic of painting, especially of emerging talent, besides reviewing concerts, plays and books. In 1927 he exhibited wood engravings with David Birch at the Arlington Gallery and held his first one-man exhibition at the London Gallery in 1938. In the previous year he made his first stage designs for Stephen Spender's *Trial of a Judge*; other designs were for operas by Benjamin Britten (the most recent being *Death in Venice*, 1973). After a visit to Paris in 1933 he turned for a few years to abstraction, returning before long to representational painting. He married, in 1935, Myfanwy Evans, the founder and editor of *Axis — a Quarterly Review of Contemporary Abstract Painting and Sculpture* 1935-7. He served as an Official War Artist 1940-2. Made a series of watercolours of Windsor Castle commissioned by the Queen 1941-2. Designed windows for Eton College Chapel 1958, for Nuffield College Chapel, Oxford, 1961, and for Coventry Cathedral 1962. Painted decorations for British Embassy to Brazil 1948 and in the same year held his first New York exhibition at the Curt Valentin Gallery. John Piper has served in many public capacities, among others as a Trustee of the Tate Gallery 1946-53 and 1954-61 and again from 1968; as a member of the Arts Council Panel 1952-7 and as a member of the Oxford Diocesan Advisory Committee since 1950. Of his many exhibitions the most recent was held at the Marlborough Fine Art in 1972. A Companion of Honour in the same year. Two books have been devoted to his work, by John Betjeman, 1944, and by S. John Woods, 1955.

BURRA, Edward
born 1905

Painter in watercolour, usually on a large scale, mostly of subjects sinister in themselves or else of everyday subjects with overtones of strangeness; occasional designer for the theatre.

Edward John Burra, born on 29 March 1905 in South Kensington, is the eldest child of Henry Curteis Burra, J.P., and his wife Ermentrude, born Robertson Luxford. The family lived at Rye, Sussex, where, apart from school and college, the artist has spent all his life. After leaving his private school he spent 1921 and 1922 at the Chelsea School of Art and the following year at the Royal College of Art. From the middle 'twenties he made fairly frequent visits to Paris and the South of France, on one occasion, in 1930, with Paul Nash, and in 1934 to Mexico, New York and Boston. Besides painting, he has made designs for five ballets and an opera: 'Rio Grande' for the Carmargo Society, in 1931; 'Miracle in the Gorbals' and 'Barabau' performed by the Sadler's Wells Company in 1944 and 1946; and 'Carmen' in 1947, 'Don Juan' in 1948, and 'Don Quixote' in 1950, performed at Covent Garden. Illustrated *Huckleberry Finn* in 1940. One-man exhibitions of Burra's work have been held at the Leicester Galleries in 1929, 1932, and 1947; the Redfern Gallery in 1942; the Lefevre in 1952, there biennially since; the Hamet Gallery in 1970 and 1971; and a retrospective, consisting of some 120 works, at the Tate Gallery in 1973. CBE 1970. *Edward Burra* by John Rothenstein was published in 1945. A film, *Edward Burra*, was made in 1972-3 by Balfour Films for the Arts Council.

HILLIER, Tristram
born 1905

Painter of landscape (often of Spanish and Portuguese cities) and occasional religious subjects. Born in Peking 11 April 1905, the son of Edward Guy Hillier and his wife Ada, born Everett. Studied at Downside, at Christ's College, Cambridge, 1922-4, at the Slade School, also attending evening classes at the Westminster School of Art, 1926-8; with Lhote; at the Atelier Colarossi and the Grande Chaumière. Travelled widely in Mediterranean countries, also in Hungary, but making his home in the South of France. Held his first of two exhibitions at the Reid and Lefevre Gallery, 1931. A member of Unit I 1933. During the war he served, 1940-4, with the Royal Naval Volunteer Reserve, being invalided out with the rank of lieutenant.

After the war he settled at East Pennard, Somerset, but spends much time in Spain and Portugal. Author of an autobiography *Leda and the Goose*, 1954. A.R.A. 1957. R.A. 1967. He has held eight exhibitions at the Tooth Gallery, the most recent in 1973.

COLLINS, Cecil
born 1908

Painter of mystical and visionary works. Born 23 March 1908 in Plymouth, son of Henry Collins and his wife Mary, born Bowie. At an early age made drawings of landscapes in Devon and Cornwall. Won scholarship to the Plymouth School of Art in 1923 where he studied until 1927, when he won a scholarship to the Royal College of Art, taking his diploma in 1931. Influenced by Greco, Blake, Picasso and Klee, also by surrealism, but more enduringly by Mark Tobey, who fostered his preoccupation with the art and philosophy of the Far East. From 1939 until 1943 he taught painting and drawing at Dartington Hall; also taught at the Central School of Arts and Crafts since 1956. In 1940 he began a series of paintings and drawings which he first called 'The Holy Fool', but he later changed its title to 'The Vision of the Fool' to accord with the title of his essay, published in 1947, in which he attacks the materialism of utilitarian standards pervading modern civilization. In 1949 he designed his first tapestry for the Edinburgh Weavers, in 1959 a big Shakespearian curtain for the British Embassy in Washington, and in 1973 he carried out a commission for an altarpiece in a chapel at Chichester Cathedral. He held his first one-man exhibition in 1935 at the Bloomsbury

Gallery. Exhibited at the Lefevre Gallery in 1944, 1945 and 1946; at the Ashmolean Museum, Oxford, in 1953; a retrospective at the Whitechapel Gallery in 1959; at the Zyghoe Gallery, Athens (from which four works were bought for the Greek national collections) in 1961; and at the Hamet Gallery in 1972. A book, *Cecil Collins, Paintings and Drawings* by Alex Comfort, with a foreword by Conrad Senat, was published in 1946.

PASMORE, Victor
born 1908

Began as a poetic painter of Thameside and other landscapes, figures and flowers, but become uncompromisingly abstract in the late 'forties, and maker of constructions. Born 3 December 1908, the eldest of the three children of Dr Edwin S. Pasmore and his wife Gertrude, born Screech, in Warlingham, Surrey. From 1922 until 1926 he was at Harrow School, then from 1927 he worked for ten years with London County Council, in the meanwhile attending evening classes at the Central School of Arts and Crafts until 1931, painting in his spare time, experimenting with fauvism, cubism and abstraction. Member of the London Artists' Association 1933, of the London Group 1934.

With William Coldstream and Claude Rogers opened a teaching studio in 1937 in Fitzroy Street, moving later that year to Euston Road, in an attempt to revive impressionism, but the School closed down in 1939 after the outbreak of war. In 1940 he married Wendy Blood and, after living briefly in Ebury Street, they settled in Chiswick, he painting Thameside scenes in a delicately Whistlerian manner until about 1947 when he returned to abstraction and moved to St German's Place, Blackheath, which remained his London home. In 1966 he also acquired a house in Malta. In 1950 and 1951 he visited Ben Nicholson and Barbara Hepworth, exhibiting with them at the Penwith Society which held the first post-war exhibition of abstract art; he also began to make three-dimensional constructions. Taught at the Central School 1949-53; was Master of Painting, Department of

Fine Arts, University of Durham 1954-61. In 1955 he was appointed Director of Architectural Design for the south-west area of Peterlee New Town, Durham. In addition he has made a number of mural paintings and reliefs commissioned for public buildings, the first being a mural for the canteen in the drivers' and conductors' 'bus garage at Kingston, Surrey, in 1950. Organized summer schools at Scarborough for study of 'basic form', 1955-7. Was an editor of *The Developing Process* to which he contributed one of its forty-eight essays on 'A developing process in art teaching', published in 1959. He served as a trustee of the Tate Gallery from 1963 until 1966. C.B.E. in 1959. Over forty one-man exhibitions of his work have been held in Europe and North and South America, including retrospectives at the Venice Biennale in 1960 and the Tate Gallery in 1965, accompanied by a highly informative catalogue.

BACON, Francis
born 1909

Figure and portrait painter. Born 28 October 1909 in Dublin of English parents, Edward Anthony Mortimer Bacon and his wife, born Christine Winifred Firth. He briefly attended Dean Close School, Cheltenham. Left home in 1926, worked in an office in London, and spent some time in Berlin and Paris. Settled in London in 1928, setting up as an interior decorator. About this time he began to paint in oil. (He had already made a number of drawings and watercolours.) That same year he showed in his studio, 7 Queensbury Mews, some of the furniture and carpets he had designed. In the winter of 1929-30 he and his friend Roy de Maistre held another small exhibition, also in his studio, showing a few oils and watercolours as well as furniture. In 1930 *The Studio* published an article 'The 1930 Look in British Decoration', a double-page feature showing his furniture, rugs and his studio. By 1931 his interest in interior decoration was ebbing and he regarded himself primarily as a painter.

In 1933 his 'Crucifixion 1933' was reproduced in Herbert

Read's *Art Now* and he showed single paintings in two exhibitions at the Mayor Gallery. In 1934 he organized an exhibition of his work in the basement of Sunderland House, which he called the Transition Gallery. Discouraged by its failure he did little painting for the next few years, devoting himself largely to gambling. During the war, unfit on account of asthma for the Army, he worked, after 1942, in Civil Defence. On account of the fitfulness of his production and a propensity to self-criticism which caused him to destroy his work, probably fewer than a dozen paintings of 1929-44 survive. But in the latter year he resumed painting in earnest and shortly showed himself an artist of a stature which astonished even his few admirers; his 'Three Figures at the Base of a Crucifixion' was shown at the Lefevre Gallery the following spring. In 1946 his 'Figure Study II' was bought by the Contemporary Art Society and he showed at several exhibitions; in 1948 his 'Painting 1946' was bought by the Museum of Modern Art, New York.

He has moved frequently from studio to studio in London, and visited South Africa, where his mother lives, in 1950-1. In 1956 he rented a flat in Tangier which he visited from time to time; he went to Italy in 1954 and he had a one-man exhibition in the British Pavilion at the Venice Biennale (which he did not visit). One-man exhibitions of his work have been held in many parts of Europe and America, including retrospectives at the Tate Gallery in 1962 (also shown, slightly modified, in Mannheim, Turin, Zurich and Amsterdam), at the Guggenheim Museum, New York, in 1964; and at the Grand Palais, Paris, in 1972.

Four monographs have been published: by John Rothenstein in 1963, by John Rothenstein and Ronald Alley (containing a catalogue raisonné by Ronald Alley) in 1964, and by John Russell in 1964 and 1971. A film, *Francis Bacon; paintings 1944-61*, was produced by David Thompson in 1961, and another film, by Michael Gill with an interview with David Sylvester, in 1966. Francis Bacon has been awarded no honours as it is clearly understood that these would not be acceptable.

COLQUHOUN, Robert
1914–62

Painter and print-maker of figures, less frequently of landscape and animals, and occasional theatrical designer. Born 20 December 1914 in Kilmarnock, Ayrshire, Scotland, eldest of a family of two sons and a daughter of Robert Colquhoun and his wife, born Janet Stewart. After attending Loanhead School and the Kilmarnock Academy, he won a scholarship in 1932 to the Glasgow School of Art. There he won a drawing prize, a post-diploma award enabling him to spend an extra year there and finally a travelling scholarship (worth £120) which funded him (with Robert MacBryde, a fellow-student who won a similar scholarship and with whom he formed an intimate and lifelong friendship) to travel in Italy and France during 1938 and 1939, returning to Scotland in consequence of World War II. After a brief period of painting and drawing in Ayrshire he served with the Royal Army Medical Corps during 1940 and 1941, but in the latter year he was invalided out and, with MacBryde, shortly afterwards settled in London, serving with the Civil Defence Force, though continuing to paint at night.

From late in 1941 until 1947 they lived in a large studio at 77 Bedford Gardens, Kensington, which became a meeting place for a large circle of friends which included poets, prose writers and fellow artists, many of them of exceptional talent. After their eviction they moved to Lewes, Sussex, where they spent almost two years making lithographs and drawings for Miller's Press. From 1949 until 1954 they lived at Tilty Mill, Essex, the home of their friend George Barker the poet and Elizabeth his wife. In 1949 they re-visited Italy. Three years later at the invitation of Massine Colquhoun and MacBryde designed costumes and décor for a new Scottish ballet *Donald of the Burthens* produced at Covent Garden in 1951, and for *King Lear* produced at Stratford by George Devine in 1953. On 20 September 1962 Colquhoun died suddenly while preparing, with MacBryde, for an exhibition of monotypes to be held at the Museum Street Gallery a fortnight later. He was buried in Kilmarnock, which he had not visited since 1946.

Colquhoun held one-man exhibitions at the Lefevre Gallery in 1943, 1944, 1947 and 1951, at the Redfern in 1950, at the Panton Gallery in 1957, at the Whitechapel (a retrospective) in 1958, and in 1963 there was a posthumous exhibition at the Douglas and Foulis Gallery, Edinburgh. The Colquhoun Memorial Gallery was opened in Kilmarnock in 1972 when the annual competition for the Colquhoun Art Prize was inaugurated. The Whitechapel catalogue is particularly informative as is the brochure prepared for the Memorial Gallery, especially about the artist's early life in Scotland.

MACBRYDE, Robert

Still-life and figure painter, occasional stage designer. Born Robert MacBride, on 5 December at Maybole, Ayrshire, son of John MacBride, a leather worker, and his wife Agnes, born McKay. Worked for five years in a factory before entering the Glasgow School of Art, where he became an intimate and lifelong friend of Colquhoun, with whom he travelled in Italy and France on a scholarship from 1937 until 1939. The outward circumstances of his life were virtually identical with those of Colquhoun, whom, however, he outlived for three years, dying in Dublin on 15 May 1966 as a result of a street accident.

FREUD, Lucian
born 1922

Painter of interiors, figures, portraits and urban landscape. Born on 8 December 1922 in Berlin, younger son of Ernst and his wife Lucie Brasch; grandson of Sigmund Freud. Brought by his parents to England in 1932, where he has lived ever since; a naturalized British subject in 1939. Studied at the Central School, with Cedric Morris at his school in Dedham and in 1942 drew part-time at Goldsmiths' College. Served during 1941 with the Merchant Marine from which he was invalided out. Won an Arts

Council Prize, Festival of Britain Exhibition 1951. Taught at the Slade School. Visited Greece in 1946 and 1947 and Paris on several occasions. Exhibitions of his work have been held at the Lefevre Gallery in 1944 and 1946; at the London Gallery in 1947 (with John Craxton); at the Venice Biennale in 1954; at the Marlborough Fine Art in 1958, 1963 and 1968, and with Anthony d'Offay in 1972, shown subsequently at the Gray Art Gallery, Hartlepool.

ANDREWS, Michael
born 1928

Painter of canvases, often very large, in which realism is given an aura of dream-like fantasy.

Michael James Andrews was born on 30 October 1928 in Norwich, the second of the three children of Thomas Victor Andrews and his wife Gertrude Emma, born Green. During 1947, his last year at Norwich School, he studied at the Norwich School of Art. After leaving school he served for two years in the Army Ordnance Corps, mostly in Egypt. From 1949 until 1953 he studied at the Slade School, where he received consistent encouragement from Coldstream, and was awarded an Abbey Scholarship and a Rome Scholarship, tenable for two years, but he spent only five months in Italy. After his return he played a part with Eduardo Paolozzi in a film *Together*, produced by a fellow-student at the Slade, Lorenza Mazzetti; it was of her that he painted his only picture while in Rome. Painting absorbs almost all his energy, although he has taught at Norwich Art School at various times, at the Chelsea School of Art 1962–4, and at the Slade 1963–6. Two one-man exhibitions of his work have been held, both at the Beaux-Arts Gallery, in 1958 and 1963. He has written little about his ideas. He contributed a number of 'Notes' to the periodical *X* no. 2, 1960 and 'A conversation with Victor Willing' to *Art and Literature* no. 2, 1964.

RILEY, Bridget
born 1931

An abstract painter, often of equivalents of conflicting forces. Bridget Louise Riley was born on 25 April 1931 in South London, the elder of the two daughters of John Fisher Riley, a commercial printer, and his wife Bessie Louise, born Gladstone. She spent part of her childhood in Lincolnshire, but the war years in Cornwall with her mother, sister and an aunt, Bertha Joyce, who had studied art at Goldsmiths' College and who first aroused her interest in the arts, encouraging her to draw and paint. From 1944 until 1946 she attended St Stephen's Convent at Taplow, proceeding to Cheltenham Ladies' College, where her growing interest in the arts was fostered by the art master Colin Hayes. From 1949 until 1953 she studied at Goldsmiths' College, concentrating on drawing. Here again she had the good fortune to awaken the encouragement of a teacher of exceptional ability, Sam Rabin. Wishing to learn to paint and suffering from a feeling of remoteness from the centre of creative activity, she transferred to the Royal College of Art, where she remained for three years. Although she learnt the elements of painting and came to know some of the leading figures in the emerging generation, she was without a sense of direction. From 1957 until 1958 she taught art at the Convent of the Sacred Heart at Harrow; she was then employed for about a year by the J. Walter Thompson advertising agency, making photo-realist illustrations. Riley's desire to be a painter was undiminished and was immensely stimulated by 'The Developing Process', an exhibition organized by Victor Pasmore, Harry Thubron and others and held at the Institute of Contemporary Art in 1959. In the same year she attended Thubron's Summer School in Norfolk, where she formed a friendship with Maurice de Sausmarez, a painter and teacher who was assisting Thubron. With de Sausmarez, who quickly perceived the nature of her talent, her friendship lasted until his death in 1970. She painted in Spain and France and initiated the Basic Course at Loughborough College of Art. In the summer of 1960 she went to Italy with de Sausmarez, visiting the art galleries and churches, also the comprehensive futurist exhibition at the Venice Biennale.

Before their visit she had assisted de Sausmarez in the preparation of the three lectures he gave at the Royal College of Art to mark the fiftieth anniversary of the publication of the Futurist Manifesto.

Early in 1961 she had begun to find her way, to an art described by David Thompson as 'dominant formal pattern under pressure of disintegration'.

Many exhibitions of her work have been held, in the United States and Europe as well as Britain. The first in London were at Gallery One in 1962 and 1963; also two major retrospectives, that at the Hayward Gallery in 1971, accompanied by an informative catalogue, and the Arts Council Touring Exhibition in 1973.

The most searching account of her work and its development is given in *Bridget Riley* by Maurice de Sausmarez published in 1970, the year of his death. She was also the subject, in 1969, of a film made by David Thompson.

HOCKNEY, David
born 1937

Painter, draughtsman and print-maker of figures, landscape and still-life. Born 9 July 1937 in Bradford, Yorkshire, son of Kenneth Hockney and his wife Laura, born Thompson. Studied at the Bradford College of Art 1953–7. As a conscientious objector worked in hospitals in Bradford and Hastings instead of National Service. Studied at the Royal College of Art, where he won several awards, 1959–62. Paid first visit to New York 1961 and two years later the first of several to California (where he taught at the University of California, Los Angeles, in 1966, and Berkeley in 1967); he has also taught at the Universities of Iowa (1964) and Colorado (1965) and elsewhere. He is exceptionally widely travelled, not only in California, where he has lived for long periods, and other parts of the United States, but in Egypt, Italy, France, Germany and Ireland. Many principal exhibitions of his work have been held in several countries, the first two in 1963 largely of student work, of paintings at the Kasmin Gallery and of prints at the Alecto Gallery. The most comprehensive of the considerable number held since — in Holland, Belgium, Italy, Germany as well as the U.S.A. and Britain — was the 1970 retrospective at the Whitechapel Gallery 'Paintings, Prints and Drawings 1960–1970', accompanied by a highly informative catalogue. Hockney designed sets and costumes for the English Stage Society's production of Alfred Jarry's *Ubu Roi* at the Royal Court Theatre in 1966 and illustrated *Six Fairy Tales* by the brothers Grimm, with thirty-four etchings, published in 1970. *Seventy-two Drawings by David Hockney* was published in 1971.

INDEX